ABOUT THE AUTHOR

Walther Kirchner is Professor of History at the University of Delaware. He received his B.A., M.A., and Ph.D. degrees from the University of California at Los Angeles. He has held teaching positions at the University of California at Los Angeles, the University of Pennsylvania, and Lehigh University. Dr. Kirchner, a research specialist in Russian history, has written *Rise of the Baltic Question, Jacob Fries' Journey through Siberia,* and *History of Russia.* He has also contributed numerous articles to leading history periodicals. Professor Kirchner has traveled extensively thoughout the world and has spent a Fulbright year in Denmark. For the years 1955–1956 he was appointed a member of the Institute for Advanced Study at Princeton.

By courtesy of the Bettmann Archive

BAS-RELIEF FROM THE ARCH OF TITUS

COLLEGE OUTLINE SERIES

WESTERN CIVILIZATION
TO 1500

WALTHER KIRCHNER

BARNES & NOBLE, INC.

NEW YORK

PUBLISHERS & BOOKSELLERS SINCE 1873

©

Copyright, 1960
By Barnes & Noble, Inc.
Fourth Printing, 1962

All rights reserved

L.C. Catalogue Card Number: 60-14634

PRINTED IN THE UNITED STATES OF AMERICA

PREFACE

The scope of European history, the diversity of achievements in classical and medieval times, the multitude of events and developments, and the wealth of ideas and beliefs born in the Western World make it impossible for any author to present without trepidation a new survey of Western civilization. Confronted with the task, he appreciates the more such advice and help as I have received from Dr. Jill Nadell of the University of Kentucky for the sections on Ancient history, from Dr. Norman Zacour of Franklin and Marshall College for those on Medieval history, and from my wife for each and every part.

W. K.

TABLE OF CONTENTS

MAPS

TABULATED BIBLIOGRAPHY
OF STANDARD TEXTBOOKS

This *College Outline* is keyed to standard textbooks in two ways.

1. If you are studying one of the following textbooks, consult the cross references here listed to find which pages of the *Outline* summarize the appropriate chapter of your text.

2. If you are using the *Outline* as your basis for study and need a fuller treatment of a topic, consult the pages of any of the standard textbooks as indicated in the Quick Reference Tables on pages xiv–xvii.

Burns, Edward McNall. *Western Civilizations, Their History and Their Culture.* 5th Ed. New York: W. W. Norton & Company Inc., 1958.
III (6–11, 23–26); IV (11–14, 16–18, 20, 26–28); V (28–29); VI (19, 29); VII (18–23); VIII (30–72); IX (72–75); X (76–138); XI (138–162); XII (162–166, 168–173); XIII (166–168); XIV (174–245); XV (244–245, 248, 260); XVI (246–273).

Easton, Stewart C. *The Heritage of the Past, from the earliest times to the close of the Middle Ages.* New York: Rinehart & Co., 1955.
II (2–6); III (6–11, 23–26); IV (11–18, 20, 26–29); V (18–20, 20–23, 29); VII (30–53, 59–62); VIII (53–58, 64–66); IX (67–75); X (76–109); XI (111–114, 117–118, 122–125); XII (109–111, 115–116, 118–121, 125–129); XIII (121–122, 132–133, 137, 138–140); XIV (129–137, 141–148); XV (148–152); XVI (152–155); XVII (156–166, 168–173); XVIII (166–168, 174–213); XIX (213–216, 229–232, 252–258); XX (198–205, 223–228, 244, 259–265); XXI (178–180, 219–223, 240–243); XXII (232–240, 248–250, 266–269).

Ferguson, Wallace K., and Bruun, Geoffrey. *A Survey of European Civilization.* Vol. I. Boston: Houghton Mifflin Company, 1958.
I (5–29); II (30–62); III (62–75); IV (76–116); V (117–129); VI (129–138, 141); VII (138–140); VIII (142–148); IX (148–152); X (152–155); XI (154–157); XII (158–163); XIII (166–173); XIV (163–166); XV (175–178, 191–192, 206–208, 213–214); XVI (178–180, 190,

192–195, 215–216, 216–217); XVII (185–188, 196–197, 209–211, 214–215, 216); XVIII (182–183, 202–205); XIX (183, 219–224); XX (183–184, 197–202, 208, 211–213, 225–228); XXI (229–230, 238–240); XXII (235–238, 246–248, 248–250); XXIII (230–235, 252–256); XXIV (240–243); XXV (245, 248, 260–261, 263–264); XXVI (257–260, 261–263, 264–265); XXVII (266–273).

Hoyt, Robert S. *Europe in the Middle Ages.* New York: Harcourt Brace and Company, 1957.

I (130–141); II (142–148); III (150–151, 152); IV (148, 151–152); V (149–150, 152–155); VI (156–161); VII (161–162); VIII (162–166); IX (166–173); X (172); XI (174–178); XII (180–181, 185–188); XIII (182–184); XIV (179, 191–195); XV (189–190, 201–205); XVI (193, 197–198, 200); XVII (196–198, 206–208, 211–213); XVIII (208–209); XIX (223–226); XXI (226–227); XXII (227–228, 244–245); XXIII (219–223); XXIV (216–217, 237–238); XXV (234–235); XXVI (213–214, 230–231); XXVII (209–211, 217–218, 251–252); XXVIII (235–236, 248–250); XXIX (231, 252–256); XXX (230–234, 247, 248, 250, 251); XXXI (240–244, 257–259); XXXII (259–273).

Savelle, Max (editor). *A History of World Civilization.* Vol. I. New York: Henry Holt and Company, 1957.

II (6–11, 23–26); III (11–29); IV (30–40, 44–53, 59–63); V (40–44, 53–58, 63–66, 72–75); VI (62–72); VII (76–111); VIII (111–138, 141); IX (121–122, 128–129, 138–140, 150–152); X (148–150); XI (152–154); XVII (142–148, 156–163); XVIII (163–166, 168–171, 213–216, 229–238); XIX (171–173, 178, 182–183, 185–187, 189–197, 202–205, 214–215, 222–223, 240–243); XX (166–168, 174–178, 196–199, 206–213); XXI (183–185, 199–202, 223–228, 244); XXII (219–222, 256–259); XXIII (246–251, 259–266); XXIV (252–256); XXV (267–272); XXVI (272–273).

Scramuzza, Vincent M., and MacKendrick, Paul L. *The Ancient World.* New York: Henry Holt and Company, 1958.

II (6–10); III (11–14, 16–18); IV (10–11, 23–26); V (18, 23); VI (18–19, 29); VII (20, 26–28); VIII (28–29); X (21); XI (21, 23, 30–31, 43); XII (31, 34–35); XIII (31–32, 34); XIV (39–44); XV (34–36); XVI (36–38); XVII (38–39); XVIII (46–48); XIX (48–51); XX (49–50); XXI (55–56); XXII (53–55, 56–58); XXIII (51–53); XXIV (59–60,); XXV (60–62); XXVI (62–63); XXVIII (63–66); XXIX (67–72); XXXI (72–75); XXXII (76–79); XXXIII (79–82, 83–84); XXXIV (82–83, 84–88); XXXV (83–84); XXXVI (89–92, 94–96); XXXVII (92–94); XXXVIII (86–98); XXXIX (98–100); XL (100); XLI (100–102); XLII (104–107); XLIII (111–112); XLV (109–111); XLVI (112–113); XLVII (113–115); XLVIII (115–116); XLIX (117–119); L (119, 125–126); LI (122–123); LII (123–126); LIII (119); LIV (119–121); LV (121–122, 128–129); LVI (129–131); LVII (125, 131–133); LVIII (134–136); LIX (136–137, 141, 144).

Stephenson, Carl. *Medieval History: Europe From the Second to the Sixteenth Century.* 3rd Ed. New York: Harper & Brothers, 1951.

I (81–130); II (131–141); III (142–150); IV (140, 150–152); V (149–153); VI (152–155); VII (151, 156–158); VIII (158–173); IX (153, 164, 167, 187); X (163–165, 168–175, 179, 180); XI (179, 182–183); XII (175–177, 185–188); XIII (182, 203–204, 235); XIV (183, 198–200); XV (201–202); XVI (202); XVII (191–192, 194, 196–197); XVIII (191, 193–194, 206–217); XIX (207–208, 211–212, 224–226); XX (213–218, 232–234); XXI (233–35, 237, 244); XXII (235–238, 248–250); XXIII (252–256); XXIV (219–223, 240–242, 246, 258–259, 270–271); XXV (259–266); XXVI (267–273).

Strayer, Joseph R., and Munro, Dana C. *The Middle Ages 395–1500.* 4th Ed. New York: Appleton-Century-Crofts, Inc., 1959.

I (134–141, 150); II (142–148, 150–152); III (148–149, 152–155); IV (156–160); V (160–165, 168–173); VI (165–168, 174–176); VII (178–180, 182–185); VIII (177–178, 185–193, 196–202); IX (193–195, 216–217); X (206–216, 217–218); XI (222–223); XII (229–233, 252–256); XIII (234–243, 246–248, 249–250, 252, 256–259, 267–273); XIV (244–245, 248, 259–265).

Swain, Joseph Ward. *The Harper History of Civilization.* Vol. I. New York: Harper & Brothers, 1958.

II (5–29); III (21, 30–75); IV (76–79, 81, 83–84, 89–96, 98–109, 111–114, 117–118, 122–123); V (80–83, 85, 88, 96–98, 109–111, 114–117, 119–121, 123–138, 141–148); VI (121–123, 128–129, 138–141, 150–152, 185–188, 196–197); VII (148–149, 152–155); IX (156–166, 168–184); X (189–196, 202–205, 213–218, 219–223); XI (166–168, 196–198, 205–213); XII (198–202, 223–228); XIII (229–265); XIV (266–273).

Swain, Joseph W., and Armstrong, William H. *The Peoples of the Ancient World.* New York: Harper & Brothers, 1959.

II (11–18); III (6–11, 23–26); IV (18–20, 26–29); V (19); VI (20); VII (29); VIII (20–23, 42); IX (30–42, 42–44); X (38, 45–48); XI (48–53); XII (54–59); XIII (59–66); XIV (67–75); XV (76–90); XVI (90–96); XVII (96–102); XVIII (103–112); XIX (114–116, 119–121); XX (121); XXI (112–114, 117–119, 121–122); XXII (122–129); XXIII (130–136); XXIV (136–141, 149–150).

Wallbank, Walter T., and Taylor, Alastair M. *Civilization Past & Present.* Vol. I. Chicago: Scott, Foresman and Company, 1960.

II (5–29); IV (30–75); V (76–128); VII (128–148); VIII (148–150, 152–154); IX (152–155); XI (156–164, 169–173); XII (165–166, 171–172, 174–183, 185–188, 197, 202–205, 209–213, 219–224, 240–243, 246–247); XIII (166–168, 183–185, 197–202, 206–209, 224–228, 244); XIV (189–196, 213–218, 232–238, 247–252); XV (260–261, 263–264); XVI (229–232, 252–259, 260–263, 264–273).

CHAPTER IN THIS OUTLINE	CHAPTER TITLE	BURNS	EASTON	FERGUSON & BRUUN VOL. I	HOYT	SAVELLE VOL. I
Introd.	On history			3–7		
I	The Earliest known Civilizations	36–40 42–46 64–65 67–72	11–12 19–24 29–58	15–17 19–22		43–56 67–72
II	Near East in the 2nd and 1st milleniums	40–42 46–63 65–67 72–133	58–137	17–19 22–25		56–65 72–98
III	Greece before 500 B.C.	140–151 156–158 165–166 170–173	179–211	26–32		99–109 119–122 131–135
IV	Greece in the Fifth Century	151–154 166–170 174–181	211–243	32–40		109–111 112–117 125–130 135–138
V	End of Greek Liberty	154–156 158–166	243–263	41–43		111–112 123–125 135–138
VI	Hellenistic Age	182–199	265–300	43–50		147–165
VII	Rise of Rome	200–207	301–320 364–369	51–54		167–171
VIII	Flourishing of the Roman Republic	207–211	320–336	54–58 59–62		171–181 184–186
IX	Establishment of the Empire	211–218 219–222	336–359 378–380 382–386	58–59 60–61		181–184 187–202 418–420
X	Imperial Rome	218–219 222–230 243–246	359–362 381–382 391–393	65–79 87–90	9–12 53–58	203–213 221–321
XI	End of the Ancient World	230–236 246–249	403–411 415–432	79–86 90–95	12–23 58–61	213–217 231–236 239–242
XII	Barbarians, Christians, and Moslems	249–255 262–268 269–289	425–461 480–498	95–100 101–114 117–125 128–134 138–145	24–52 61–99 100–116 118–120	236–239 245–257 271–277 420–429
XIII	Early Feudal Age (741–1000)	255–261 299–312	503–520 524–549 551–562 622–628	125–127 135 145–157 158–170	116–118 120–175 175–206 285–297	257–261 411–412 429–450 471–474

to pages.

SCRA-MUZZA	STEPHEN-SON	STRAYER & MUNRO	SWAIN (HISTORY OF CIVIL-IZATION) VOL. I	SWAIN (PEOPLES OF THE ANCIENT WORLD) VOL. I	WALLBANK & TAYLOR VOL. I
11–12					2–10
14–26 27–43 46–51			35–47 49–54 55–62	17–22 39–46	33–39 42–51
43–45 51–71 72–101 101–114 118–136			47–48 54–55 62–75 80–89 93–101	22–37 47–62 111–113 117–118 146–149 151–166	39–42 51–60 98–102 188–190 194
136–199 200–207			101–107 121–126	167–171 175–206	102–106 112–115 118–119
208–294			75–78 107–115 126–132 139–144	206–260	106–112 115–117 119–123
295–315 324–342			115–116 132–137	261–281	117–118 123–124
343–393			116–120 129–130 137–139 144–147	283–313	124–128
395–434			154–160 212 225–226	315–337	129–134
435–503	5		160–184 213–215 216–217 226–227	338–380	134–140 149–154
504–589	6		184–193 217–219 221 263–265	381–423 445–452	140–143 154–155 195–198
590–719	7–27 36–42	24–30	193–211 215 219–237 252–259 265–280	452–512	143–149 155–160 199
719–728 732–734 736–747	27–36 42–43 44–49 60–64	1–23	237–242 280–289	513–525	199–207
	49–59 64–117 118–133 159–160	30–90	216 242–245 289–313 403–412 442 548–552	526–529	207–216 221–227 246–256 368–370
	133–158 177–193 198–211 217–219	90–142 146–156 161–174 180–184	336 413–436 457–460 552–553		311–334 336–342 227–228 234–235 240–241

CHAPTER IN THIS OUTLINE	CHAPTER TITLE	BURNS	EASTON	FERGUSON & BRUUN VOL. I	HOYT	SAVELLE VOL. I
XIV	Beginning of a New Millenium	312–313 321 336–339 341–345	520–524 562–566 572–577	136–137 171–180 183–188 197–198 200–201 213–217	210–224 228–244 259–266 298–304 333–336 393–400	261–268 456–458 460–462 477–478 507–510 654–655
XV	Flourishing of the Middle Ages (12th C.)	289–296 317–320 322–330 348 356–358 360–361	566–569 578 580–584 630–632	188–193 198–200 201–205 217–218 223–237 238–251 252–260 261–264	224–225 245–258 266–284 306–324 336–337 381–387 407–411 505–507	283–288 451 458 462 474–493 521–528 535–539 541–542
XVI	"Greatest of Centuries" (13th C.)	313–315 320 322 332–338 347–355 358–359 361–365	568–572 578–580 584–591 593–600 635–648 673–704	193–196 205–212 218–222 260–261 264–272 364–365	337–347 354–380 387–392 400–406 412–418 423–439 442–448 462–474 479–491 507–516	289 451–452 459 462–463 497–504 511–519 528–546
XVII	Eve of the Renaissance (1275-1350)	315–316 320–321 345–347 360 379	602–607 664–672 748–753	275–278 280–282 286–292 301–306 311–319 311–322	419–420 439–440 448–461 474–478 491–523 542–547 564–567 592–596 599–601	453 459–460 463–469 493–495 504–505 554–558 579–581
XVIII	Early Renaissance (1350-1453)	316 367–376 379–381	607–616 734–735	278–280 282–285 292–300 306–310 322–334 338 345–347 351 366	516–517 521–531 535–540 547–562 567–573 574–591 596–599 601–609	289–290 453–456 581–584 589–590 605–606 656–657
XIX	On the Threshold of the Modern Age (1453-1492)	388	735–737 750–758	343–345 354–361 362–364 367–369	503–505 517–518 531–535 540–541 562–564	456 460 560 598 657–661

to pages.

SCRA-MUZZA	STEPHEN-SON	STRAYER & MUNRO	SWAIN (HISTORY OF CIVIL-IZATION) VOL. I	SWAIN (PEOPLES OF THE ANCIENT WORLD) VOL. I	WALLBANK & TAYLOR VOL. I
	193–197 219–234 256–258	156–161 174–180 184–215 226–239 348–352	337–338 436–440 443–444 448–454 460–463 577–579		228–231 241–243 342–349 370–372 402–404
	212–216 235–240 250–255 258–260 292–296 310–333 342–345	215–226 239–276 277–290 296–301 343–347	338 438–439 441–442 464–480 484–487 553–570 585–591		231–238 349 353–357 374–375 382–385 404–408 414–415 422–423
	240–250 260–291 296–309 333–342 346–373	290–296 301–305 306–343 352–413	339–340 480–484 487–498 516–530 570–576 579–585 628–629		349–353 357–359 373–374 375–381 388–391 415–417 423–425 428–429
	373–397 398–401 419–420 433–441 464–466	414–443 457–461 467–475 496–501 506–508 514–516	491–495 498–500 536–537 591–611 613–614		359–361 385–387 409–412 418 425–427 434–441 465–466
	401–414 415–419 420–432 441–452 453–464 466–470	443–456 461–467 475–488 501–506 510–513 516–544	341–342 601–606 610–613 614–628 630–634 637–648 670		361–362 412–413 431–449 460–470 239
	471–491	456 488–496 508–510 544–549	606–609 672		413–414 419 420–422 430–431

WESTERN CIVILIZATION
TO 1500

ON HISTORY

THE STUDY OF HISTORY has not always meant to man what it means to him today. Perhaps at all times, curiosity has induced him to seek to "remember what has happened"; and at some times, the desire to perpetuate great events and noble deeds has impelled him to write down what he witnessed. But it is only our own age, influenced by present-day attitudes, which has looked to history as to a science which can reveal and explain the trends underlying human life and human affairs. It is a question whether or not history can be regarded as a science, and it may well be that future generations will deprecate our efforts. Yet, in the age in which we live, history serves as more than a remembrance of times gone by and of past efforts of man; it serves as a guide for our actions, which shape the future.

Divisions of History. Western historians have divided history into three parts: Ancient, Medieval, and Modern. Into the chapter of Ancient History fall all events up to the decline of the Roman Empire—i.e., approximately up to the fourth or fifth century A.D. Medieval History comprises the events from then until approximately the end of the fifteenth century. What has happened since constitutes Modern History.

This division of history was established centuries ago and has often been challenged. Some feel that it would be more logical to divide history just as we divide our calendar, namely, into a period B.C. (before Christ) and a period A.D. (*anno domini*—year of the Lord). Others would prefer a division according to the main stages

of man's rational development—as expressed by his scientific interests, his organization of labor, and his mastery over natural forces;
they suggest a first, primitive stage which ended approximately in
the fifth century B.C.; a second, higher stage from then to about the
twelfth century A.D.; a third, lasting until the eighteenth century;
and the stage in which we live, which would make up a fourth era.
Still other historians, asserting that the traditional divisions do not
take most of the non-European cultures into consideration, propose
still other "periodizations," the purpose of which would be to make
the divisions meaningful in terms of world history. However, since
dates and periods are not much more than aids contrived to help
organize an unbelievably vast amount of information so that it may
be grasped and interpreted, it may be as well to maintain the
established divisions into Ancient, Medieval, and Modern History;
for this periodization has proved serviceable—at least for Western
civilization. It has an inner justification insofar as it corresponds
to the various stages in the growth of Western civilization; Ancient
History comprises the areas around the Eastern Mediterranean
where the earliest high civilizations flourished; Medieval History
includes all of the European continent; and Modern History encompasses the whole of the globe.

Beginnings of History. More difficult than establishing generally
acceptable divisions of history is the task of fixing a date for the
"beginning" of history. Peculiarly enough, although we constantly
move farther and farther from the earliest civilizations, we come
to learn more and more about them. Remembrance may fade, but,
as the work of archaeologists and historians proceeds, records (carved
in stone or brick, written on pergament or tree bark, or embodied
in utensils for daily use and monuments erected by ancient generations) become increasingly available. Judging by the results of this
work we may say that the beginnings of history must lie somewhere
in the fifth millennium B.C. From about that time date the earliest
artistic achievements worthy of superior cultures, the first decipher-
able records of man's higher rational development, and the beginnings of political and social organizations which deserve to be
called "states."

Can we speak of this period also as the beginning of "Western"
civilization? Obviously not, if by Western civilization we mean
the civilization of the European peoples, i.e., the Germanic, Ro-
mance, and Slavic nations. Their history begins, properly speaking,

only with the medieval period, or at the most with the history of Ancient Greece and Rome. Yet, the more we learn about ancient times, the more we come to realize that a close connection existed between Europe and earlier civilizations in Syria, Mesopotamia, Egypt, and Asia Minor. The heritage of these regions bordering on the Eastern Mediterranean was strongly felt, especially in Greece, and was, indirectly, transmitted by Greece to Western civilization. We may therefore be justified in including some of the Ancient Near East into an account of Western civilization.

Concepts of History. The questions of periodization of history and of the beginnings of history are closely interwoven with our philosophy of history. Many different philosophies have been proposed, reflecting alternatingly the optimism or the pessimism of each age in which they were conceived.

CONCEPTS OF "PROGRESS" AND "RETROGRESSION." The most widely accepted contemporary view postulates "progress." Those who hold this view insist that mankind, or at least Western man, has developed from humble beginnings in ancient times to certain heights in the present and that he will continue to advance. But they have come to realize that this progress is traceable chiefly in man's rational and material life and less so in his ethical and moral development. Actually both Greek and Christian traditions have maintained quite an opposite view, namely, that retrogression rather than progress marks man's development. Thus, the Greeks spoke of the earliest age as a "Golden Age" and considered subsequent stages as less happy; their own age they termed the "Iron Age." Similarly, Jews and Christians have put Paradise at the beginning of their story; later and present stages of mankind have brought suffering and death. Indeed, no solution exists in the Christian view until the end of man and of his history comes with the Day of the Last Judgment. Even rationalist thinkers of recent centuries have been inclined to see primitive man as the "noble man" and have attributed to the coercion exercised by law and civilization of modern ages the blame for having morally corrupted mankind.

CONCEPTS OF CONTINUITY AND CYCLICAL MOVEMENTS. Advocates of progress and retrogression, imaginative as they are, have often ignored the facts taught by history. More sagacious investigators have approached the problem on a more scientific basis. Searching the past, some of them have come to the conclusion that fundamentals have not changed in the stream of history; man is what he has always been, and no more can be traced throughout history than an eternal recurrence of all human aspirations and activities— without beginning, aim, logic, or meaning. Others have maintained that mechanical or economic laws govern the path of history; once these laws are understood, we might even be able to predict future developments. Still others have interpreted history in terms of repetitive cyclical movements, each having its own fulfillment, and all sharing a common pattern. For, according to them, each individual civilization has a beginning, a period of maturity, and an end —like the life cycle of man which encompasses the stages of birth, growth, decline, and death. They have come to the conclusion that Western civilization itself is now declining and that another cycle will shortly supersede it. Lastly, some thinkers have tried to combine this theory of cycles with the philosophy of progress and have insisted that there is a spiral, rather than disconnected cycles, and that the spiral shows an upward direction.

Significance of Historical Studies. All philosophies of history seem to have one thing in common: the assumption that history is not only the story of past events but that it is also a thought process in the present. Herein lies the value of history—a value which, however, can be achieved only through a scientific and sober presentation of facts and through clear and disciplined thought based on these facts. If facts are thus presented and thought thus given, history cannot fail to have meaning for our lives of today and to exercise a powerful influence upon our actions.

CHAPTER I

THE EARLIEST KNOWN CIVILIZATIONS

T HE EARLIEST KNOWN civilizations were developed in regions to
the southeast of Europe. In Europe itself Neolithic (New Stone-
Age) man—ancestor of the various modern races of Western civilization—appeared about 5000 B.C.; but "historical" data about him
do not exist. It is man living in the Near East—in Syria or in the
fertile valleys of the Nile or the Euphrates and Tigris—who furnishes us with the first indications of man's historical existence. By
the time he enters our field of vision—*ca.* 4500 B.C.—man in the
Near East had passed the Stone Age. He had ceased to be dependent
upon hunting and had learned to build houses and to domesticate
certain animals. He knew how to cultivate the soil, to make tools
and weapons, to build ships, to fashion earthenware, and to weave
cloth. He manufactured copper utensils (but he had not yet produced bronze) and he used gold and silver. He had developed
political organizations and laws and had begun to live in towns.
He owned property, produced and traded merchandise, and built
ornamental altars to gods and elaborate tombs for the dead. Records
of that age are extremely scarce. One of the oldest evidences is a
seal in the form of a cylinder, with images on it; its age has been
estimated at about 6500 years, and it was found in Syria somewhat
north of present-day Antioch. Yet, notwithstanding the fact that
Syria was a centrally located area at the crossroads of great trade-
ways and that, possibly, it was there that the first grain was planted
and the first brick made, not even Syria furnishes us with much
additional information. Her two great towns, Aleppo and Damas-

5

cus, are more than 4000 years old, but we know nothing of their beginnings. We must therefore turn to Mesopotamia and Egypt in the fourth millennium in order to get our first glimpses of the precursors of Western civilization and of the oldest civilizations known today.

EGYPT AND SUMER UP TO THE
SECOND MILLENNIUM B.C.

The beginnings of Egyptian and Mesopotamian history go back to the fifth millennium. In both the great river valleys of the Nile and the Tigris-Euphrates, small communities or kingdoms arose. Royal offices—based on law and exercising political, religious, and economic duties—were set up, and with the help of advanced tools and perfected techniques the peoples of both areas learned early to control their natural surroundings to a certain extent. Men in both areas learned to exploit available resources through irrigation and canal building, to increase the fertility of the land so as to make settled agricultural life possible, and to enforce laws which would guarantee the maintenance of these achievements and further the common welfare. They seem to have been acquainted, as early as 4000 B.C., with primitive furnaces in which to melt iron (probably from meteors) and form it into utensils. They developed a calendar, which implied observation of nature; and the art of writing, which implied scholarship. Whether or not significant and direct connections existed between Egypt and Mesopotamia at that time cannot be determined; the parallels are interesting. Yet, Egypt led a fairly isolated existence; owing to her location, she enjoyed a modicum of peace from outside disturbances, except for rare Negro invasions from the south, and still rarer attacks from pirates in the Mediterranean on the Nile Delta. Mesopotamia, on the other hand, found herself in the midst of much action and agitation; she carried on brisk trade with distant regions, experienced much intermingling of races, and suffered from numerous invasions.

Egypt from 3500 to 1800 B.C. Our information about Egypt becomes more detailed for the time after 3500 B.C. The originally independent communities along the Nile began to draw closer to one another, a process of unification began, and first two kingdoms, then—by *ca.* 3200 B.C.—one single kingdom was formed. With it began a period, lasting for more than a thousand years, during which Egypt was to bring forth enduring monuments of a high civilization. This period is divided into two parts: The Early Kingdom (*ca.* 3200–2300 B.C.) and the Middle Kingdom (*ca.* 2000–1800 B.C.).

EARLY KINGDOM. The Early Kingdom begins with the rule of the so-called "First Dynasty," founded by the mythological figure Menes (*ca.* 3200). He resided in Thinis on the middle course of the Nile and is credited with having achieved the process of unification. Under his successors, the country gained in strength and the rulers (called pharaohs) accumulated power, reaching a climax with Cheops (or Khufu, *ca.* 2650 B.C.) of the Fourth Dynasty. By that time, the capital had been moved to Memphis, close to the delta of the Nile; from Memphis, by means of rigorous centralization, the pharaohs exercised strict control over the whole country. Cheops, best known of the great pyramid builders, was hated for his regimentation and harsh exploitation of the people.

The decline of the Early Kingdom set in with Pepi II (*ca.* 2300 B.C.) of the Sixth Dynasty. He extended the sway of Egypt far up the Nile to the second cataract of this river, but during his long rule the central authority of the pharaoh could not be maintained; an autonomous landholding nobility asserted itself and various rebellions of slaves occurred. Disintegration followed.

Governmental and Societal Structure. The pharaoh was identified in earliest times with the falcon-headed sun god Horus, and later with the god Ra. He was ruler and lawgiver and possessed absolute and divine authority. As supreme landlord, he levied elaborately systematized taxes in kind and service, regulated agriculture, and exercised control over the water system which served periodically to irrigate the land with the waters of the Nile. He ruled with the help of a steadily growing bureaucracy (consisting of nobility and priests, but also of numerous scribes recruited from the common people) and of governors (often royal princes), who supervised the execution of the laws in the various districts or "nomes," into which the country was divided. Most of the farmers were free—at least during the early dynasties—and possessed cattle and their own plows and hoes. Later, the nobility succeeded in monopolizing much of the land and cultivated it with the help of slaves. Yet, strict class stratification did not exist; social mobility prevented a rigid structure, and many rose from low to high estate. Women seem to have had an equable place in society; monogamy was the rule, even though the rich occasionally took several wives.

Skills and Learning. Ancient Egypt was comparatively densely populated. There were a number of towns besides Memphis, the capital, and trade and artisanship flourished. Textiles, jewelry, papyrus, glass, and metal objects of gold, silver, and copper were produced. In the schools, scribes instructed children in writing and reading, mathematics (including algebra and geometry), mechanics, astronomy, and medicine, and prepared them for government service. Scholarship was also promoted. As early as about 2800 B.C., a calendar of 365 days per year had been invented. A system of writing was evolved using hieroglyphs (picture writing). At first, the pictures represented only complete words or concepts, but later (before 3000 B.C.) they also acquired symbolic value for individual sounds. For the development of writing, Egypt profited from the availability of the papyrus plant, which provided far more satisfactory material on which to make records than stone, brick, or clay tables, as used elsewhere, could furnish.

Art. The Egyptians have left to posterity an extraordinary artistic heritage. Paintings and masterpieces of sculpture have been found in temples and tombs, and representations on textiles, pottery, and numerous other objects of daily life bear witness to the greatness of Egyptian civilization. No general statement would, however, seem adequate to describe the art of Egypt, for the period of Egypt's artistic creations spanned more than two millennia, and notwithstanding a considerable degree of conservatism the Egyptian taste and approach to beauty changed in the course of the centuries. All one could point out by way of generalization would be, perhaps, a rather persistent trend toward large size, a very special, unvaried calm and dignity in the highly stylized representations, and a particular sense of balance which the paintings, sculptures, and architectural masterpieces of the Egyptians, their temples, columns, and tombs, convey. There persisted throughout an element of symbolism, which reflects the unchanged grandeur of their artistic conceptions and gives their creations a timeless character. Among their extraordinary achievements were the pyramids. The first was constructed *ca.* 3000 years B.C. by Imhotep, adviser, physician, and architect of the pharaoh. Others, more daring in technique, followed. Like the great European cathedrals of the Middle Ages, the pyramids, temples, and tombs probably served economic purposes, creating work in time of need; but this objective was transcended by more important motives. Primarily, pyramids were an expression of the Egyptian attitude toward life, death, and existence beyond death, and they served the glorification of the divine, the exaltation of the pharaoh, and the beautification of man's surroundings.

Agriculture, Industry, Trade, and Law. The majority of the Egyptians lived by means of agriculture. They raised wheat, barley, vegetables, and grapes, as well as cattle and fowl; horses were unknown in the Old and Middle Kingdoms. Of course, agriculture depended upon seasonal irrigation of the desert by the waters of the Nile, and the maintenance of the irrigation system was one of the chief burdens of the farmer. A minority engaged in industry, mined copper on the Sinai peninsula, worked stone and made bricks, and produced cloth and articles of glass and bronze. They made pottery, adorning even simple daily utensils with lovely colors and paintings. They made writing materials out of the papyrus plant growing on the banks of the Nile, and they produced luxury items for the small wealthy class which lived in richly furnished mansions in the towns.

External trade does not seem to have played a large role in Egypt; it was essentially restricted to supplying neighbors, such as Nubia. Some trade connections extended to overseas regions, including Syria and Crete; Syria was a much needed producer of wood from the cedars of the Lebanon. Since money did not exist, barter was the basis of all trade. Laws (eventually codified) regulated both trade and agriculture. A census of the land was repeatedly taken. During the first few dynasties, justice seems to have been dispensed fairly equitably to all classes, but growing stratification of society, which came with more complex living conditions under later dynasties, terminated the practice of equality before the law.

Religion. Religion permeated all phases of Egyptian life. In early times, it concerned itself less with man's ethics than with man's fate—especially after death. Hence the furnishings and splendor of the tombs of kings, nobles, and the rich, and the mummification of their bodies. Later, religion embraced broader aspects of man's spiritual life and inspired literary and artistic works. Eventually, the priests, who had been under the control of the pharaohs and had attended mainly to services in the temples, achieved political power also and prominence such as their brothers in other regions often enjoyed.

The supreme Egyptian divinities were successively Horus, Ra, and Amen—all of them identified with the sun. Osiris, who represented the Nile, held a special place as judge and ruler of the dead; but myths concerning him later became intermingled with those of Horus and Ra. Isis, goddess of motherhood and fertility, was sister and wife of Osiris. Worship of these highest gods was supplemented by veneration of lesser, local deities. Many of the gods were represented as animal or part-animal forms.

MIDDLE KINGDOM. The glory of early Egyptian culture was interrupted when, in the twenty-third century B.C., after the death of Pepi II, central authority broke down and prolonged political troubles ensued. The nobility gained wide autonomy and the country was torn by strife among local rulers. Invasions from the south and north contributed to a worsening of conditions. Devastating famines occurred. Only with the Eleventh and Twelfth Dynasties (*ca.* 2000–1850 B.C.) did peace return. Order was then re-established by a revived strong central authority, and once more the nobles had to obey the royal will and be satisfied with serving as members of an unified administration.

Political and Economic Organization of the Middle Kingdom. In the times of the Eleventh and Twelfth Dynasties, and especially under Pharaoh Amenemhet III, absolutism reached its peak. The capital was moved from Memphis to Thebes, far up the Nile near the center of the country. The central government resumed control over the water supply, lifeline of the country, and extensive irrigation projects were again undertaken. The area of arable land was extended by bringing under cultivation the desert to the southwest of the Nile Delta. A canal was constructed connecting the Nile and the Red Sea and the Nile was made navigable beyond the first cataract. By these measures, as well as by maintaining internal order and expanding the country eastward and southward, the pharaohs succeeded in furthering trade and industry. They even tried to restore the social balance which had been upset in the time of troubles at the end of the third millennium. Although preserving the existing system of slavery, they settled free people on the land, checked the arbitrariness of the nobles, and protected the craftsman.

Cultural Organization. Culture in the Middle Kingdom showed signs of what philosophers of history such as Oswald Spengler or

Arnold Toynbee have considered a "mature" stage of a civilization. Artisanship, painting, and sculpture did not evince the same creative impulses which earlier ages had brought forth. Perhaps we can trace continued perfection of workmanship (especially in the minor arts), less formalism, and greater realism, but new ideas and depth of artistic feeling seem to have been somewhat lacking. More than before, emphasis was placed on size; and attention shifted from art to science. Mathematics and practical activities such as construction and mining flourished. Literature—another expression of a mature society—came to play a wider role. Prose stories, histories, travel accounts, and religious and secular poetry were composed, folk tales were collected, and philosophical works were written. As for religion, the god Amen came to replace Ra, and in connection with his worship religion began to emphasize ethical standards.

Decline. Toward the end of the Twelfth Dynasty, degeneration and effeminacy became increasingly noticeable; military prowess declined. The successors of Amenemhet III proved to be incompetent. Collapse came when foreign invaders, known to history as the Hyksos, attacked the country. Equipped with horses, a resource unknown to the Egyptians, they conquered the land, annihilated the old nobility, and established their own "barbarian" government.

Sumer. A development not unlike that of the Nile Valley took place in the lands enclosed by the Tigris and Euphrates rivers comprising Mesopotamia ("between the rivers"). Here, too, nature favored the early growth of civilization. Probably about 3000 B.C.—somewhat later than in Egypt—the numerous small and independent Mesopotamian communities began to consolidate into one kingdom. This kingdom was dominated by Sumerians (of unknown origin) who had invaded Mesopotamia in the fourth millennium and after whom the country is named "Sumer."

Government. The early government of Sumer did not enjoy the same stability which contemporary Egypt possessed. Central authority remained so weak that individual states, such as Ur, Akkad, and Lagash, retained a large measure of independence. Their government was in the hands of local kings or priests who exercised both economic and political control, though some of them may have been elected by popular assemblies. At various times, one or the other of these local rulers overthrew the central Sumerian government. Thus, at various times the kings of Ur, Lagash, Akkad, or other regions succeeded in making themselves masters of the whole area. But tensions remained and were increased by struggles over economic control—especially of the water supply and irrigation. Moreover, difficulties resulted from the steady influx of nomadic Semitic tribes. These eventually became numerous enough to impose their language upon the entire area.

RULERS. A number of outstanding rulers appeared in Mesopotamia in the course of the third millennium. There was Messanipada (*ca.* 2600 B.C.), during whose reign trade flourished, reaching from the Indian Ocean to the Mediterranean Sea. About a century later reigned Eannatum (*ca.* 2500 B.C.). Originally, his rule encompassed no more than the northern parts of the country; but, being a mighty conqueror, he soon extended his sway over most of the south. Great monuments, temples and sculptures, mark the path of his victorious armies. Perhaps the most famous ruler was the Semitic upstart Sargon of Akkad (*ca.* 2350 B.C.). He put an end to internal strife which had preceded his reign, once more unified Mesopotamia, established firm central authority, and conquered additional territory up to the shores of the Mediterranean. After his death, anarchy returned. Barbarian invasions followed and not until about 2100 B.C. was independence restored to Mesopotamia—this time by the rulers of Ur. Under them—and especially under Dungi or Shulgi (*ca.* 2000 B.C.)—the arts of peace flourished again. Laws were codified and enforced. New canals were built, the irrigation system was repaired, and beautiful temples were erected.

The authority of the Mesopotamian rulers, similar to that of the Egyptian pharaohs, rested upon their claim to a position equal to that of the gods. They were commanders of the army, arbitrators of all political disputes, and, indirectly, owners of all property. They controlled the irrigation system, which was the basis of Mesopotamian prosperity. Their weakness, in contrast to the Egyptians, lay in their failure to develop an effective and reliable bureaucracy. They remained dependent upon local kings, priests, and a feudal nobility—a situation fraught with danger inasmuch as the army was composed of mercenaries who often proved to be untrustworthy.

LEARNING. The Sumerians studied mathematics, astronomy, and medicine. They knew how to alloy metals (adding tin to copper in order to manufacture bronze), and they worked metals into everyday utensils. By 3000 B.C. or thereabouts, they had succeeded in constructing a wheel and could use this invention to build wheeled carriages and improve the manufacturing of pottery. They were skilled construction engineers and built in brick as well as stone. They invented a numerical system and worked out a correct calendar. They also invented a system of writing, called "cuneiform" (wedge-shaped), and with reeds entered their wedge-shaped signs on clay tablets. They practiced a type of cuneiform writing long before 3000 B.C., but in the course of time they simplified the signs, adopted symbols for individual syllables and sounds, and eventually created a remarkable literature. Libraries were built, numerous records were kept, and engraved cylinders serving as seals for documents were produced. Among the works of literature still preserved is the *Epic of Gilgamesh*. It contains legends of gods, kings, and heroic events, some of which show marked similarities to those recorded in the Old Testament.[1] The *Epic of Gilgamesh* constitutes an invaluable source of information about Sumerian life, beliefs, and ethics.

ART. To judge from surviving monuments, the Sumerians were not so proficient as the Egyptians in the fine arts; scarcity of raw materials and economic backwardness may be partly responsible for this fact. Nevertheless, their sense of beauty, their artistic genius, and their craftsmanship are attested by numerous works. They created fine sculptures, they built elaborate palaces and temples, and their metalwork rivalled in beauty and perfection some of the best creations of ancient times. The sound of their music has, of course, vanished, but representations on monuments indicate that the Sumerians appreciated music and possessed instruments such as the lyre and the flute.

COMMERCE AND LAW. The central location of Mesopotamia favored foreign trade. Some historians believe that, at the time of Sargon, Mesopotamian connections extended as far as South America; certainly, traders reached India, Egypt, North Africa, Syria, and Asia Minor. Lacking any type of coined money, they exchanged goods on a barter basis. They exported fine jewelry and woven goods and also tools, arms, and slaves, and they imported metals and other necessary materials. Society was clearly stratified along feudal lines; the population consisted of a priestly caste which enjoyed a privileged position, ordinary citizens who were free, and slaves who in the course of time seem to have become more numerous. A sizable class of artisans and merchants existed, but the largest group

[1] Sections of the Old Testament probably derive from Sumerian sources.

were the peasants; despite the importance of trade, agriculture formed the basis of economic life in Mesopotamia as in Egypt. Law was codified at various times—a most revealing codex, which throws light on social conditions, dates back to about 2000 B.C.

RELIGION. In view of the dominant position of the priest, religion was bound to play an important role in Mesopotamia. Sky, sun, earth, water, and other forces of nature were worshipped. Statues of gods were made and vast pyramidical, stepped buildings—ziggurats—were erected and adorned with temples and sculptures. Religion permeated all thinking in Sumerian culture to the extent that the Sumerians assigned even to abstract ideas (gods, spirits, natural forces, religious concepts) a place in daily life and in the hierarchy of society. The Mesopotamians were preoccupied with questions of immortality and resurrection, but they never reached the depths of transcendental religious thought explored by the Egyptians or the Jews.

OTHER CULTURES BEFORE 2000 B.C.

With the progress of excavations and of the science of archaeology we have come to realize that at least in the third millennium, if not earlier, other advanced civilizations existed. This is not only true for Near Eastern lands, including Syria and Asia Minor, but also for at least one corner of Europe—the island of Crete at the southern end of the Aegean Sea. Available evidence indicates that Crete possessed an organized political life with powerful rulers and that it carried on trade with Asiatic lands and Egypt. In Crete was developed a remarkable architecture, and Cretans (possessing, like the Sumerians, the potter's wheel) produced industrial as well as agricultural goods for exchange. But the remnants so far discovered of Cretan, or "Minoan," civilization for the period before 2000 B.C. are too few to permit a description of life and arts in Crete which would add substantially to our knowledge of those ancient civilizations which can be regarded as forerunners of our own.

CHAPTER II

THE NEAR EAST IN THE
SECOND AND FIRST MILLENNIUM B.C.

AFTER 2000 B.C., new peoples, whose achievements became meaningful to Western civilization, enter our field of vision. History becomes more varied, more dynamic. For the fourth or third millennium, scarcity of sources makes conditions appear static. To be sure, historical evidence may be manifold, consisting of written documents; engravings in stone, clay, and metal; pictorial representations; tools and other objects used in daily life and found in tombs and temples; excavated houses; and a great variety of other evidences of human life, thought, and institutions. Yet, despite the multiplicity of sources, it remains difficult for the historian to gain a feeling of that evolutionary movement, that constant change, which is implied in history. Nothing "is," and everything is in the process of "becoming." From the second millennium onward, our information is, however, more detailed, and we begin to get a dynamic picture.

THE SECOND MILLENNIUM

The geographical area which embraces almost all the known civilizations of the second millennium is still circumscribed by the same triangle within which moved the civilized peoples of earlier times. The points of the triangle lie in Egypt, Mesopotamia, and

Crete. Within the area appear now Babylonians, Hittites, Phoenicians, Hebrews, and Assyrians; only Achaeans or Aegeans—forerunners of Greek civilization—moved outside the triangle. But not all the cultures which developed in the second millennium were indigenous; some were superimposed by invaders from Central Asia and Europe. Numerous migrations took place, and groups speaking Aryan, Semitic, and other tongues intermingled with native peoples and, once settled, produced works and ideas important for the Western world.

The Babylonians. Soon after the turn of the second millennium, Babylonians (so named from Babylon, the Sumerian capital they conquered) appeared. They were Amorites, a Semitic people living west of Mesopotamia, who invaded the country and, about 1950 b.c., put an end to the old Sumerian Empire. The Babylonians seem to have had little culture of their own to offer but, once established, they took over and cultivated the heritage of preceding Sumerian generations. The shattered unity of the area was re-established, a reliable bureaucracy was instituted, and by the time Hammurabi, Babylon's greatest ruler (1792–1749 b.c.), came to the throne, trade and agriculture once more flourished.

Society. Under the Babylonians, we find the structure of society acquiring certain feudal traits; class stratification was pronounced. Priests enjoyed a privileged position. They acted as judges, teachers in the schools, and officials in the bureaucracy. They were among Babylon's foremost students of nature, practiced astrology and divination (by inspecting the entrails of slaughtered animals) and predicted the future. Their superior factual knowledge, their prestige as prophets, and their status as judges and teachers gave them a position in society which, especially after the death of Hammurabi, they could exploit for the sake of gaining political and economic power. A second layer of society was made up by a landholding nobility; its influence rested on its hold on agriculture, which remained the chief source of wealth of Mesopotamia and which prospered again when, owing to royal supervision, irrigation once more functioned and the network of canals was extended. However, the nobility's control of the landed estates was made dependent upon its rendering military or administrative service to the ruler. Then, there was a class of freeholders, who not only farmed their plots but also enjoyed, as in Sumerian times, factual ownership of them. The fourth and last class consisted of slaves.

INDUSTRY AND COMMERCE. Under the protection of a powerful government, industry and trade regained their former importance. City life revived; the production of metal objects, weapons (swords, shields, and bows and arrows), jewelry, woven materials, earthenware, and building materials (especially brick) increased; and although coined money did not yet come into use and trade remained based on barter, elaborate business methods were evolved: "corporations" were organized, prices regulated, and formal sales contracts were engraved on brick. Trade extended to the eastern limits of Asia and to the western parts of the Mediterranean Basin.

LAW. In the eighteenth century B.C., under Hammurabi, a famous law code was drafted. It was based on existing customs and stipulations and regulated all aspects of social life—public affairs, professional affairs, business affairs, and family affairs. It divided the populace into noblemen, freemen, and slaves, setting forth the rights and duties of each class and extending the protection of the law to all—including slaves. It favored monogamy, protected the rights of women, but, in order to encourage a high birth rate, legitimized the offspring of plural wives. With the concept of strict retaliation underlying the ethics of the lawgiver, the code, though it contained some humanitarian and enlightened elements, made many crimes punishable by death.

LEARNING, EDUCATION, AND RELIGION. The Babylonians knew how to construct arches and vaults resting on high columns; and they built more ziggurats. Like all peoples who must sail the seas or cross deserts, they excelled in mathematics and astronomy. They introduced a 354-day calendar and divided the day into twelve hours. They studied geography and medicine. In well-developed schools they taught writing (cuneiform), and their government supervised and regulated many scholarly activities. Their religion prescribed veneration of various gods and goddesses, most of whom were attached to individual localities. Highest among them was Marduk, the local god of the capital, Babylon. Their religion emphasized purity of heart and a belief in immortality.

FALL OF BABYLON. The lack of a strong and independent political power at a time when priests dominated the affairs of the state proved disastrous for Babylon. Military strength declined and the empire was weakened by attacks from north and south. About 1550 B.C., it fell prey to the Hittites and others. Using horse-drawn war chariots, the Hittites overwhelmed the Babylonian foot soldiers, who lacked the mobility and advanced techniques which their enemies possessed.

The Hittites. The Hittites were "barbarians" of Indo-European origin. In the late third millennium they had conquered large parts of Asia Minor, whence they penetrated into Mesopotamia and, subsequently, also seized Syria, then under Egyptian rule. They did not retain full control of Syria, however, but divided it with Egypt and concentrated on ruling Mesopotamia. A warlike people, they seem to have possessed little culture and contributed little more to Mesopotamia than an efficient ruling caste. In Hittite times, Babylonian art and artisanship declined. Life became cruder, even though (as so often in history) the conquerors were eventually conquered by the higher civilization of the defeated people. Like other northern Aryans, the Hittites placed the main emphasis on agriculture; but they also learned to engage in industries (especially those using iron mined in the mountains of their homeland in Asia Minor) and to promote trade. Governmental administration under the Hittites lacked some of the Oriental features which characterized Egyptian, Sumerian, and Semite governments. Kings were not regarded as gods; they had to obey the laws, and, being often mere military chieftains, were bound by reciprocal feudal obligations to their followers. Their laws were not so despotic and barbarous as those of many Orientals. Hittite rule in Mesopotamia lasted until the twelfth century B.C.

The Phoenicians. By the time Hittite strength waned, other peoples, too, had built civilizations which left a permanent imprint on later Western civilization. Among these peoples were the Phoenicians. Their history goes back to the fourth millennium, but we know little about them until the second, when they came successively under Egyptian, Babylonian, and Hittite domination. When Hittite power declined, they gained independence, which lasted, however, only until the ninth century.

COMMERCE. Like other Semitic peoples, the Phoenicians excelled as traders. In this lay their significant role in history, and they owed it largely to the geographical location and the topographical features of their country. In their narrow, mountainous strip of land on the eastern coast of the Mediterranean, they found little opportunity for agriculture; but owing to excellent seaports (notably Sidon and Tyre), they could become, toward the end of the second millennium, the foremost navigators of their time. They established colonies as remote as Cadiz in Spain, traded with Gaul and Britain (from which they imported tin), and through their widespread activities carried Egyptian and Babylonian civilization to many areas of the Mediterranean coasts. Later (*ca.* 850 B.C.), they founded Carthage in North Africa, and it is possible that in the seventh century their sailors rounded the southern tip of Africa.

GENERAL CULTURE. The Phoenicians were famous as dyers of cloth and as workers of metal; they produced fine armor, glass, and pottery, and they provided the Near Eastern empires with much needed timber. But perhaps their chief and most lasting contribution lay in their devising, on the basis of older models, a more practical alphabet (the word "alphabet" is derived from the Phoenician) than other peoples possessed. It was composed of twenty-two letters representing sounds, and it proved a far more efficient tool for writing than hieroglyphs and other elaborate symbols representing whole words or syllables.

Arameans and Hebrews. Besides Babylonians and Phoenicians, two other Semitic peoples merit consideration for their contributions to later Western civilization. One of these peoples were the Arameans. They lived in the area of Damascus and, just as the Phoenicians were renowned for their overseas activities, so they became famous as overland traders. They established contacts between distant parts of the world and therewith initiated cultural interchanges. Their language came to be widely spoken; as far as we know, it was also the language Christ used.

The Hebrews' significance lies, of course, in the influence they exercised upon Western ethics and religion. Originally, they had been, probably, Bedouins living in the dessert. In the course of the first half of the second millennium they settled in Palestine. Some appear to have migrated to Egypt later, and it is presumed that their descendants returned from Egypt and reoccupied Palestine. This country had, in the meantime, fallen to Canaanites and Philistines (from whom the name *Palestine* is derived). A government of a united, yet very small country was established by Saul, and therewith the Hebrew state became a power in the Near East. Saul's successor David (*ca.* 1000 B.C.) conquered Jerusalem, extended the borders of the country to the shores of the Red Sea, and secured the frontiers against foreign invaders. Culturally, David's rule was important for its firm support of prevailing monotheistic trends. He, in turn, was followed by Solomon (*ca.* 950 B.C.). With

Solomon came a period of peace, prosperity, cultural flourishing, building and lively trade, but also of Oriental luxury, arbitrariness, and despotism. After his death, revolts (which had been averted during his lifetime owing to his remarkable wisdom) broke out, and the unity established in Saul's time was destroyed. Nevertheless a foundation had been laid for that body of laws and religious tenets which, in the following centuries, was codified in the "Old Testament."

The Assyrians. Egyptians and Sumerians are important primarily because of their artistic and scholastic legacy, Phoenicians and Arameans because of their economic and intellectual achievements, and Hebrews because of their religious and ethical concepts. The Assyrians, who "enter history" in the last part of the second millennium, added little to these accomplishments; it is their genius as empire builders which taught lessons to later ages. They were related to the Sumerians, and they had settled on the lands along the upper Tigris. As early as the eighteenth century they had freed themselves from Hittite rule, and in the twelfth century they started on a long career of conquest, gaining most of Mesopotamia. Under Tiglath-pileser I (*ca.* 1100 B.C.), they extended their rule westward in the direction of Syria. Though small in number and inferior in culture to their conquered enemies, they understood how to preserve a powerful commonwealth by means of harsh discipline, ruthless destruction of all opposition, constant improvement of military organization and weapons, and effective, bureaucratic administration.

The Aegeans. Recent discoveries have thrown much new light not only on the high civilizations of the Ancient Near East, but also on the earliest high civilization of Europe, the "Aegean" civilization. It comprised southern Greece and the islands and Asiatic littoral of the Aegean Sea. Into this region infiltrated Achaeans, Ionians, and Dorians (peoples about whose origin we have little information), who probably came in waves between 1800 and 1100 B.C. from the Danube region or perhaps even from areas north of the Danube. They spoke Aryan tongues, settled as an upper caste in the newly won territories, and ruled the indigenous peasants, artisans, and traders. The fusion of their traditions with those of native civilizations laid the basis for new and original achievements.

AEGEAN CIVILIZATION. Crete, Mycenae on the Peloponnesus, Troy on the Asiatic continent (which was located close to the Dardanelles), and a number of islands formed major centers of Aegean civilization. Their governments were generally in the hands of kings, who in some places were elective officers. Priests did not play the same role as in Sumer, in Egypt, or among the Semites. The nobles constituted a military caste, retained considerable independence, and lived (e.g., on Crete) in well built stone palaces. Below them in the social scale were free peasants, artisans, and merchants, but unlike Oriental cultures, these groups exercised an influence upon government through popular assemblies. The lowest class was that of slaves, but during the early periods of Aegean civilization they were apparently few in number. Women were treated on a more nearly equal basis with men than in Oriental countries.

Crete. Within the area of Aegean civilization, the island of Crete held a special place. The Minoan culture there reached its peak between 1800 and 1500 B.C. By then, the island was enjoying its most prosperous times. It benefited from connections with Egypt and Phoenicia—an advantage which Cretan merchants, experienced as they were in seafaring, retained for many centuries. Large towns developed, and the ruling classes lived in luxury, as demonstrated by the art treasures which have been preserved. Vast palaces were built (the most famous being that of the legendary king Minos at Knossos) and were adorned with graceful sculptures and frescoes. Skillful craftsmen excelled in making fine jewelry and beautifully decorated pottery. Music seems to have flourished, but achievements in literature were apparently insignificant; great works in philosophy or religion from Crete are not known; only records of business transactions have come down to us.

Mycenae. Around 1400 B.C., Crete was invaded from the Greek mainland and became part of Mycenaean culture—named after the town of Mycenae. This culture, which lasted until about 1184 B.C. (the year now generally accepted as the date of the destruction of Homeric Troy), was the result of cross-fertilization between the civilization of the Greek mainland and that of Crete and other islands in the Aegean. Mighty buildings (among which stands out the acropolis of Mycenae itself) and extravagantly furnished tombs were created, which were embellished with exquisite works of painting and sculpture and which have yielded huge treasures of silver, gold, and bronze objects, such as decorated armor and jewelry. Windows and bathrooms exhibit technical proficiency. Shipbuilding, trade, and travel flourished; Mycenaean traders could

ANCIENT NEAR EAST

NUBIA extended from
First Cataract of the Nile
southward to Khartoum
in the Sudan

be found, like the Phoenicians, anywhere from the Pillars of Hercules (modern Gibraltar) to the littorals of the Black Sea and the Gulf of Persia. Mycenaean civilization also produced legends of mythical heroes, which have been transmitted to us by Greek writers. Religion (with some rites of probably northern origin) did not assume, however, forms which could contribute to the spiritual treasures of later generations.

DECLINE OF AEGEAN CIVILIZATION. In the twelfth century, new invasions of Greece took place. By that time, Aegean civilization was declining. Overpopulation in essentially agricultural Greece had led to incessant internal strife; control of the seaways had weakened; and, eventually, an attack on Troy ruined the manpower resources of the region. Troy, rich owing to the wealth of nearby silver mines and the control of trade via the Dardanelles into the Marmara and Black seas, was captured and destroyed (a fate encountered several times in its history). But the losses of the Greeks (or "Achaeans," as Homer calls them) were great, and when a northern people, the so-called "Dorians," arrived, the Aegeans were unable to withstand the attack and were conquered.

The Dorians attained no memorable civilization; they brought physical prowess, intelligence, and some rather primitive religious cults from the north; they proved incapable, though, of raising the culture they found in the conquered territories to greater heights. Feudal traits in the existing institutions were strengthened; freemen, however, began to decrease in proportion to slaves, and gradually freedom disappeared. Eventually, bitter internal struggles again rent the whole area of Greece and the Aegean islands.

The Egyptians. While one civilization after another came and disappeared in the course of the second millennium, Egypt, despite many disasters, continued to play a constant and unique role. The Hyksos invaders of the eighteenth century never gained sufficient influence to break the great traditions of the country. Exercising their power from the delta of the Nile, they could never claim the domination of all Egypt.

THE "NEW KINGDOM." After two hundred years, the Hyksos rulers were overthrown by Ahmose I of Thebes (*ca.* 1570 B.C.) and the ancient unified kingdom was revived. Ahmose restored Thebes, far south of Memphis and the delta, as the capital of the realm, and with him began the "New Kingdom." He replaced the mercenaries by an indigenous army, and with its help and that of a rejuvenated bureaucracy began to rule firmly the two kingdoms of Upper and Lower Egypt. He enforced strict obedience and, after having gained full control, he turned to external conquests. His work was continued by outstanding successors, including Thutmose III (fifteenth century B.C.), Amenhotep III and Ikhnaton (both in the fourteenth century B.C.), and Ramses II (thirteenth century B.C.).

Thutmose III and Amenhotep III. Under Thutmose III and Amenhotep III, the absolute rule of the pharaohs was vigorously maintained. The bureaucracy governed the country according to established and codified law that represented the will of the pharaohs; and the nobility, the priests, and the army were compelled to obey their orders. The foreigners, who as mercenaries and slaves had infiltrated the country under Hyksos rule, were settled on the land and, having gained a modicum of security, were absorbed. The frontiers of the country were pushed southward and eastward, war booty flowed into the treasury, and lively trade relations were established with Hittites, Phoenicians, and numerous tribes of Syria, Crete, and other regions. Luxury once more increased, and the construction of monumental temples, great palaces, and splendid tombs again bore witness to the might and pretensions of the pharaohs.

Ikhnaton. The imprint of strong rulers is often such that subsequent generations direct their whole attention to preserving their work, whereby timely reforms are precluded. In Egypt, such conservatism was furthered after Amenhotep III's death by the priests of the ram-headed god Amen, who in the time of the Hyksos had come to be identified with the sun; and priests exercised steadily growing political influence. The dangers threatening the country were, however, recognized by Ikhnaton, a pharaoh who ruled during the late fourteenth century. Sympathetic to, and stimulated by, foreign examples which were known to him through the contacts built up in the preceding century, he sponsored radical reforms. He moved the capital northward of Thebes to Akhetaton (modern Tell-el-Amarna, halfway down the Nile toward Memphis), redivided the country, and gave up those conquests (especially overseas) which constituted a drain rather than a gain. He interested himself in the lower strata of the population, had new towns laid out, and distributed land among free peasants and serfs. He sponsored schools and learning, furthered the sciences, and inspired literary work and the fine arts, which exhibited new and original trends in the direction of greater naturalism. He turned his attention also to questions of religion and priesthood; he abolished the cult of Amen and, with the exception of Osiris, judge of the dead, that of the various local deities; and he instituted the veneration of a single god, Aton, who was related to the former Ra, the sun disk. In doing so, he pursued the political objective of reducing priestly power and the economic aim of appropriating priestly wealth; but he seems to have been prompted also by new spiritual insights. The Aton cult tended in the direction of monotheism, and its ethics were of a higher order than those connected with Horus and Amen.

DECLINE OF THE NEW KINGDOM. Preoccupied with such vast schemes, Ikhnaton neglected other aspects of his office. He failed to defend the frontiers vigorously enough and lost not only useless but also valuable territories. The army was allowed to deteriorate; bureaucratic regulations superabounded, excessive luxury and corruption spread; and a dependable ruling group to continue Ikhnaton's work was not recruited. After his early death, disorganization and decadence set in. More border lands fell to invaders; many of his reforms (including the cult of Aton) were abolished; and under Tutankhamen, last ruler of the Eighteenth Dynasty, the Amen priests regained their old power. To be sure, Egypt still succeeded for another two hundred years in defending herself against outside enemies; and particularly Ramses II's rule (1292–1225 B.C.) marked a revival of Egyptian power and splendor. After concluding an alliance with the Hittites, Ramses was even able to regain some of the territorial losses. But then, beginning in the time of Ramses III of the Twentieth Dynasty (1195–1167), the security of the country came to be again dependent upon mercenary troops. Soon thereafter, Egypt fell prey, first to these hired foreign soldiers, and subsequently to successive conquerors from the outside. With the year 1085 B.C., the "New Kingdom" came to an end.

THE FIRST MILLENNIUM

The history of the Near East in the last millennium before Christ is most absorbing in itself, but it has less immediate significance for Western civilization than earlier periods. In the first place, Europe—through Greece—emancipated herself from Eastern influ-

ences and, notwithstanding cultural contacts with Eastern neighbors, charted a course of her own. In the second place, much of
the former vitality of the East, expressed in its manifold artistic
creations, was lost in the last millennium B.C. What caused such a
decline is a subject of dispute. Perhaps, after thousands of years, the
Eastern civilizations had "grown old"; or material changes, perhaps
in climate or soil, had undermined their strength. Perhaps, originality and initiative had shifted to other peoples, who had learned
from Eastern experiences and overshadowed their masters. Or perhaps, by sheer accident, great creative minds became scarce in the
Orient.

Egypt. The decline of civilization in the Near East is very noticeable in Egypt. Under the domination of Assyrians, Babylonians,
and Persians, who for long periods made themselves masters of the
country, few great works (judging from those that have come
down to our own times) were produced. Only in the seventh and
sixth centuries B.C., when Egypt had regained independence and
the Twenty-Sixth Dynasty—Psamtik I and his successors—ruled,
did a certain revival occur. Arts, in particular sculpture, flourished
again; metal goods and pottery of considerable beauty were again
created; and the study of natural sciences progressed. The country
prospered under a capable administration and its influence was felt
beyond its borders. Foreign settlers, especially Greeks, came and
contributed their share to the revival. Yet, spiritual vigor, marked
by originality in thought and artistic creation as opposed to imitation of old models, can scarcely be detected.

Assyria. Of somewhat more immediate interest for the growth
of Western civilization than the history of the Nile Valley during
the first millennium is that of Mesopotamia. There, the Assyrians
(who after the death of Tiglath-pileser I had experienced two
centuries of eclipse) once more awoke to the challenge of great
tasks. In the ninth century they invaded Syria and conquered
Damascus and Phoenicia; in the eighth century, they captured
Babylon and seized Israel. In the seventh century while successfully defending their northern boundaries against threatening Cim-
merians, they extended the southern boundary of their empire deep
into Egypt. They established their capital in Mesopotamia and,
after various changes, finally fixed it at Nineveh.

ASSYRIAN CULTURE. The Assyrians have not left a great cultural
heritage. Schools and libraries flourished during the reigns of

Tiglath-pileser III and Sargon II in the eighth century and Sennacherib and Ashurbanipal in the seventh century, but they depended upon the Babylonian religious and scholarly legacy. However, the Assyrians did develop some remarkable new forms of sculpture and, especially, bas-reliefs; in their animal plastics, they evinced a realism very distinct from the geometric patterns and symbolic representations of other peoples, and these plastics have remained one of the glories of the ancient world. The Assyrians also achieved considerable technical proficiency, as evinced by the aqueducts which they constructed.

ASSYRIAN POLITICAL ORGANIZATION. Of continued importance, too, was the example set by the Assyrians in the art of empire-building. Constituting but a small minority in their dominions, they had to face special tasks. They solved them by force. A powerful, brutal military establishment was built up; weapons—many made of iron —were developed to perfection; and by terroristic tactics obedience was enforced. The administration was put into the hands of harsh, efficient military governors, solely responsible to the king and drawn either from the princes of subdued nations or from the Assyrian nobility. Military measures to hold down the conquered peoples were combined with shrewd economic policies: foreign merchants were invited; transit trade was aided; and taxes and tolls were fixed at a moderate level so as to stimulate commerce and enrich the treasury of the king. Coins were used as a means of exchange to replace the more primitive barter system.

The Chaldaeans. The vast expansion of their dominions proved to be the undoing of the Assyrians. Having reached out too far, they could not maintain their empire. Constant rebellions of individual provincial administrators occurred, and between 650 and 520 B.C. Egyptians, Babylonians, Persians, and other peoples freed themselves from their hated rulers. In the course of the revolts, the Assyrian towns and many of their art treasures were destroyed. In 612 B.C., Nineveh was taken by the Babylonians (or "Chaldaeans" or Aramaic origin) and razed.

The Chaldaeans, who founded what has come to be known as the Neo-Babylonian empire, soon in turn extended their sway beyond Mesopotamia into Judaea and Syria. Their rule lasted little more than fifty years. Yet, under Nabopolassar and Nebuchadrezzar, they inaugurated an era of remarkable accomplishments. It was again a period of elaborate building; mighty fortifications and palaces, with the famous Hanging Gardens of Babylon, were erected; new works of construction for the improvement of agriculture were built; and scientific investigations, especially in astronomy, were successfully carried on.

The Persians. The next masters of Mesopotamia were the Persians, a people whose ruling caste belonged to the Indo-European group. They defeated their neighbors, the Lydians, who had once participated with them in revolts against the Assyrians and who in the meantime had tried to build an empire of their own, and they took prisoner Lydia's fabulously rich King Croesus. He had ruled a country extending from the Black and Aegean seas to the Mediterranean in the south and the Halys River in the east—a country of considerable culture and wealth, in which the first coined money, made of gold, was used. The Persians also defeated their other former allies, the Medes. Moreover, they subdued the Greek cities on the Aegean coast of Asia Minor. Finally, in 539 B.C., they conquered Babylon.

PERSIAN CULTURE. Thereafter, during the span of almost a century, a succession of four Persian kings—Cyrus II, Cambyses II, Darius I, and Xerxes—ruled over one of the most powerful and civilized empires. The arts, inspired by the examples of many regions, flourished; Babylonian and Assyrian traditions were preserved. A religion, preached about 600 B.C. by Zoroaster (Zarathustra) and his disciples, emerged which embodied ideas of immortality, truth, and justice and explained the world in terms of an eternal struggle between good and evil. It combined these ideas with ethical concepts that paralleled in many respects the tenets of Christianity and Confucianism. It became Persia's official religion.

PERSIAN GOVERNMENT. The Persian kings established their capital at Susa, not far from the Persian Gulf. Their realms extended from the borders of India to Egypt—the latter country being conquered in 525 B.C. by Cambyses, who made himself pharaoh. As customary among most Oriental peoples, the will of the king reigned supreme; in Persia it was enforced on both land and sea by highly trained military forces and by a special guard of "Ten Thousand Immortals." The empire was subdivided, and it was administered by a carefully organized bureaucracy which, at least from the time of Darius on, was subjected to strict supervision by the central government. Through travelling inspectors, who also dispensed justice, the government checked on the proper execution of the king's laws.

As opposed to the Assyrian rule by force, the Persians showed a co-operative attitude toward conquered nations, allowing them a measure of native law, their own officials, and a light tax load. Great postal roads were constructed, the canal connecting the Nile and the Red Sea was restored, a good monetary system was introduced, and lively commerce developed again. Nevertheless, the bureaucratic empire degenerated until it was conquered in 331 B.C. by Alexander the Great.

The Hebrews. The various civilizations of the Ancient Near East have made lasting contributions to the Western world in the fields of art, handicraft, science, law, and government. In the area of religious beliefs (aside from Persia and the teachings of her great philosopher Zoroaster) only one country had a permanent—and, indeed, overwhelming—influence on Western civilization: the land of the Hebrews. Under Solomon's successors, the Jewish country had been first divided into two parts—Judaea and Israel—and then each part was torn by internal quarrels and by wars between the two regions. In 732 B.C., after conquering Damascus, the Assyrians made the two Hebrew states tributary and, ten years later, took over the entire northern region of Israel. The southern division, Judaea, was conquered in 586 B.C. by the Babylonians, and Jerusalem was destroyed. Many inhabitants, especially the rich, influential, and skilled men, were abducted, and their children were not allowed to return until the times of the Persians, who gave them permission to do so in 536 B.C.

It was just during this period of political dissolution that a unique religious codex was evolved. From Elijah in the ninth century B.C., Isaiah and Jeremiah in the eighth and seventh centuries, and Ezekiel and Daniel in the sixth century, to Ezra in the fourth century, a long line of great religious leaders and prophets preached unwaveringly the idea of a single god, Yahweh, a god of justice, sometimes even of mercy, who punished the sinful and rewarded those who acted rightfully and obeyed the divine law. Though constantly challenged by worshippers of foreign gods and foreign customs, they staunchly upheld monotheistic views. In the course of the centuries their teachings were written down and eventually formed the content of the Old Testament, which, together with Christian teachings, ever since has constituted not only the chief code of ethics of Western civilization but also the main inspiration in Western creative arts and literature.

CHAPTER III

GREECE BEFORE 500 B.C.

WIDE VARIETY DISTINGUISHES Greek civilization from almost any preceding or subsequent civilization in Europe or the Near East. Seldom has the Western world seen such a blossoming of thought and art as the tiny Greek country produced within the short span of about two or three centuries.

What accounts for the splendor of Greece? An infinity of factors must have contributed to it: the advantages of a moderate climate; the mixtures of peoples; the diversity in living conditions made possible by the presence, within a small area, of mountains, plains, valleys, inlets of the sea, and islands; the inspiration derived from the beauty of land and seascape; the contacts with old civilizations; the economic opportunities afforded by a geographic location favorable to trade; and many other advantages. Yet, the decisive element must have been the extraordinary number of individual men and women of genius. Among scores who might be named were Socrates, Plato, Aristotle; Homer, Sophocles, Aristophanes, Sappho, Anacreon, Pindar; Phidias, Praxiteles; Pericles, Alexander, Thucydides; Pythagoras, Thales, Hippocrates, and Euclid.

THE POLITICAL SCENE

The political history of Greece centers primarily around two towns—Athens and Sparta—and their institutions. Other towns (e.g., Corinth and Thebes), the various islands off the coast of Asia Minor, and the colonies (e.g., Syracuse in Sicily, Tarentum in southern Italy, and Panticapaeum on the Black Sea) essentially followed the lead of the two main centers. Athens and Sparta never created empires such as the Assyrians, Babylonians, and others had built earlier, or such as Rome was to establish later. It was on a very limited scale that they developed the various forms of political organization which were to become models for all future generations.

The Greek World. The Greek world comprised not only Greece proper, including Macedonia, but numerous islands of the Aegean Sea and many other, more distant territories as well. Greek colonization of these outlying parts occurred in waves, beginning in the ninth century B.C. and reaching one climax late in the eighth century and another at the end of the seventh. The Greek colonizers, leaving their overpopulated territory to seek arable land and opportunities to trade, established settlements to the west in Sicily, southern Italy, southern France, and Spain; to the south in Egypt and along the whole northern coast of Africa; to the east on the shores of Asia Minor; and to the north around the Black Sea. In their new homes, they engaged not only in agriculture and trade, but also, as in Spain or Asia Minor, in the exploitation of mineral wealth. The colonies were independent of their various mother states, but they maintained close contact with them. They spread Greek ideas and distributed Greek products abroad, and took back to Greece foreign ideas and foreign merchandise.

Government and Evolution of Governmental Structure. The Greeks created governments very different from Oriental despotism. Their monarchies were limited and short-lived, and even their tyrannies were moderate. A landed nobility, such as the Assyrians or Persians had evolved, did not secure a lasting hold on their governments, nor did their priests ever gain much political power. Ultimately many of their states achieved a measure of democracy.

MONARCHY AND OLIGARCHY. In the beginnings of Greek history the chief system of government was monarchical. The king represented tribal unity; he was *primus inter pares* within a tribe, and each tribe was based on, and derived its cohesion from, "a sense of common ancestry, common language, and common religion, a realization of common military and economic interests and a geographical proximity."[1] The king exercised political leadership and

[1] Jacobsen and Lipman, *Political Science* (College Outlines Series, rev. ed. 1955), pp. 708.

performed priestly functions. Even when not actually elected by assemblies of freemen, he was generally subject to their control. By the eighth century, however, the royal powers had declined, for the nobles had gained control of the land (which had been under communal ownership) and had seized the direction of public affairs. Soon, they, too, had to share some of their new power with the commercial classes, which benefited from the fact that the geographical location of Greece was highly favorable to trade. An oligarchy based on birth as well as wealth, they took over the government.

TYRANNY. Greek political institutions underwent a further change when trade expansion stimulated the growth of industry and thereby increased not only the number of unskilled laborers (e.g., men to work the mines) but also the ranks of the skilled artisans. Soon, the artisans, growing discontented with their status, joined the impoverished peasants in demanding political and social reforms. In some parts of Greece, the ensuing conflicts resulted in government by tyrants; during the seventh and sixth centuries B.C., "tyrannical" rule prevailed not only in various states of Greece proper, but also in a number of colonies and on many Aegean islands. Among the famous tyrants were Periander of Corinth, Polycrates of Samos, and Peisistratus of Athens.

Frequently the tyrants were wealthy upstarts. Having seized the government by illegal means and violence, they needed broad support in order to maintain themselves in power and therefore often catered to the lower classes. They enacted laws advantageous to the masses, divided estates among needy peasants (whereby they simultaneously deprived their aristocratic opponents of their chief resources), and instituted programs to encourage trade. They thus provided work for the artisans as well as profits for their merchant friends. Dependent as they were upon commerce, the tyrants generally preferred peace to war. They took pride in the embellishment of towns, displayed pomp, and entertained their subjects with theatrical performances and with games (at which valuable prizes were distributed). However, inasmuch as they ruled without a legal basis or traditional sanction, they often had to contend with bitter opposition and were driven to commit acts of brutality. Their governments rarely endured for more than one generation. Some of the tyrants were murdered or exiled; others retained power until death, but, for lack of capable heirs, failed to establish dynasties.

Eventually, the whole concept of tyranny, associated as it was with illegality and arbitrariness, took on an opprobrious connotation.

THE CITY-STATE OR POLIS. Another form of government, the city-state (or *polis*), was to become important in subsequent Grecian history. Originally, a polis constituted an "association of kinsmen," a community of houses, shops, and markets, built around a fortification or a temple. But this narrow character of a polis was soon lost; the city-state expanded to include neighboring hamlets, and eventually losing much of its significance as a practical political unit, it became an ideal concept which embraced all free men of the same kinship, no matter whether they lived in the main town, in neighboring dependencies, or in far-away independent colonies. Common rights of citizenship, inherited by generation after generation, and bonds of sentiment provided a lasting link between the members of a polis. Occasionally, several city-states would form a federation, choose a famous shrine at which to venerate a common deity and under its protection seek place among the members, co-operation against enemies, and commercial prosperity.

Two city-states, Sparta and Athens, stand out as examples of Greek governmental structure. Each made momentous contributions to Western civilization.

Sparta. Sparta was a town in Lacedaemonia on the Peloponnesus. Lacedaemonia's rugged coast provided no good harbor facilities, and Sparta's citizens depended upon agricultural work. Sparta had flourished in Mycenaean times; Homer names it as the home of Menelaus and Helena. Probably in the eleventh century, it had fallen to Dorian invaders who deprived the natives of the rights to the land and forced them to cultivate the soil for the benefit of the new masters. In the eighth century, they extended their sway into neighboring Messenia. Numerous revolts followed; however, by the beginning of the sixth century the conquerors had succeeded in imposing a political system which guaranteed stability. The establishment of this system has been popularly attributed to a legendary king, Lycurgus, but more probably it developed gradually. It laid the basis for Sparta's power. Toward the end of the sixth century, a Peloponnesian League under Spartan leadership was established.

SOCIAL CLASSES. The Spartan system provided for rigorous social stratification. The privileged ruling class (or *Spartiates*), including less than a tenth of the population, was composed of descendants of the Dorian invaders. Though divided into various groups, they were all free citizens. A second class was made up of the *perioeci*, descendants largely of the native population before the Doric invasion. They were small landholders, tradesmen, and artisans. They enjoyed rights of citizenship only in their home communities, but were subject to military service. The third, or largest class, was that of the *helots*, who belonged to the conquered peoples and had the status of serfs. They were attached to the soil, compelled to till the land and surrender to the Spartiate landowners a sizable share of their produce as well as to provide auxiliary military service. They could be freed (especially for bravery in war), in which case they entered the *perioeci* class. Lastly, there were slaves, mostly prisoners of war, who were the property of their masters and could be bought and sold.

EDUCATION. A martial spirit permeated the life of the ruling caste, the Spartiates. It was instilled in them during their childhood. Infants who appeared to be physically unfit were killed shortly after birth—a practice which eventually resulted in a dangerous shortage of population. At the age of seven, male children were taken from home and reared by the state. They underwent rigorous military training, were hardened to hunger and pain, and learned to share an equal, de-individualized life. At the age of thirty, they became full citizens and thereafter had to devote themselves to military and administrative service; trade was forbidden to them as something beneath their dignity. They could marry only with the consent of the state. Not until the age of sixty were they given full freedom and were permitted to become members of a "Council of the Old."

POLITICAL AND MILITARY INSTITUTIONS. Sparta had two kings, who belonged to two different ancient royal houses and were chosen by lot. They acted primarily as priests and as generals of the army. Depending upon their ability they could exercise more or less influence. Chief political power lay with the Council of the Old which initiated legislation and exercised supreme administrative and judicial functions. A popular Assembly, composed of Spartiates over thirty years of age, had the right of final approval for measures proposed by the Council of the Old. In the course of the sixth century, an elective office—that of five "ephors"—gained importance. Gradually, the ephors superseded in power the Council of the Old and even assumed the right to remove a king.

In accordance with its social and economic status, each class contributed its share to the military strength of the country. The army was a well-disciplined, heavily equipped force. It not only served in foreign wars but attended also to police duties, maintaining the existing class structure and holding the subjected segments of the population in check.

ECONOMIC AND CULTURAL LIFE. The militaristic character of the state did not prevent Sparta from bringing forth substantial economic and spiritual achievements. A number of facts reflect the economic achievements. Since Lacedaemonia possessed iron deposits, clay, and timber, the *perioeci* manufactured iron goods and a great variety of pottery and wooden articles. These products were artistic as well as practical. Trade was carried on with the Greek cities in Asia Minor and even with distant Persia, and both production and commerce were stimulated by fairs and festivals held periodically in Sparta which brought together peoples from many regions.

As to cultural advances, they were reflected in music and poetry. The arts of singing and dancing were cultivated, and Homer's works were memorized by children. Outstanding Spartan poets were Alcman, a Lydian who lived in Sparta, and Tyrtaeus.

Athens. Athens (in Attica) had the advantage of a favorable location. Excellent port facilities for overseas trade were available; the countryside was rich in grain, olives, wine, and honey; and deposits of iron, clay, and silver existed in the vicinity. Resources also included marble quarries in the homeland and gold mines in the colonies. Since the Doric invaders, who had captured Sparta, had spared Attica, which lay off the main path leading to the Peloponnesus, the Ionians who had settled in Attica before the fifteenth century B.C. (and who were of the same race as those who inhabited the islands of the Aegean and many cities of Asia Minor) retained control of the land.

SOCIAL CLASSES. There were in Athens the usual classes—the nobility, merchants, artisans, and peasants. Slaves were proportionately more numerous than in Sparta, but it was a rather common practice for Athenians to free their slaves. In addition, there were the "metics"—foreigners welcomed to Attica for their skills or trading interests and allowed to live there permanently, though without enjoying the rights of citizens.

POLITICAL INSTITUTIONS. In early times Athens, like other Greek towns, was ruled by kings. In the course of the centuries, a well-established landholding nobility wrested control from them and reduced the royal office to a chiefly representative function—that of high priest. Men elected from the ranks of the nobility itself, called "archons," took over the high judicial and administrative tasks. The influence of the archons, too, declined when, at the beginning of the seventh century, their number was fixed at nine and their term of office was limited to one year. Eventually, the nobility was in turn deprived of its privileged status by the prosperous merchants. Despite these shifts in governmental power, landed wealth remained, however, the principal factor determining the political status of an individual citizen.

SOCIAL CHANGE AND REFORM IN ATHENS. The changing phases of Athenian institutions and their foundations (birth, landed property, monetary wealth) contrasted with the more static conditions of agricultural, militaristic Sparta. Various constitutions and law codes, drawn up to increase the rights of the lower strata, gave the institutions of Athens a fluidity lacking in those of Sparta.

Reforms under Draco and Solon. Late in the seventh century, friction and social upheaval were rife. In order to stem the tide of class struggles and preserve the virtues of early times, a severe code of laws was issued under the guidance of the aristocrat, Draco; it prescribed the death penalty for many offenses against the *status quo*.[2] But within less than a generation, in 594 B.C., changes were introduced by Solon. He had excelled as a general, merchant, and poet. Despite his aristocratic background, he sought to break the power of the landed aristocracy by limiting the amount of land anyone could own and by extending civil rights to the lower classes. He divided the citizenry into four tribes (excluding metics and slaves) on the basis of the income an individual derived from the land he owned. Every citizen's status within his tribe determined the taxes he had to pay and the rank he held in the various formations of the well-trained, powerful army. Only the first of these tribes had the privilege of providing the archons; but men from the three upper classes could be appointed to a newly established "Council of 400," and all four classes had the right to participate in the popular Assembly, which discussed matters brought before it by the Council and which elected the archons. Archonate, Council, and Assembly were supplemented by a People's Court, which supervised the administration of the archons and constituted an element of "checks and balances." Besides making these constitutional ar-

---

[2] Actually, we know little about Draco, even though his name has become synonymous with harsh, cruel laws.

rangements, Solon also eased the peasants' debts, abolished enslavement for debt, and made provisions for the admittance of non-Athenians to citizenship. He promoted industry by laws furthering exports and restricting imports, encouraged silver mining, and established a uniform currency and a simplified system of weights and measures.

Reforms under Peisistratus. Solon's reforms were as inadequate as those of Draco to give the desired stability to the Athenian state. Within thirty years, Peisistratus (who was related to Solon) made himself tyrant of Athens. Like all tyrants, he gained power with the help of hired soldiers, judicious bribery, and the buttressing of his authority through promoting the interests of the lower classes and filling all key offices with his merchant friends. Yet, at least formally, Peisistratus maintained Solon's laws. He continued Solon's attacks on the old aristocracy by dividing estates; he supported the merchants by building roads, encouraging the immigration of metics, and establishing colonies; and he courted favor with the masses through festivals and through the adornment of the city with palaces and temples. His sons, who succeeded to power, were, however, incompetent: one was murdered (514 B.C.), the other expelled (510 B.C.). Even though Athens had enjoyed prosperity under Peisistratus and his sons, this revolt against the tyrants was celebrated in subsequent centuries as a testimonial to the Athenian love of freedom.

Reforms under Cleisthenes. After the disappearance of the tyrants, the process of democratization went on. Attempts of the aristocracy to regain power were defeated, and around 508 B.C., under the influence of the statesman Cleisthenes, another reorganization took place. The four-class system based on heredity, property, and tribal connections was maintained only for purposes of taxation; otherwise, it was replaced by new divisions. These were so devised as to reduce the importance of old ties of kinship and local allegiance, to prevent a resurgence of the aristocracy, and to build among all citizens new loyalties to the state as a whole. Citizenship rights were further extended; every male over twenty years of age received the right to vote in the Popular Assembly. The highest offices, as well as membership in the Council (increased to 500), were opened to all citizens and evenly distributed among the various divisions; archons, members of the Council, and military leaders were chosen by lot, and all offices were made subject to rapid rotation. Moreover, *ostracism* was introduced, whereby the voters could impose a ten-year period of honorable exile on anyone whom they regarded as a threat to the existing political order.

THE SOCIAL AND CULTURAL SCENE

In the period before 500 B.C., the Greeks not only laid foundations for new types of political organizations, but also economically and culturally struck out on paths of their own; and just as their political thought has retained validity for more than two thousand years, so have many of their philosophical and scientific speculations and most of their artistic creations stood the test of time. Perhaps it is the rationality and logic of their thinking combined with their sensitivity and taste that account for the merits of their work. Ionians and Dorians, homeland, islands, and colonies—they all contributed to the legacy which Greece has left. Every part took pride in the contributions of any other part, thus bearing witness to the common aspirations which animated the Greek world and to the firm links which, despite the variety of traditions and institutions, bound it together.

Economic and Social Conditions. A varied and for a long time healthy economy, built up by an industrious and (in regard to material luxuries) not too demanding people, underlay the cultural evolution of Greece. Agricultural pursuits were of prime importance, but industrial production and trade grew as time went on. They soon constituted, together with language and culture, the most vital link connecting the various parts of the Greek world; however, they also contributed to wars, not only with foreign competitors but also among the Greek states themselves.

INDUSTRY AND AGRICULTURE. The growth of an advanced economy was stimulated by the introduction of a monetary system. The Greeks did not rely on barter, but early took over from the Lydians the policy of minting money. Their currency consisted generally of silver coins. Their sound monetary system played a vital role in the expansion of their commerce and of large-scale manufacturing. Soon the Greeks excelled in the making of fine pottery (often beautifully decorated), of iron goods, bronze articles, woolen cloth, and marble. Their shipbuilding industry grew similarly; ports were constructed and sciences necessary for seafaring were studied. Mining operations were expanded and unavailable minerals were introduced from Asia Minor as well as from Spain, Britain, and elsewhere. Business methods improved; merchants organized trading companies and sponsored progressive commercial laws. Breaking the Phoenician monopoly on overseas trade, they began to export large quantities of Grecian products and to import other products, especially grain, fish, and raw materials. Substantial profits were derived from the slave trade.

Agriculture adapted itself to commercial needs. Since increased specialization and manufacturing made Greece, and particularly Athens, dependent upon imports and exports and since arable land was scarce, early diversification of agriculture could not be maintained. The production of wheat, flax, barley, fruits, vegetables, and cattle (a type of production suited to a small population) had to give way to the specialized production of olives and wine for export.

SOCIETY. Increased trade was largely responsible for the shifting of governmental power in commercial centers from landholding aristocrats to wealthy merchants, from peasants to artisans; it led to a decline of conservatism and to progressive democratization. Wherever commerce flourished, it speeded up social mobility, i.e., the transfer of people from one class to another. Moreover, it contributed to changes in the status of the various classes. On the one hand, although the old aristocratic families often retained their special standing, the merchants and even the artisans came to share in various privileges. On the other hand, the conditions of peasants and slaves deteriorated; farmers had a hard time with a growing burden of debts; slaves (perhaps a quarter of the population) generally led an increasingly miserable existence in the mines, in the shipyards, on the farms, and in household service.

The Humanities. The same diversity characteristic of the political and social life of the Greeks was also a feature of their philosophy and art. The early great thinkers and artists (almost all of whom were children of the sixth century) were citizens of many different parts of the Greek world—products of widely differing conditions. Some of them came from Attica or the Peloponnesus; others came from the colonies. Most of the leading figures came from the Ionian islands or the Asiatic coast, where they had been in touch with Oriental traditions.

PHILOSOPHY AND SCIENCE. The Greeks made no formal distinction between philosophical thought and natural sciences; the term "philosophy" included not merely speculative theory, but practical observations and discoveries in the fields of mathematics, physics, astronomy, medicine, and zoology. Among the greatest philosophers was Pythagoras, who was born in Samos and brought up in southern Italy. Though we possess no actual writings of his, we know that he was not only one of the most outstanding mathematicians of all times, but also an eminent idealistic philosopher, who through his mystic teachings strove to reform the moral, social, and political life of his compatriots. Three other great scientists and philosophers came from Miletus: Thales, Anaximenes, and Anaximander. They believed that the universe is composed of a single, basic substance which they sought to identify. Thales concluded that it must be water, Anaximenes that it is air, and Anaximander that it is a prime, eternal, and indestructible matter which, by incessant movement, gives birth to every object and living being and to which everything returns. In the course of their speculations all three arrived at many insights of importance for the evolution of science. Thus, Thales' astronomical observations led to a correct prediction of an eclipse of the sun in 585 B.C., and Anaximander's geographical descriptions furnished information required for an understanding of the size and locations of the various countries and their distances on the globe. Still other scientist-philosophers of lasting importance were Xenophanes of Colophon and Heraclitus of Ephesus. Like the philosophers from Miletus, Xenophanes searched for an identification of prime matter, believing it to be earth; and he speculated about the shape of the universe, which he conceived as spherical. He also occupied himself with religion, postulating one god—a universal deity as opposed to the numerous anthropomorphic deities of popular Greek worship. Heraclitus, on the other hand, emphasized the purely rational character of life and nature. He conceived all phenomena to be subject to a law, or *logos,* which is above and in all things. He insisted that the world is in constant flux, that there is eternal change, and that everything leads through war or struggle to its own opposite and back to its original form. This theory of change was rejected by Parmenides, most famous of the metaphysicians, who taught that things either are or are not, but that there is no "becoming," no eternal change.

ART. The profound and noble character of Greek thought was matched by the beauty of Greek art. During the seventh and early sixth century B.C., Greek sculpture, with its stylized geometrical patterns influenced by northern traditions, combined rhythm and strength, while the paintings on Greek vases, despite a similar formalism, evinced a special grace and simplicity in conception. The temples, too, reflected strict, mathematical thought; yet, despite the perfection of their proportions, they did not leave the impression of artificiality, but of an intuitive sense of harmony. The earliest style of temples emphasized the severe, simple Doric column; it was followed by more elaborate Ionic patterns (which were influenced by Asiatic models), and eventually by the light and cheerful Corinthian style. The temples were adorned with friezes with elaborate bas-reliefs and high-reliefs; they also contained murals, none of which, however, have survived. Though built to honor the gods, the temples did not reach up toward Heaven like the great Gothic cathedrals of the Middle Ages. Even when large in size, they stood firm, close to the ground. Horizontal, not vertical, lines predominated and mirrored the special interest of the Greeks in the affairs of the world.

LITERATURE. The same concern with worldly and human affairs which Greek art shows, helps to explain the trend of Greek literature, which flourished in an age when nothing comparable was created by other civilizations. The Greeks were proud of their language; it constituted a link between their widespread lands, and it set them apart from the outside world of barbarians—people who spoke a variety of tongues (bar-bar). Its sound and rhythm possess a special beauty. The verse meters created by the Greeks set standards for thousands of years; and their lyrics, praising wine, music, and love, their epics in honor of gods, battles, and heroic deeds, and their prose describing or criticizing the events of the day, enchant, inspire, and "evoke awe and pity." Transcending the immediate subject matter with which their literary works deal, they constitute eternal comments on the meaning of man's life and fate. Two Homeric epics (the *Iliad* and the *Odyssey*) have come down to us from the ninth or eighth century B.C. Only slightly later, Hesiod composed his *Theogony,* a cosmogony based on Greek myths about creation. The same author wrote *Works and Days,* a book which contains descriptions of contemporary modes of living. Probably from the seventh century B.C. date Aesop's *Fables* and Sappho's and Alcaeus' lyrics. Other, somewhat later, Greek poets include Anacreon of Samos, likewise famous for lyrical poetry, and Tyrtaeus of Sparta and Solon of Athens—noted for battle hymns as well as tender songs. Most of these works possess strong individualistic traits, which distinguish them from the known literature of earlier civilizations.

MUSIC. From the myth of Orpheus, whose playing wrested concessions even from the god of the nether world, we gain some inkling of the place music held in ancient Greece and the power it exercised on the Greek mind. Unfortunately, only a few fragments of actual compositions have come down to us. We know that the rhythms were similar to those in poetry, that choral song was cherished, that voices were often accompanied by instruments, but that polyphonic music was rarely produced. Among the instruments were the lyre, the flute, the harp, and cymbals. Music was considered a fundamental part of a man's education, and it played a central role at the great Greek festivals, when prizes were given to the best musicians.

GAMES AND FESTIVALS. In their philosophy, the Greeks strove to achieve the aim of self-knowledge, *gnothi seauton;* in their arts, they sought harmony, *kalon kàgathon.* Both ideals inspired their games and festivals. These meant far more than mere amusement or sports or than a stimulus of trade or than an opportunity for statesmen to negotiate with friends and enemies. They were expressions of the Greek view of life, of their unity, of their belief in the beauty of mind as well as body. For the duration of the games, a general truce reigned; from all parts of the Hellenic world, participants came under safe conduct and found hospitality—this most sacred obligation of a Greek citizen. We can trace such festivals from the eighth century on. Perhaps the most famous are the Panhellenic Olympic games and the games of Corinth and Delphi. The feast days brought competition in athletics, music, dancing, and poetry; and at the beginning and end of each festival, religious celebrations were held. Vase paintings, sculptures, and surviving literature bear witness to the significance of the Greek games.

Religion. The Greeks adhered to a polytheistic religion. Their gods were superhuman rather than divine, and there was little emphasis on ethics or morals. The religious thought of the Greeks constitutes, indeed, the one area of human experience in which subsequent ages have had little to learn from them; only art and literature have gained from the imagination displayed by their mythology.

DEITIES. The chief deities were Zeus, Athena, Aphrodite, and others—most of them well known from Homer's works. Some of the traditions connected with them were handed down from Mycenaean times; others go back to Oriental precedents. With the passage of time, new gods were added—among them Dionysus, the god of wine. Aside from these gods who were supposed to dwell on the Olympus, there were half gods, like Hercules, and numerous local deities. Each family honored some one god as its special protector, and many communities were devoted to the service of a parochial god, in honor of whom the leading aristocrat performed a priestly office.

MYSTERY CULTS. A greater depth of religious experience was achieved through various mystery cults, which sprang up in the sixth century and later. In an atmosphere conducive to transcendental speculations, the members of such cults attempted to fathom the problems of death, immortality, and transmigration of the soul, and to search for the meaning and aim of life and the path to virtue. As in a number of Oriental religions, the cults included various magical rites, devoted especially to deities such as Demeter and Dionysus, or even to legendary mortals such as the singer Orpheus. They were celebrated only by small groups of individuals initiated in secret ceremonies. Often the worshippers indulged not only in religious speculations, but also in ecstatic and licentious rituals.

ORACLES. Greek religious ceremonies were supplemented by the practice of divination. Priests inspected the entrails of animal sacrifices and predicted the outcome of public or private enterprises. "Oracles" were consulted. The most famous oracle was that near Delphi in central Greece, which gained a unique power in the national life because it was consulted not only in numerous private matters (such as family problems) but also in grave political issues. A priestess (the Pythia), sitting on a tripod over the vapors of the Delphian hot springs, uttered sentences; these were induced by trances, simulated or real, or prompted by—generally rather conservative—priests of a nearby temple of Apollo. Many of the Pythia's pronouncements were enigmatic and contradictory; yet they did influence decisions at various turning points in Greek history—during the Persian Wars and on other occasions.

EARLY GREECE

CHAPTER IV

GREECE IN THE FIFTH CENTURY

BEFORE THE FIFTH CENTURY, most of the outstanding achievements of Greek civilization originated on the Ionian islands and in the Greek cities on the Asiatic shores of the Aegean Sea. In the fifth century, however, the cultural center of Greece shifted to Athens. It was there that, during the "Periclean Age," architecture, literature, history, and philosophy came to flourish; and it was then that Greek culture reached its culminating glory and that noble thought turned the experience of life into a treasure for all times. But the fifth century was also a century of strife and human anguish. It opened with wars between Greece and Persia and it closed with civil wars. It witnessed the triumph of Athenian democracy and the work of Athens' greatest statesman, Pericles, but it also brought the imperialism of Athens, her infringement on the liberties of weaker communities, her exploitation of her allies, and the ultimate collapse of her democracy. It saw the heroism of the Greeks in a struggle with an outside enemy, but also their brutality and perfidy in a struggle with each other. Like every society, Greece offered a twofold, contradictory picture.

THE POLITICAL SCENE

The reality of Greece's political life, even in the times of Greek glory, has provided the world with anything but a model for imitation. The parochial political institutions of Greece have little purport for countries with huge masses of citizens and for ages shaped by modern technology, because they were adapted to the needs of small city-states where a comparatively large percentage of the citizenry could play an active part in national policies, personally contribute to lawmaking, personally take a share in the administration, and have personal access to those in power. But Greek institutions did not even fulfill adequately their purpose within the framework of Greek surroundings. The *agora,* or market place, was in no way like the serene atmosphere associated with Socrates; it was the El Dorado of slavedrivers and of dirty, loud-mouthed peddlers accustomed to cheating customers. The law court, with corrupt and venal judges, was a center of perjury. The politician betrayed his country and the orator used his talents for furthering selfish aims. Women were discriminated against in every field. Homosexuality was a common and accepted form of behavior. Noble temples and public buildings were surrounded by ugly, ill-smelling houses, and the artist entrusted with erecting inspiring monuments absconded with public funds. Even in wartime, as in the desperate struggle against Persia, the individual only seldom subordinated his interests to the common good.

The Persian Wars (492–479 B.C.). The fifth century began with a great enterprise in the area of foreign affairs: war with Persia. The Persian Empire had grown during the preceding hundred years and had conquered Lydia and incorporated various Ionian towns in Asia Minor and on the islands of the Aegean. The Persian king had then turned his attention farther westward and, primarily to protect his realms against possible Scythian invasions from the north, had reached out beyond the Bosporus into Europe proper—into the Danube region and into central Thrace. This second step alarmed the Greeks even more than the subjugation of their Aegean compatriots. Many Greek city-states drew closer together; following the example of Sparta and her Peloponnesian League, they formed other leagues, and co-operation was also established between the two leading Greek centers—Sparta and Athens.

PRELIMINARIES OF WAR. The next phase in the rivalry between Greece and Persia was a revolt of the Ionian cities which, incited by the tyrant of Miletus, rebelled despite the fact that Persian rule was rather mild. They received naval aid from Athens, but were defeated; and the Persians, provoked and warned, thereupon (in 492 B.C.) again sent an army across the Hellespont—this time in order to occupy the coast of Thrace and subdue Macedonia. In the following year, they dispatched ambassadors to Athens and other continental Greek cities and demanded their submission. The envoys met with a firm refusal; indeed, Sparta as well as Athens committed the outrage of murdering the Persian envoys, and war resulted. Perhaps this war was not the great decision between East and West for the salvation of culture which ancient Greek and many modern writers have tried to make of it; perhaps the battles were not so gigantic, fearful, and brilliant as they have been portrayed in Greek accounts; and perhaps many Greeks did not consider Persian rule as so grave a threat. Indeed, there were numerous Greek collaborators, often whole city-states, and the Persians would probably never have attacked, had they not felt sure of Greek disunity. But at least the descriptions of the struggle of small, divided Greece against mighty Persia have been an inspiration for all future generations. Countless were the acts of devotion and selfless fulfillment of duty reported to us, and both ordinary citizens and leaders accomplished memorable deeds.

First Campaign. Immediately upon rejecting Persian demands, the Athenians began to prepare for war. Under the leadership of a capable general and statesman, Miltiades, they increased their military forces, improved their tactical strength through a reform of their infantry formation (the phalanx), and entered into negotiations with Sparta for aid. When in 490 b.c. the Persians launched the expected attack, they were ready. Without waiting for Sparta, which was busy with a festival, they counterattacked and, in the famous battle of Marathon, completely defeated the Persians.

Intermission. A ten-year period of respite ensued. During this time, revolts following the death of the great Persian king Darius in 486 b.c. and the accession of his son Xerxes delayed Persian preparations for a new invasion, which were not completed until 480 b.c. In the meantime, Athens, too, prepared anew for war. Leadership passed from the hands of Miltiades into those of two younger statesmen: Aristides, defender of old aristocratic ideals, and Themistocles, a partisan of democratic trends. Both worked devotedly, but increasingly at cross purposes, until, in 483 b.c., Aristides was ostracized. A man of integrity but of perhaps somewhat narrow views, he had advocated conservative military defenses, while Themistocles, ambitious and enterprising, had favored the risky and expensive strategy of relying for the defense of Athens upon the construction of a powerful navy.

SECOND CAMPAIGN. The new invasion by the Persians occurred in 480 B.C. The first encounter was that at the Thermopylae, a mountain pass leading into central Greece, where the mighty Persian army was stopped by a small band of Greek defenders under the Spartan king Leonidas. Together with three hundred men, Leonidas sacrificed his life in one of the most renowned battles of history. Once the Thermopylae were cleared, the Persians moved on into Attica, devastated the countryside, and forced the Athenians to give up their capital, which was burned. At this juncture, the Spartans, supreme commanders on land, advocated withdrawal south to the Isthmus of Corinth; but the Athenians objected and, as supreme commanders on the sea, risked a naval battle. At Salamis, they succeeded in destroying the Persian fleet and forced the Persians to retreat. The following year saw the defeat of the Persian rear guard at Plataea by the Spartan phalanx under Pausanias, and another Athenian maritime victory, this time at Mycale. A number of Ionian cities were liberated, and in 478 B.C. control of the straits dividing Asia and Europe was gained with the capture of Byzantium. Although no peace was concluded, this ended the struggle in Europe.

Postwar Period (478–445 B.C.). War had brought ruin to large areas of the Greek mainland. Material reconstruction, both of buildings and agriculture proceeded quickly, but social difficulties (stimulated by a leveling process which the Persian Wars, like all wars, had brought about) could not be so promptly adjusted. They caused a long period of troubles in Sparta, and they led to thoroughgoing changes in Athens.

SPARTA. After the end of the Persian wars, Sparta, though spared from invasion during the war, found her institutions threatened. The danger came from two sides: from some people who intended to replace the existing order by one-man-rule; and from others who, on the contrary, sought broad, democratic forms. Those desiring one-man-rule were led by Pausanias who, after having achieved victories in the field, aspired at making himself monarch. For this purpose, he even negotiated with the former enemy. But his attempts came to naught. He was convicted, and his compatriots let him starve in a temple in which he had sought refuge. The democratic forces were also defeated. Following a terrible earthquake in

464 B.C., they instigated a revolt of the helots against the Spartiates. With great difficulty, the revolt was crushed. Altogether, it took Sparta more than fifteen years to restore the traditional order.

ATHENS. In contrast to Sparta, Athens did not maintain her existing social structure intact. Her path led to further democratization. Significantly, this was achieved regardless of whether defenders of the aristocratic faction or protagonists of the popular forces were at the helm.

Leadership in Athens. The leading figures in Athens after the Persian wars were Themistocles, Aristides, Cimon, and, finally, Pericles. Themistocles led the work of reconstruction for almost six years, but he was ostracized in 472 B.C. and eventually went to Persia, where he died, a traitor to the Greek cause. Aristides, who dominated the political scene after Themistocles' departure, died five years later, and was followed in the leadership of the aristocratic party by Cimon. Cimon was a very capable man, but one of excessive ambition, and he, too, was ostracized—in 461 B.C. He survived his exile and returned, but in 449 B.C. died during a campaign which he led against Persia. The next important figure was Pericles. He came from a leading aristocratic family and was a man of energy and ability, of broad knowledge, and of taste. A good orator, with marked demagogic talents, he allied himself with the democratic forces. To be sure, Athenian democracy remained imperfect in his time, and men of wealth and high birth kept their hold on the direction of affairs; but there was a constant drive toward broad popular rights.

Democracy in Athens. Under the leadership of these four men, a transformation of Athenian institutions took place. Citizenship rights were extended to almost all the free population—which meant that, since women, metics, and slaves were not included, about a quarter of the total population came to enjoy such rights. The voting age was lowered, and the Assembly, which met not less than forty times a year, gained in influence. Government positions were opened to all citizens. The court system was improved; the aristocratic Areopagus, the highest court in Athens, was stripped of many of its administrative functions, and these were given to the Council. Magistrates were made liable for their acts; and the practice of paying officials for their services was instituted so that others besides the wealthy could hold public office. Payments were made even to those who merely attended a public festival.

Internal Policies. Public works were undertaken, such as the construction of temples and other buildings, whereby many of the unemployed were afforded an opportunity to earn a living. The tax system was changed to improve the lot of the poorer classes of the population. The fortifications of the town were strengthened, the navy was rebuilt, and new harbor facilities at Piraeus were installed. Military bases were erected in the lands of the allies, and the power thus gained was used to promote the economic policies of the state.

Economic Policies. Athenian trade expanded. The competition of commercial towns, such as Aegina, was eliminated by force; that of others, like Corinth, was reduced by boycotts and other economic measures. Athens secured domination of the straits leading to the Black Sea, founded new colonies, such as Amphipolis in Thrace and various towns in Sicily, and settled citizens abroad. Unlike the Spartans the Athenians pursued a policy, not of self-sufficiency, but of expansion. More and more of their agriculture was oriented to serve the needs of external commerce. They concentrated on the production of wine, fruits, olives, and oil. But grain (much of which), like the large quantities of fish needed, came from the Black Sea region) was imported; so, too, was lumber. Exports included metals, marble, wood, and ceramic products.

External Policies. Dependence upon foreign trade and a desire for economic dominance necessitated an aggressive external policy. The period between the Persian and the Peloponnesian wars constituted an era of Athenian imperialism. Exploiting the prevalent anti-Persian sentiments, Athens induced various Greek city-states and Aegean towns to form the "Delian League" and, taking the lead in it, gradually secured almost complete control over them. Although a constitution provided for proportionate rights for all members, Athens imposed arbitrary taxes, assumed jurisdiction over the allies, and refused to grant citizenship to the peoples of the empire; in Pericles' time, the government had the funds of the League (which had originally been deposited in Delos) transferred to Athens and soon began to use them, as if they were tributes, to finance Athenian shipbuilding programs and pay the wages of Athenian workmen. In a variety of ways, Athens exploited the League as a means of expanding Athenian economic influence.

Force supplemented persuasion and bribery whenever necessary to help Athens impose her will on the allies. Having defeated, in 466 B.C., Persia's Phoenician allies in the naval battle of Eurymedon and secured dominance in the Aegean Sea and in large areas of the eastern Mediterranean, Athens gradually extended her power into Euboea, stationed a garrison in the town of Megara on the Gulf of Corinth, seized the island of Aegina, sent troops into Boeotia, and eventually also took possession of the Chersonese. But this ruthless expansionist policy engendered hatred, fear, and, finally, one war after another. First, there came a new campaign against the Persians. It was brought to a successful conclusion when, after victories gained by Cimon, Pericles signed a peace treaty which ended Persian interference in Greek affairs. Then, there came other campaigns—these directed in turn against Greek sister states. They, too, brought some successes, as Boeotia and Phocis were subdued. But in 447 B.C., Athens suffered at Coronea a grave defeat which induced a number of tributary towns to secede. Two years later, Pericles was forced to conclude a thirty-year truce. Athens lost some of her conquests on the continent, but retained superiority on the seas and with it domination of her colonies and the Ionian islands.

Prelude to Civil War (445 B.C.–431 B.C.). The truce did not last; quickly, Athens resumed her aggressive policies. Fearing new revolts within the empire and the continued enmity of Sparta, the Athenians sought new alliances, erected new military bases, and accumulated a large war fund. They finished their main fortifications, the "long walls," which connected the city with its life nerve, the harbor of Piraeus. Pericles even attempted to have a wall built across the Isthmus north of Corinth, planning to combine defense aims with the objective of gaining control of the trade in the Gulf of Corinth and reducing the city itself. He also supported rebellions against Corinth. When, in retaliation, Corinth encouraged a revolt of the town of Potidaea against Athens, Pericles attacked and defeated the Corinthian forces in battle. Such infringements not only endangered the liberty of others but also violated the truce established in 445 B.C.; and when, in addition, Athens engaged in an economic boycott of the small town of Megara, Sparta (joined by Corinth, Thebes, and other Greek towns) assumed the role of defender of "Hellenic liberty." In 431 B.C., war began.

The Peloponnesian War (431–404 B.C.). Pericles had long prepared for war, militarily and financially. The war was bound to decide the issue of hegemony in Greece, and Pericles seems to have welcomed rather than feared the decision. Actually, the war did decide the issue—and the decision turned against Athens.

FIRST DECADE OF WAR. The Peloponnesians started by invading Attica. Pericles suffered the devastation of the Attican countryside and, according to plan, evacuated the inhabitants behind the new city walls. There, they could be provisioned with the help of the supplies which Athenian supremacy on the seas was to guarantee. The plan worked, and it is probable that new invasions thereafter would have been equally unsuccessful. But as a result of the over-crowded conditions in Athens, a terrible plague broke out in 430 B.C., killing a third of the population, with Pericles himself a victim in 429 B.C. During the ensuing years, even though Pericles was succeeded by Cleon who was an able leader from the artisan class and won a number of victories, the power and prestige of Athens steadily deteriorated. A loss of manpower weakened the army and the food supply became scarce; eventually, the Spartan general Brasidas inflicted on Athens a severe defeat in the sea battle off Amphipolis (in Thrace), in which Cleon was killed.

DEFEAT OF ATHENS. Following Cleon's death, the aristocratic party under Nicias gained the upper hand in Athens. This party favored peace and in 421 B.C. succeeded in concluding a ten-year truce. But even as Greece began to recover from the ravages of war, the Athenians broke this truce, just as they had broken the truce of 445 B.C. Persuaded to do so by the brilliant but unscrupulous young aristocrat and demagogue Alcibiades, they resumed their imperialistic policies. Not only did they seize the island of Melos, which was a Peloponnesian colony (after the island surrendered, they slaughtered nearly all the defenders), but, disregarding the warnings of Nicias they also undertook to support a revolt in Sicily against a regime friendly to Sparta and Corinth. Straining all their reserves, they equipped a mighty expedition and sent it to Sicily. The expedition failed in an attack on Syracuse in which the entire Athenian army, including Nicias, perished. In the meantime, Alcibiades had deserted to the enemy and, following his counsel, the Spartans resumed their attacks. They established a permanent base of operations in the Attican countryside, secured financial assistance from Persia, and won a number of victories. In the face of disaster, Athens restored oligarchic rule and welcomed the return of Alcibiades. His organizing ability and audacity enabled Athens to gain a few new victories, but a last great success in a naval battle (406 B.C.) near the islands of Arginusae was followed the next year by a crushing defeat of the Athenians at Aegospotami by the Spartan general Lysander. The Spartans then moved on to Athens, laid siege to the city, and forced its surrender. In the name of "liberty for Greece," they destroyed its military power and defenses and reorganized its government. They installed a new oligarchic regime under thirty pro-Spartan "tyrants" and put a garrison in the town. Thus ended the war.

Reorganization in Athens. The Thirty Tyrants, led by the aristocrat Critias, ruled with brutality. They exiled or killed their opponents, and not until 403 B.C. could a revived democratic faction under a new leader, Thrasybulus, get rid of them. Even then, democracy, which had proved disastrous for Athens and the rest of Greece, was not fully restored; nor could plans advocated by Thrasybulus for a revival of the Athenian empire be carried out, for Sparta as well as Thebes kept a close watch over their defeated enemy.

GREEK THOUGHT AND ART

Not until the fourth century when great thinkers were to appear who described and evaluated the experiences of Greece in politics, finance, and administration, and who thought through the art of government and gave lasting meaning to the ephemeral—not until then could the political life of ancient Greece become a treasure for all times. Greek law did not provide standards to emulate, for the Greeks, unlike the Hebrews or the Romans, failed to develop either on the basis of religious and ethical concepts or on the basis of practical precedents a code of law which could serve as a permanent guide. Their legal decisions were arrived at individually, "ad personam," in line with momentary trends, convictions, and judicial inquiry. It is therefore to the fields of science, philosophy, art, and literature that we must turn in order to find the greatness of fifth-century Greece: the evolution of the scientific concept of the "atom"; the Hippocratic standard for the medical profession; the Socratic rules of ethics and self-understanding; the perfection of the Greek ideal of harmony in art; and the achievements of the dramatists. It is through such achievements that Greece has served, uniquely, all future generations.

Science. Greek scientists of the fifth century, instead of treading new paths, carried on the search for reality and for the origin of life along the lines laid down by their predecessors. Like their predecessors, they failed to develop instruments (on which modern science is accustomed to rely) but concentrated, as before, on speculation and logical mathematical deduction rather than on observation.

MATHEMATICS AND PHYSICS. Notwithstanding the shortcomings of their methodology, the achievements of the Greeks were remarkable—especially in arithmetic, geometry, astronomy, and cosmogony. Speculating on matter and the substance of the universe, Anaxagoras, the first great philosophy teacher in Athens, formulated remarkably clear ideas about the nature of the sun. He also taught that all matter consists of an infinite number of minute particles, and that a spiritual force imposes order upon their chaotic arrangement. His contemporary, Zeno of Elea, preoccupied with Heraclitus' law of eternal change, expounded the opposed belief in the world's essential stability. A third contemporary, Empedocles of Agrigentum in Italy, continued the search of Thales and Anaximenes for the "building stones" of nature. Instead of the oversimplified answers of his predecessors, he suggested the hypothesis that four "elements" constitute these materials and that by alternatingly separating and uniting they produce the various forms of matter. Toward the end of the century, a fourth great scientist, Democritus, took a step beyond these theories. He postulated that many different, indivisible material particles, or "atoms," make up the cosmos, and that even the soul consists of such particles.

MEDICINE. Interest in the study of nature, as reflected in these investigations, led to remarkable advances in medicine. Hippocrates (d. 377 B.C.) was the outstanding physician, whose great contribution consisted of his denial of supernatural causes of disease and his advocacy of the study of natural remedies. He showed the way toward scientific diagnosis of illness; he gave expression to the highest ethics of the medical profession.

Philosophy. Speculation about the nature of the universe was followed by systematic inquiry into the nature of man. Empedocles, who was not only a scientist but also a teacher and a prophet, taught a religious philosophy based on belief in transmigration of the soul. More influential than his teachings were those of the "Sophists"; and even more significant were the ideas of Socrates.

THE SOPHISTS. The Sophists sought to gain self-knowledge and self-fulfillment. Their most outstanding exponent was Protagoras, who considered man the measure of all things; he therefore subordinated the demand for ethical behavior to the right of man to develop his gifts and fulfill his aspirations. Later, the Sophists became famous for their critical ability and their skill in rhetoric and shrewd dialectics.

SOCRATES. The tendency of the Sophists to fence with words and to use ingenious arguments in their logic was condemned by Socrates who was the most famous of the philosophers, though known to us only through the writings of others. He taught men that they should doubt unsupported statements and should develop their ability to analyze them critically; he insisted on the clarification of ideas by means of rational answers to rational questions. He searched for absolutes—for truth, virtue, beauty, and ethical standards. He emphasized the Greek ideal of self-control, and he believed in a divine principle and an unfailing inner voice which can direct man's actions along the path of morality. Although devoted to the laws of Athens and serving dutifully in various civic capacities, he was accused of impiety and corrupting the youth; and in 399 B.C., in his seventieth year, he was convicted and forced to take poison.

Education. In the fifth century B.C., Greece had many schools. Children, especially those of the wealthy, were taught to read and write. Boys often had broad educational opportunities, learning to recite poetry and to master at least simple problems in arithmetic, to play instruments or sing, to develop physical health and skill through sports and games, to study rhetoric and prepare themselves not only for a profession or trade but also for the responsibilities of citizenship. Girls, generally, received little education beyond reading and writing, except for gymnastic training and instruction in household arts and music; marriage was considered their goal. A woman could obtain a divorce, though, and in such a case was even allowed to keep her property. Women seldom participated in public affairs. They had none of the privileges of citizenship but all could attend theaters and festivals, which provided the Greeks with an important means of general education.

Arts. Much of the art of Greece has disappeared, some as recently as the times of Turkish rule in Greece. Yet, quite a few original works have survived, and these together with descriptions, architectural ruins, and reconstructions and Roman copies give us a feeling for the beauty and majesty of fifth-century Greek art. The most notable examples are the public buildings of Periclean Athens (especially the Acropolis with its Parthenon, Propylaea, and Erechtheum); the buildings around the *agora;* the theaters; and the town walls. These structures were built with a rare sensitivity for natural surroundings, purposeful use, and esthetic value. The Greeks combined mathematical calculation with artistic design to give their works strength and grace and to make them live up to their ideal of harmony. Among the supreme artists who created these works were the architects Callicrates and Mnesicles; the painter Polygnotus, whose work, has, however, perished (we know of him through written tradition); and the great sculptors, who used marble, bronze, gold, and ivory—especially Phidias (renowned for his statues of Athena in Athens and of Zeus in Olympia), Myron (who created the "Discus Thrower"), and Paeonius (who sculptured a famous *Nike*, "Winged Victory"). Many of the sculptures evince a higher degree of attention to anatomical details and closeness to nature than those of earlier centuries, but they do so without losing the "ethos," i.e., the character and transcending ideal nature which marked the more symbolic expressions of past ages. Deep artistic feeling also distinguished Greek creations in the minor arts, such as coins and gems.

Music and Literature. Just as important as the artistic works of Greece in the fifth century B.C. were its great written works. In the preceding centuries music and literature were closely connected, but now a gradual separation of the two took place.

Music. Music began to develop its own independent characteristics. A musical theory was created, scales, rhythms, and harmonies were worked out, and notation was invented. The range of instruments increased.

Poetry. Some of the simplicity and purity of early Greek poetry, which was speaking directly to the listener, was lost in the more elaborate and artful works of the poets of the fifth century. Yet, this was the century of Pindar, most celebrated writer of odes, whose influence on subsequent ages was perhaps greater than that of any other Greek poet except Homer. Still, Greek poetry contributed less than history and the drama to the great literary achievements of the time.

History. History was conceived in terms of both art and science; it was both subjective and objective, both a dramatic art and a cold investigation of impersonal forces, both a study of necessity and a portrayal of human character. The two foremost Greek historians were Herodotus and Thucydides. Herodotus came to Greece from

Asia Minor and travelled widely, remaining only a few years in Athens. In his *Historia* ("Inquiry") he described the Persian Wars "that the great deeds be not forgotten." By endeavoring to find unbiased sources and maintaining an objective attitude about his own countrymen, he hoped to teach future generations a moral lesson. His works include also accounts of his travels. Thucydides was a native Athenian who led an unsuccessful expedition during the Peloponnesian War, was consequently exiled, and then wrote a history of that war down to 411 B.C. He, too, despite his admiration for Athens, retained a large measure of objectivity concerning the Athenians and their institutions—realizing that greed and lust for power are as potent factors in the course of events as natural forces and idealism. He analyzed events scientifically, presented his story dramatically, adorned it through the eloquence of his style; and he has left a legacy which has served as a model for all later generations.

DRAMA. The drama flourished as shown in the works of three great writers of tragedy: Aeschylus (*The Persians, Orestes*), Sophocles (*Oedipus Tyrannus, Antigone*), and Euripides (*Iphigenia in Tauris, Medea*). Only a few works of each of these have survived; and the works of other dramatists of this period have been lost. Greek drama, containing also some of the most beautiful lyrical passages ever written, portrays the eternal conflict between Fate and Man; it comments in critical or approving tones on matters of the day and on eternal problems; it analyzes character, guilt, and punishment, and, like the religious festivals during which the plays were presented, it seeks to purify the souls of men by evoking in them fear, awe, and pity. Its form was strictly prescribed: as a rule, a play had to exhibit unity of time, place, and action; there were no more than three actors on the stage, in addition to a chorus (reflecting the earlier close connection between music and poetry), whose task it was to comment on the meaning of events.

Greek comedy differed from tragedy in its approach, but not in its essence. Thus, the greatest master of Greek comedy—Aristophanes (*The Birds, Clouds, Lysistrata*)—merely chose a lighter form to arouse in his audience the same emotions and attitudes as tragedy. Greek comedy often emphasized criticism of the contemporary society. The works of Aristophanes reflected his deep insight into human behavior as it exists at all times—a universal quality which has given his comedies their permanent value, even though much of their significance for events of his time may escape the modern reader.

The Art of War. Since the fifth century b.c. was a century of conflict, it is not surprising that, while the arts of peace flourished, the Greeks also became proficient in the arts of war. Sparta, Athens, Thebes, Macedonia, and other states of Greece developed their own techniques of combat. They perfected their heavy-armed infantry, the phalanx, invented new formations and orders of battle, devised more efficient weapons, increased the speed and fighting power of their ships, and improved naval tactics. Moreover, they inspired every citizen with a martial spirit and with devotion to his *polis*. In almost all states, the whole population, including alien residents, contributed, each according to his financial and professional status, to the fighting forces. Every boy was trained early, through athletics, to steel his body; and every youth served in the armed forces.

Fifth-century Religion. Greek society, which was interested in all things human and therefore devoted itself to rational inquiry, produced little worthy of note in the realm of metaphysical speculation. Some of the philosophers theorized that a divine power or a spirit had given order to the universe and guided its action; just as Parmenides and Pythagoras had done in the sixth century, so Empedocles devoted himself in the fifth century to the study of questions pertaining to the soul, faith, and a divine plan. The fact that the mystery services (which centered around the cycle of the seasons—fructification, death, and resurrection) became more widespread may indicate a certain intensification of religious feelings; but a transcendental religious system was not developed; and a clergy in the modern sense was not organized. No book of religious revelation was written. The cults of the old gods of the Olympus or of the various local gods, the traditional religious ceremonies, and the customary public practice of divination were maintained, and the oracles, such as the oracle of Delphi, retained their influence. A great new religious festival, the Panathenaea, was introduced, but it, too, reflected the habits of the past rather than new perspectives.

CHAPTER V

THE END OF GREEK LIBERTY
(404–336 B.C.)

WITH THE END of the Peloponnesian War and the fall of Athens, a new age in Greek history began. Greece continued to produce works of astounding beauty in architecture and sculpture (and probably also in painting and music); and it was only then, with the contributions of Plato, Aristotle, and Euclid, that Greek philosophy and science attained their highest development. But in the political sphere, the prestige of Greece declined. Economic changes, including a great expansion in commerce and banking and the growth of a wealthy "bourgeoisie," hastened the disintegration of the society which had been able to defeat the mighty Persian Empire and which had persisted through a quarter of a century of civil war. The old simplicity in habits and manners was replaced by a love of luxury which sapped the strength of the country. The initiative and imagination of earlier times was lost. Even where democratic institutions endured, they proved no safeguard against the domination of society and the direction of the public will by a small group of ambitious aristocrats, rich merchants, or professional politicians and demagogues.

POLITICAL CONDITIONS

The greatest changes in Greek political institutions occurred, necessarily, in Athens, which had been the leader of Greece in the fifth century. Sparta showed fewer signs of change; there, as so often happens, victory led to petrification of existing institutions rather than to a healthy evolution. Thus, Sparta's role as a leading power was brief; within less than a generation, Sparta was defeated by Thebes, and within less than another twenty-five years, all Greece fell under the domination of Macedonia.

Eclipse of Athens. After defeat by the Spartans, Athens recovered rapidly in economic affairs. Agriculture in Attica was restored and improved methods of cultivation (especially crop rotation) were introduced. As the shipping industries recovered, Athens regained the role of leading banker and trader. In fact, standards of living were possibly higher than they had been at the time of Athenian supremacy. But inflation started, class differences became more accentuated, slavery (despite the freeing of many individual slaves) increased, and social unrest was widespread. Even though social mobility made it possible for men from the lower classes to rise, many of them, disillusioned with political conditions and induced by lack of faith and of interest in local affairs, decided to leave Athens. A new emigration movement set in, which soon spread to other parts of Greece. Thousands settled in Italy, southern Russia, Asia, and Africa; other thousands hired themselves out as mercenaries; and other thousands, who had been slaves, escaped. Eventually, as the population of Athens, of Attica, and then of all Greece diminished, agricultural productivity declined —a consequence which, in a vicious cycle, led to further depopulation.

Hegemony of Sparta. With Athens' power waning, Sparta gained hegemony in Greece. But Sparta's political heritage and provincialism did not make her fit to guide the country's political reconstruction. Handicapped by her rigid constitutions, maintained without change, internal development stagnated. Reform programs were defeated which capable, though perhaps overambitious generals and statesmen like Lysander and, after him, Agesilaus tried to introduce. Moreover, Sparta's foreign policy aroused apprehension and fear. Sparta engaged in expansionist maritime undertakings, insisted upon keeping garrisons in many towns of Greece, often supported oppressive oligarchic parties in the various city-states, and imposed conservative economic and social policies. In 380 B.C., the Spartans used force against rebellious Mantinea, and in the same year committed the outrage of occupying the citadel of the town of

Thebes, which had supported the revolt. In view of Sparta's ambitions various federations were formed against her. One such federation, the Corinthian League of 395 B.C. (composed of Thebes, Corinth, and Athens and supported by Persia), disintegrated in 387 B.C.; another, the Olinthian League, was broken up in 379 B.C. and a third, the Second Athenian Confederation, fell apart for fear of a renewed Athenian imperialism. Only a fourth—the Boeotian League, led by Thebes—was destined to succeed.

International Redistribution of Power. In the meantime, the decline of the whole of Greece continued until it reached a point at which the balance of power shifted to overseas territories.

SICILY. One of the areas which fell heir to continental Greece's former position was Sicily. Greek colonies there benefited from the influx of artisans, peasants, and scholars. Sicily became a great cultural center, excelling in the arts, philosophy, and science. The area also became a center of trade; Sicilian merchants competed with those of Athens and Corinth and assumed leadership in the struggle with the Phoenicians, whose mighty colony Carthage sought to encroach on Greek territory. Foremost among the Sicilian towns was Syracuse. Unlike two earlier Sicilian Greek colonies (luxury-loving Sybaris in the seventh century B.C. and hard-working Messina in the sixth century B.C.) Syracuse built a strong commonwealth and, under the able tyrant Dionysius I (d. 367) acquired a small empire, which extended beyond Sicily into southern Italy.

PERSIA. The chief beneficiary of the civil strife in Greece was, however, not Sicily but the Persian Empire. Persia profited in three ways: like Sicily, she could secure capable emigrees and mercenaries; she could reassert her domination over most of the Greek Ionian cities; and she could keep her traditional enemy weak. Victories which the Spartan Agesilaus had won in 396 B.C. were the last important triumphs of Greece over Persia. Thereafter, Persia alternated in siding for and against Sparta, thereby managing to perpetuate disunity and weakness in Greece. In 387 B.C., after one of Greece's internal wars, Persia was even accepted as arbiter in Greek peace negotiations.

Hegemony of Thebes. No solution of Greek troubles materialized when the Boeotian League under Theban leadership defeated Sparta. Two capable generals and statesmen, Pelopidas and Epaminondas, emerged in Thebes. Owing to the courage of the former, Thebes recovered her lost citadel; owing to the diplomatic ability of the latter, she gained the support of various small towns and an alliance with vacillating Athens. The Thebans then called a general peace conference; and when this conference failed because of Spartan intransigence, they attacked and utterly defeated Sparta in 371 B.C. in the battle of Leuctra. At the head of a brilliant army trained in new military tactics, Epaminondas then successfully invaded the Peloponnesus, dissolved Sparta's Peloponnesian League, freed the long-subjected Messenians, liberated the helots, and thus destroyed the very foundations on which Spartan power had rested. But compared with Sparta Thebes had even less of a program for the reorganization of Greece, which could have given permanence to Theban supremacy gained on the battlefield. The role of Thebes as a "great power" was shortlived; for Athens, perennial rival, quickly put an end to it. The Athenians formed a new Peloponnesian League and, in alliance with the former enemy, Sparta, crushed the Theban forces in 362 B.C. in a battle near Mantinea, in which Epaminondas was killed.

Panhellenism. A century of strife had thus successively brought Athenian, Spartan, and Theban leadership. But each state, individually, had failed to bring internal peace to Greece and to keep the country strong against external enemies. Collectively, they had likewise failed. Nevertheless, very few of the Greek leaders worked wholeheartedly for a thorough change and the establishment of a system providing for co-operation. The majority continued to uphold the ideal of individual suzerainty; and before the forces in favor of a union could make their influence widely felt, the problem of unity was solved—but at the expense of freedom, and by an outsider, King Philip II of Macedonia.

The Macedonian Conquest. In 359 B.C. Philip became ruler of Macedonia, a country which for a hundred years had enjoyed many economic and cultural ties with Greek city-states, yet was less advanced in trade and arts and was considered half-barbarian by its southern neighbors. In his youth, Philip had spent several years as a hostage at Thebes, where he had become well acquainted with Greek ways and institutions. A capable ruler, he employed the first ten years of his reign to strengthen his position in his own country and to extend his rule not southward, but northward. In that area, and chiefly at the expense of Athenian colonies, he gained important resources by annexing harbors, mines, and agricultural lands; he then turned his attention to Greece proper.

PREPARATION FOR CONQUEST. Shrewdly, Philip took advantage of the differences between those Greeks who advocated the preservation of the traditional small, independent city-state and those who aspired to establish a federation. Despite passionate denunciations (Philippics) by the great Athenian orator and patriot Demosthenes, he convinced many that unity under Macedonian leadership was preferable not only to independence for individual city-states, but also to a Greek federation. He gained the support of Demosthenes' great opponents Aeschines and Isocrates, and, with the help of lavish bribes, he acquired further adherents. By 346 B.C., Philip had secured a seat and vote in an all-Greek Council and had been chosen president of the Pythian games.

SUBJECTION OF GREECE. Eight years later, Philip deemed the time ripe for a final blow: Sparta was weakened militarily by loss of manpower and population, economically by the freeing of Messenia and the helots, and spiritually by the abandonment of the old Spartan traditions; Athens was being ruined by internal strife, by Persian interference, by the Macedonian conquest of her gold mines in Chalcidice, and by the threat to her supply lines from the Black Sea; and Thebes' ephemeral strength was gone with the defeat she had suffered at Mantinea. Consequently, Philip decided to strike. With his splendid cavalry and Macedonian phalanx, he defeated the Greeks decisively in 338 B.C. at Chaeronea, shattering the league which, under the persuasion of Demosthenes, Athens had built jointly with Thebes. He followed up his victory by a display of force as well as of generosity. He occupied Thebes, ravaged the Lacedaemonian countryside, and placed governors in strategic spots throughout Greece; but he appeased Athens by granting her a favorable treaty and refrained from attacking Sparta, which had not participated in the league against him. He then formed a Panhellenic League, of which he made himself president.

Thus ended Greek liberty. Philip's rule in Greece was, however, short. In 336 B.C., within two years of his conquest, he was murdered, and it was left to his son Alexander to consummate his plans.

GREEK CULTURE IN THE FOURTH CENTURY

The German philosopher and poet Gottfried von Herder once said that "the owl of philosophy flies at dusk." Was it the dusk of Greek civilization that began with the fourth century, which produced Greece's great philosophers Plato and Aristotle? Witnessing other facets of civilizations which are often considered signs of dusk or decay—emphasis on business activities and money, stress on individualism, and interest in scientific instead of metaphysical and religious questions—many historians will agree with Herder. Yet, so important were the Greek contributions in science (Euclid), art (Praxiteles), oratory (Demosthenes) and so vast were the political and military achievements of Alexander the Great that, notwithstanding the political collapse of the typical Greek *polis,* it hardly seems justifiable to regard the period after the Peloponnesian War as one of dusk or decline. At the most, we may speak of that period as an age of maturity.

Arts. In the fine arts, the fourth century brought greater mastery of technique and strong secular interests. Yet, the old Greek sense of beauty was not sacrificed to technical skill, nor did the Greek artists allow their creations to become mere imitations of nature or reproductions of earlier models.

PAINTING AND SCULPTURE. The two most celebrated painters were Zeuxis and Apelles. Hardly any of their works have survived, but we know that they were widely imitated by subsequent generations. Among the sculptors, the foremost were Praxiteles and Scopas. Their works exhibited not only the same charm, rhythm, and harmony which characterized those of the fifth-century masters but also a new element of animation, emotionalism, and humanism, which modified the majesty of earlier representations. Among themes depicted in their sculpture was that of the nude female body—an innovation inasmuch as preceding generations had abstained from presenting it in favor of the male figure.

ARCHITECTURE. The architectural works of the fourth century emphasized (in accordance with the changed tastes of a new generation) monumental size and elaborate ornamentation and sometimes were lacking in that harmony of proportion which was characteristic of architecture in the Periclean Age. Great examples of fourth-century architecture are few in number in Athens, but more numerous on the Peloponnesus, in the Ionian cities of Asia, and in the colonies. The Mausoleum in Halicarnassus, a new temple of Artemis in Ephesus, and Alexander's tomb in Alexandria illustrate the main trends.

Literature. The literary works of the fourth century, like the works of art and philosophy, reflected the maturity of Greek civilization. Prose superseded lyrical poetry and drama as the most important form. Aristophanes' life span extended into the beginning fourth century, but no new writer appeared who could match the great fifth-century authors of tragedy and comedy. Similarly, the foremost historian, Xenophon (a disciple of Socrates), can hardly be considered an equal of Herodotus or of Thucydides. Nevertheless, in his *Hellenica,* he has given a vivid account of Greece from the point where Thucydides had left off; and in his *Anabasis* he left a moving description of the spectacular retreat of ten thousand Greek mercenaries who, under his leadership, attempted to get back to the homeland after their campaigns in Persian service. Another historian, Theopompus, related in a light but critical vein the history of his contemporary Greece, interspersing his presentation with sharp political comments. Besides the foregoing types of literature, there were numerous works of rhetoric, many of which have survived in written form. The most famous orator was Demosthenes, whose speeches, even in printed translation, still impress us with their fire, power, and persuasion.

Philosophy. The greatest achievements of the age were the writings of Plato (a disciple of Socrates) and Aristotle (a disciple of Plato). Both were interested and active in politics, and both used politics as a starting point for a broader investigation of man, of society, of nature, and of reality beyond observable natural facts (metaphysics). Compared with their legacy the work of other philosophical schools (such as that of the Cynics) which flourished in the fourth century was of minor significance.

PLATO AND ARISTOTLE. In the tradition of Socrates, both Plato and Aristotle taught clear, methodical, logical thinking and ethical behavior. They occupied themselves in studying the problems of virtue and beauty, justice and immortality. Plato in his *Republic,* and Aristotle in his *Politics,* offered solutions for the problems of organizing society so that the individual would be able to develop his capacities and society would gain peace, stability, and self-fulfillment. Both turned their attention to ethics, esthetics, logic, and history—indeed, to almost all areas of knowledge and experience. Of special concern to them was the inquiry into the nature of reality. Plato came to the conclusion that concepts ("ideas") constitute reality and that the world of our senses is but a reflection of a reality beyond it. But Aristotle, who was an industrious student of nature, regarded the world around us, including both its forms and its material substance, as the reality. He compiled the studies of his predecessors, classified their observations and his own in the fields of botany, geography, and physics, and worked on scientific methodology. He saw in reason the means for an understanding of all problems, including those of ethics; and he regarded the divine power as a thought, as a moving force in the universe, as "being" in its ultimate form, and as the aim toward which everything strives.

CYNICISM. Of the various other philosophical schools, the school of the Cynics merits special attention. This school was organized by Antisthenes, who was also a student of Socrates. Cynicism embodied essentially negative elements: disregard of worldly goods and pleasures, abstraction from conditions around us, and lack of faith in a divine power. Its most famous representative was Diogenes. He and his followers were sincere seekers after virtue, and through abstinence and acceptance and valiant endurance of all the vicissitudes of life, they sought to show by examples how to deal with the problems of mankind.

CHAPTER VI

THE HELLENISTIC AGE

IN 338 B.C., PHILIP of Macedonia subjected Greece; in 336 B.C., his
son Alexander destroyed Thebes; in 214 B.C., the Romans
engaged in the first Macedonian War; and in 146 B.C., they destroyed
Corinth. These dates, spanning two hundred years, mark the path
of the disintegration of the Greek commonwealth and the end of
Ancient Greek History, properly speaking. But the Hellenic spirit
and its creative powers survived; they broadened and—consciously
furthered by Alexander the Great, by Greek emigrants, Greek mercenaries in foreign service, and later by Rome—became cosmopolitan. They came to comprehend the homeland, the colonies, the
newly established Greek centers in the Near East, and the Roman
Empire, and eventually fused even with barbarian thought and art.
The period during which this happened is the "Hellenistic Age."
Despite all the depth of thought and beauty of art in the times of
Pericles and the narrow city-state, it was only in the Hellenistic
Age that Greece's all-embracing influence on Western civilization
was established.

ALEXANDER THE GREAT AND HIS SUCCESSORS

Politically and economically, the Hellenistic Age meant for
Greece a period of almost uninterrupted warfare and violent social
change. First came eleven years of conquest under Alexander the
Great. Then, after his death, came thirty years of struggle for power
among his successors. Finally, there came reassertion of Macedonian

overlordship; but stability did not return. The populations suffered—
at least within Greece herself, and economic preponderance shifted
from one place to another. Athens and Sparta sank down to the
level of provincial towns, and new economic centers grew up in
Corinth, Ephesus, Antioch, Byzantium, and Rhodes.

Alexander the Great. Alexander was a pupil of Aristotle.
Arrogant, irrascible, brutal, and occasionally indulging in drunken
bouts, he was yet a man of valor, breadth of vision, youthful
ambition, and enthusiasm; and it is because of these traits that he
has inspired generation after generation. When after his succession
to the throne rebellions broke out in Greece, he destroyed, as a
warning, the city of Thebes, which had acted as leader of the revolt.
Firmly in power, he then turned to the unfinished plan of his
father and the great task for whose sake many Greeks had reconciled themselves to Macedonian rule—an all-Greek war on Persia.

Conquest of the Persian Empire. Within the ten years 334 B.C.
to 324 B.C., Alexander conquered the greatest empire that had yet
existed. In two battles—at the Granicus River (334 B.C.) and at
Issus (333 B.C.)—he defeated vastly superior Persian armies; he
took, though only after many a long siege and the perpetration of
gross brutalities, all the ports on the eastern Mediterranean, including the famous Phoenician port of Tyre; and he occupied Egypt,
where he made himself pharaoh. When the Persian king Darius
III offered him half the Persian Empire and the hand of his
daughter, he rejected the offer, attacked anew, and did not rest
until in a third great battle, at Gaugamela (331 B.C.), he had
destroyed Persia's military might and captured Darius' enormous
treasures; and when, shortly thereafter, Darius was assassinated,
Alexander ascended the throne of the Great Kings. From Susa, the
Persian capital in Mesopotamia, he then pushed his conquests even
farther—into Bactria, across the mighty Hindukush mountains into
Turkestan, the Caspian and Oxus regions, and on to Samarkand.
He then crossed the Khyber Pass into India, defeated opposing
armies there, marched along the Indus River to the Persian Gulf,
and finally returned to Susa.

Alexander's Failures. Where would Alexander's ambition have
led him, had not a sudden fever prematurely claimed his life in
323 B.C.? Would he have been able to hold together the empire he
had conquered? Judging from the fact that he alienated the sympathies of his own Macedonians and that his policies caused

mutinies in his army, plots against his life, and a dangerous revolutionary spirit in Greece, he seems to have lacked political acumen. He heightened Macedonian and Greek resentment by adopting Oriental manners and dress, contracting marriages first with one, then with another, foreign princess, and insisting upon being shown divine honors such as those the pharaohs and Mesopotamian rulers had enjoyed. Moreover, he showed no more than limited administrative abilities. He created no new institutions which promised permanent usefulness. He was forced to preserve Persia's imperial organization and keep Persians in high and subordinate positions, and his grandiose plans for the future, sponsoring mixed marriages between Greek soldiers and barbarian women, met with no more than fleeting success.

ALEXANDER'S ACHIEVEMENTS. Nevertheless, Alexander's conquests resulted in great positive achievements. Hellenic civilization was disseminated and a cosmopolitan spirit was fostered. Roads connecting distant lands were built, a common law and a common currency were initiated, trade increased, and prosperity followed in its wake. To a certain extent, the major part of the civilized Western world was welded together. A special contribution of Alexander consisted in the founding of more than seventy cities, over twenty of which were named after him. Some of them, like Alexandria in Egypt, were peopled with Greeks and could carry on Greek culture at a time when former centers were disintegrating.

The Diadochi. With Alexander's death, the political edifice he had so recently erected, broke down. Soldiers mutinied, subjected peoples rebelled, and ambitious generals, desirous of becoming his successors, began to fight among each other for the supreme position. Not until a score of years later, after the battle of Ipsus in 301 B.C., was the basis for a new order laid. By then, the most able among Alexander's successors, called the "Diadochi," had been killed; Antipater, Alexander's governor in Europe, had died; Alexander's little son had been murdered; and Antipater's successor Antiochus had perished. The remaining Diadochi contented themselves with partial rule, and thus—aside from a number of small semi-independent states—three large separate kingdoms emerged: Egypt, Syria, and Macedonia.

EGYPT. The Egyptian throne fell to the lot of a Macedonian general, Ptolemy (d. 283 B.C.). Despite much internal unrest, he and his descendants retained the crown of the pharaohs until the time

ALEXANDER'S EMPIRE

—— Limits of Alexander's Empire   —— Alexander's Route

of the Roman conquest. They ruled capably though harshly, assuming once more the godlike position which the ancient pharaohs had held. Like their predecessors, they reserved for themselves numerous trade monopolies, ownership of all landed property, control of irrigation, and regulation of industrial production. They kept many of the old laws of the land, and they saw to it that some of the ancient glory of Egypt returned. They beautified towns, built great new temples, and erected fine sculptures. They protected settlers and traders who came and brought prosperity and spread Hellenic culture while themselves absorbing Oriental habits. It was preferably upon Greeks, or Hellenized Orientals, that the Ptolemies conferred administrative and military positions. Alexandria became one of the culturally and economically most flourishing cities, not only of Egypt, but of the entire Hellenized world; and through the cult of Serapis and other mystery services, Egypt gave even new religious impulses to Hellenic civilization.

SYRIA. The Macedonian general Seleucus (murdered 281 B.C.) became ruler of the large territory extending over Asia Minor, Syria, and Mesopotamia. He, his son Antiochus, and their successors based their power on the land between the two rivers; but, like earlier dynasties, the Seleucids experienced grave difficulties in holding together the highly diversified and exposed empire. Soon, its most eastern parts, Bactria and Parthia, had to be given up, and constant wars had to be waged with neighbors over the possession of Syria and Asia Minor. Centralized governmental control as in isolated Egypt was not achieved. The Persian subjects fought all concentration of power in the hands of the Seleucids, and further disunity was created by the Seleucid's own policy of separating the civil from the military administration in the provinces. They attempted to "divide and rule," yet they fostered only disrespect for law and played into the hands of the local landholding nobility. Moreover, they, like the Ptolemies, alienated sympathies by giving preferential treatment to Greek settlers. Revolts resulted, and in the course of the third century, great trading centers, such as Antioch and Pergamum, made themselves practically independent.

MACEDONIA. In Macedonia, Greece, and Alexander's other European possessions, General Antipater (d. 319 B.C.) established his own rule after Alexander's death. He efficiently crushed (in 323 to 322 B.C.) a revolt led by Athens and known under the name of the Lamian War, abolished the rest of Greek autonomy, and installed new oligarchic regimes controlled by himself. His successor, Antigonus (d. 301 B.C.), and Antigonus' heirs continued Antipater's policies, and at no time permitted re-establishment of Greek independence. Rebellions, such as that sponsored in 251 B.C. by the Achaean League of the Peloponnesian states, were broken, and only Sparta, which finally introduced various social reforms, could maintain an uneasy autonomy. However, control of Greece did not include that of Sicily. The Greek colonies there remained independent of Macedonian rule and increasingly oriented themselves toward Carthage and Rome.

Economic Conditions under Alexander's Successors. Despite political disruption after Alexander's death, the economy of the Hellenic world flourished. The closer connections between far-apart regions and the wider markets offered opportunities of unaccustomed dimensions to the merchants—not only in old centers, like Athens and Corinth, but especially in new ones, like Antioch, Alexandria, and Rhodes. Oriental products, luxury goods, jewelry, and spices went through their hands and were exchanged for the traditional Greek specialties—metals and metal objects, marble, agricultural products, and textiles. Shipbuilding and shipping activities reached new heights; and improved methods in banking and financial administration (which benefited from lessons learned from the Orient) stimulated production and trading activities.

GREEK ART AND THOUGHT IN THE HELLENISTIC AGE

Even though most of the Hellenic world obeyed despots and dispensed with democratic institutions such as had constituted the pride of Pericles and his time, Greeks continued to create cultural monuments of unique value. To be sure, the art of the time has been criticized for "decorativeness," shallowness of feeling, lack of inspiration, and megalomania. Yet, in the midst of barbarous struggles and political disintegration, some of the noblest works of all times were produced. The Hellenized Near East, in particular, where town life and commerce flourished and wealth was accumulated, excelled, under the sponsorship of splendor-loving rulers, in the sciences, art, literature, and in all other fields of learning. Likewise, the Greek colonies in the West (especially Syracuse) brought forth great thinkers and artists.

Sciences. During the late fourth and the third and second cen-

turies B.C., rapid progress was made in mathematics and natural
sciences. A sharper separation of philosophy and science, of speculation and observation, and a new emphasis on experimentation
may account for the advances which were made. Heraclides and
Aristarchus figured the distances from the earth to the moon and
sun and came to realize that the earth is round and revolves around
the sun. Eratosthenes, astronomer and geographer, studied the inclination of the eclipse and calculated the circumference of the earth.
He also gave descriptions of foreign lands—descriptions based on
actual travel accounts which had been stimulated by Alexander's
expeditions to India and Central Asia and by other ventures—
some northward along the European and others southward along
the African coasts of the Atlantic Ocean. Euclid, in his *Elements,*
laid down fundamental principles for geometry and arithmetic
which have remained valid through more than two millennia. Hip-
parchus calculated, like Aristarchus, the earth's distances from sun
and moon, measured the exact length of the year, and investigated
trigonometric functions. Archimedes computed the value of π,
stated the "law of floating bodies," and invented various types of
machinery. He set an example in the practical application of
science. Botany was furthered by the studies of Theophrastus, who,
notwithstanding his metaphysical leanings, scientifically described
and classified plants. Medical studies were stimulated by Egyptian
scholars; emphasis was placed on anatomy and research. After dis-
secting human bodies, Herophilus observed the circulation of the
blood and investigated the nervous and muscular systems. Scientific
therapy to an ever-increasing degree replaced magic, charms, and
incantations. Agricultural advances were ushered in by the wide
application of the three-field system.

Although according to modern standards much of Hellenistic
science was erroneous, its impact upon future times was immense.
Owing to the surpassing authority enjoyed by Hellenistic scholars,
both their valid statements and their errors lived on. Both shaped
Western thinking, retarding medieval and modern sciences in some
directions and advancing them in others.

Libraries and Schools. With increase in knowledge came an
increase in the production of books. More was written, more copied
from older texts; and libraries, like the famous one of Alexandria,
were founded and became centers of learning. Simultaneously, the
school system was broadened. The art of reading was taught to

widening circles of students, the Greek language was spread, and new fields of study were opened up. Much of the teaching centered, however, around problems of style and grammar, and entailed criticism rather than original thought.

Literature. In creative writing, we find less originality in form and less depth in ideas than in earlier centuries. Emphasis was placed on tradition. Although much of Hellenistic literature may have become a model for poets who lived almost two thousand years later, the artful lyrics written by men like Theocritus or Callimachus or the plays of Menander tended primarily to entertain, and often satisfied no more than ephemeral tastes. Many of the works are full of wit, satire, criticism; thus, Menander's portrayal of the way of life among the merchants of Athens is lively and realistic; but a tendency toward shallowness prevailed. In history, too, we miss great, moving works. Alexander's expeditions furnished much material, but those who described them were only too often inclined to embellish events rather than investigate, describe, and interpret them. Not until Polybius in the second century did a historian emerge who to a certain extent returned to the scientific and artistic standards of Herodotus and Thucydides. While living as a hostage in Rome, Polybius wrote his *History,* which covers the last century of Greece before the Roman conquest. A Stoic, he composed it as a lesson in statecraft and a testimony to the inexorable path of events.

Art. Trends similar to those in literature can be traced also in Hellenistic art and architecture. A vigorous realism, perfection of technique, sober observation, and a sense for the dramatic characterize the works of art, which sometimes were lacking in sincerity and restraint. Nevertheless, notwithstanding justified criticisms by purists, the great sculptures of the Hellenistic period, which include the "Nike of Samothrace" and the "Laocoön," endure as monuments of a civilization providing an unending source of inspiration. Of the great works of architecture and of painting and mosaic, unfortunately only a few, such as the Pergamum Altar with its famous frieze, have survived. But we know that, for example, the Pharos Lighthouse near Alexandria was considered a Wonder of the Ancient World; and we also know that great progress was made in city-planning, in the laying out of broad streets and parks, and in the erection of theaters and other public buildings.

Religion and Philosophy. In the midst of vigorous activity, there was, however, no evidence of creative faith. Religious beliefs were wanting, and thinking observers, aware of the signs of cultural decay, sought consolation in philosophies which led away from participation in public affairs, emphasized resignation, and looked for satisfaction and self-fulfillment of the individual.

RELIGION. With the decline of the small city-state and community, local deities had lost their meaning; cults of family patrons were destroyed with the breaking up of old family traditions, and old Olympian gods could no longer fill man's religious needs either. Perhaps the Orphic, Eleusinian, and other mystery cults, with their search for an understanding of creation, soul, and life after death, came closer to satisfying emotional needs, but their orgiastic and superstitious elements deterred many. Of the Oriental religions, Zoroaster's teachings could have brought a new life-giving element into the Hellenic world; but disciples of the master had perverted some of Zoroaster's original thought. Thus, philosophy—with its rational approach to the problems of mankind—substituted for religion.

PHILOSOPHY. Two schools of philosophy stand out: the Epicurean, founded by Epicurus in the late fourth century B.C., and the Stoic, founded by Zeno, a Phoenician, early in the third century B.C. Both were concerned chiefly with ethics, with the pursuit of knowledge, virtue, and the right way to live. The Epicureans did not acknowledge a divine power which would reward virtue. They trusted only their senses and were skeptical of man's ability to understand, to know. If they advocated justice, courage, and moderation, they did so to increase enjoyment of life and reduce pain and suffering, which are unavoidable on this earth. Since they rejected general ideas and proposed that everyone choose his own way of conduct to fit his own needs, their teachings were later abused and led to indulgence in every available pleasure. The Stoics, on the other hand, looked for a divine law and order. To submit or adapt oneself to such an order and to bear with strength and dignity what it imposes—that they considered the right way to live. Virtue meant for them gaining mastery of oneself, ignoring pain and pleasure, being in accord with the laws of the universe and, with the help of reason, in sympathy with other men.

The teachings of Stoics and Epicureans summed up the *Weltgefühl* of the Greeks at the time the Hellenistic world merged with the Roman Empire.

CHAPTER VII

THE RISE OF ROME

IT IS OFTEN REITERATED that whereas the chief contributions of the Greeks to future Western civilization consisted in their scientific and artistic achievements which display clarity of mind, moderation, a sense of beauty and harmony, and a love of freedom and truth, Rome's contributions were of a more practical kind. They are supposed to have to do with societal structure, with government and law, with the construction of roads, aqueducts, and baths—in general, with the ability to adapt material conditions to man's use. On the other hand, an almost opposite argument can be proffered: that the Greeks, with their interest in life and their application of reason to life's problems, brought forth "a (practical) rule by which we can live"; and that the Romans, with their respect for virtue and character, set up ideals for the conduct of man regardless of material advancement. Roman history shows that the Romans were great not only for what they accomplished in the organization of society but also for what they established as the aim of human existence.

EARLY ROMAN CIVILIZATION

Unlike most important centers of antiquity (Ur, Babylon, Memphis, Thebes, Tyre, Troy, Athens, Alexandria, Byzantium) and even unlike other Italian towns (Tarentum, Syracuse, Naples), Rome was founded at a location which seemingly held little promise for future greatness. Situated on the banks of an insignificant river, without proper port facilities on the sea, amidst a not too fruitful land, and lacking special strategic advantages, the city nevertheless grew and came to dominate, first more highly civilized surrounding nations, then all of Italy, then most of the areas of ancient cultures, and, finally, large parts of the barbarian world. Geography, climate, trade, and religious fervor fail to explain this astounding development. Was it "fate" or "accident," or was it perhaps the genius of individual Roman men which accounts for Rome's path toward eminence and empire?

Mythology and Legend. What we know of Rome's earliest developments has come down to us mostly through myths and is supported by few archaeological data. However, the myths have importance: not only what has happened, but also what is believed to have happened is a force in history. Roman belief in a legendary past helped to shape the destiny of the Roman Empire, and Roman myths have provided unending inspiration for later writers, painters, sculptors, and warriors.

MYTHOLOGICAL ACCOUNTS OF ROMAN ORIGINS. According to myth, the Trojan hero Aeneas, after long travels subsequent to the fall of Troy, established a colony at Alba Longa in Latium and married a native princess, Lavinia. Twelve generations later, in 753 B.C., his descendants Romulus and Remus, once suckled by a she-wolf, founded the city of Rome. Until 509 B.C., this city is supposed to have been ruled by a succession of seven kings, who enacted laws, established religious traditions, built temples, fortifications, and water systems, trained an efficient army, and extended Rome's borders. The mythology includes also the story of the murder of Remus by his brother; the rape of the Sabine women; the purchase of the Sybilline books in which predictions of the future were entered; the suicide of Lucretia, violated by the son of the last of the seven kings, Tarquin Superbus; and this king's expulsion by the hero of liberty, Brutus.

LEGENDS OF THE EARLY ROMAN REPUBLIC. Stories depicting Roman life during the age of the kings are continued in the legends of the early Republic. There was Horatius Cocles who singlehandedly defended a Roman bridge against invading Etruscans; Scaevola, who demonstrated to a victorious and awed enemy his and his compatriots' indifference to pain and death by stretching his hand into a tray of burning coals and seeing it charred; and Coriolanus, a haughty patrician leader, who first saved Rome from attacking enemies, then, disappointed in his expectations for gratitude, deserted to this very enemy, and, finally, moved by the pleas and the pride of his old mother, returned although he knew that he had forfeited his life.

Historical Facts. What can be historically ascertained with regard to Rome's early developments is more prosaic. In the second millennium, several waves of northern invaders entered Italy and occupied the rich Po Valley in the north and the fertile western slopes along the Mediterranean coast. They mixed with native populations and with Greeks, with Celts from Gaul, with Phoenicians from Asia, with Numidians from Africa, and with other eastern, southern, and western peoples.

VILLANOVAN CIVILIZATION. By 1000 B.C., Italy had produced a civilization which was named after Villanova, a town north of present-day Florence. Villanovan civilization belonged to the Iron Age; it lasted in Italy until about the eighth century B.C. Various tribes, foremost among which were the "Latins," represented this civilization. The Latins may have been the people who introduced iron into Italy; they left to future Rome a rich legacy in societal institutions, setting models for family life and local government. They founded towns such as Alba Longa, their capital, and Rome itself. Another people belonging to the Villanovan civilization were the Etruscans; as time went on, they developed, however, a culture of their own.

ETRUSCAN CIVILIZATION. Although excelling as farmers, the Etruscans, too, founded towns. As early as the tenth century B.C., Tarquinia and Veii had arisen, and it was around these places that Etruscan civilization was built.

Industry and Commerce. Etruscan towns became famous for the manufacture of fine metal objects, weapons, textiles, and pottery. Mining activities were lively and were further stimulated when, with the conquest of the islands of Elba and Corsica (both rich in iron deposits), additional resources became available. Commerce grew accordingly. Soon, Etruria constituted an essential trade link between the Germanic regions north of the Danube and the Mediterranean areas inhabited by Italians, Greeks, and Phoenicians.

Society and Culture. Production methods in Etruria being advanced, a considerable amount of social stratification existed, and Etruscan concepts of kingship and aristocratic rule fructified later Roman political thought. Likewise, Etruscan religious customs and arts were of influence in Rome. Etruscans borrowed both religious and artistic ideas from archaic Greece, but soon added their own strong individual traits. In the sixth century, Etruscan art reached a first climax. At that time, Etruscan work in fresco painting and sculpture and modeling of bas-reliefs equalled the best work of other countries, and Etruscan craftsmen created exquisite ornaments and jewelry. Perhaps Etruscan literature, too, was highly developed; however, no definite statement can be made because, while we can read the Etruscan alphabet which is related to archaic Greek, we have only in few instances succeeded in establishing the meaning of the words.

Fusion of Etruscan and Roman Institutions. Etruscan civilization lasted until the third century. Thereafter it was no longer distinguishable from that of Rome, with which it had gradually fused. From the seventh century on, when Etruscans conquered Latin Rome, Etruria and Rome were intimately linked. The mythological seven kings of Rome represent Etruscan rulers. They organized government along Etruscan tradition which they followed when raising the military strength of the city, building water systems, and promoting commerce. Under their domination, Rome grew and was adorned with temples, in which gods of Etruscan origin— such as Jupiter, Juno, and Minerva—were venerated. They ruled for more than one hundred years, until the Romans expelled the last Etruscan king, Tarquin Superbus, and established their independence. This change meant at first a setback for the development of central Italy, for it not only led to two decades of war between Romans and Etruscans, who (as the stories of Horatius and Scaevola suggest) almost succeeded in re-establishing their rule, but it also brought economic and social hardships. Insecurity and loss of unity between town and hinterland worked to the disadvantage of both Rome and Etruria. Rome showed a sharp decline as a trading center; Etruria was cut off from the sea at the mouth of the Tiber. In both areas, suffering and revolts ensued.

Roman Civilization at the Time of the Establishment of the Republic. When the Etruscan rulers had been driven out of Rome, a republic was instituted. Leadership fell to the "patricians," a hereditary class composed of wealthy, landowning Romans of old Latin stock. The mass of the population, including all other freemen, whether peasants, merchants, or artisans, were called "plebeians." Some of these were men of wealth and landed property, whose families, however, did not count among the traditional Roman gentry; others were poor. In addition, there were slaves. These varied in numbers throughout the centuries, accounting at times for one-quarter of Rome's total population.

GENS AND FAMILY. The patrician and plebeian classes were subdivided into units called "gens," and a gens was composed of families. Each family was a firm entity directed by the father (*pater familias*), who exercised power over life and death of the other members, acted as priest before the family deities, administered the (originally indivisible) family property, and represented the family in gens and class. Upon him and his example depended that traditional honor and virtue which are supposed to have constituted one of the main foundations of Roman greatness.

GOVERNMENT. Upon the establishment of the Republic, executive power was vested in two annually chosen "praetors" (or, soon, "consuls"). Unlike the former kings, they did not have power over life and death; moreover, at the end of their terms, they were held responsible for their acts. In times of grave emergency, a special official, a "dictator," could be appointed who, during a six-months period, exercised absolute authority.

The fathers of the patrician families constituted an advisory body, the "Senate," which had at first 300 members. The same group monopolized the important offices. All other free Romans constituted an "Assembly"—the Assembly of the Centuries, which debated matters of administration and of war and peace, and which served as a court of last appeal for capital offenses. It soon nominated or elected the highest magistrates and made laws. Its members were divided, according to property qualifications, into five groups; voting was done by groups so as to guarantee the decisive influence of the wealthy, who composed the first two groups.

MILITARY ESTABLISHMENT. Classification by group, and thus property, determined everyone's share of the military burden and his place in the army. Each unit of the army was formed collectively by a number of families. The consuls acted as commanders. Plebeians did not have access to the highest posts.

RELIGION. The family and governmental system were intimately connected with religion and permeated by religious rites. Gods and spirits (*numina: penates* and *lares*) watched over home, hearth, farm, and family, as well as over crops, and over the state itself. To the priests fell both religious and state functions. Augurs, who inspected the entrails of sacrificed animals or watched the flight of birds and studied the calendar, determined favorable times for action and thus indirectly influenced policies. A high priest with life tenure (*pontifex maximus*), who enjoyed great authority, set feast days and ordered religious services. Temples were built and diverse ceremonies were invented. But, as in Greece, ethical codes of behavior or transcendental views were not connected with the Roman deities.

THE BUILDING OF THE REPUBLIC

Rome's history during the two hundred fifty years following the end of the monarchy is one of economic growth, of social struggle within, and of expansion abroad. It is often represented as a coherent story which, when compressed on a few pages, may leave the impression that the foresight and persistence and the courage and endurance of Rome's citizens led the city on a straight path to territorial greatness and a new social order. A rather different picture, reflecting a more meaningful history, emerges when we consider the events by short spans of time. For what over a long period may appear as a straight path then turns out to be a complex process, which was never consciously planned and which might as easily have brought Rome's ruin as Rome's rise.

Rome in the Fifth Century. With the fifth century begins Rome's life as a republic. The importance of this century for Rome lies neither in territorial and commercial expansion nor in the creation of notable works of art. What is memorable is the social and political system which the Romans built—a system which was to serve them in the more than three centuries during which the insignificant city grew into the capital of a world empire.

Territorial Growth. Throughout the fifth century, Rome carried on desperate struggles to stave off reabsorption by her neighbors. The struggles were crowned by the undertakings of the dictator Cincinnatus against the Latin Sabines and, later, those of the dictator Camillus against the Etruscan Volscians. War against the Volscians eventually brought the conquest of Veii. Owing to this success the tiny territory of Rome was enlarged—although by no more than a still smaller strip on the right bank of the Tiber—and Rome improved both her strategic position and her agricul-ural basis. However, the conquest of Veii was achieved only with the help of some of Rome's Latin neighbors whose intention it was not only to aid but also to control any expansion of the city.

COMMERCE. With respect to commerce, too, Rome achieved little during the fifth century. As long as she had enjoyed close connections with Etruria, many foreign traders had come; after she had established her independence, traders rarely found it profitable to visit the town. Reduced to a comparatively primitive agricultural economy, Rome had to begin all anew to attract commerce.

SOCIAL CONDITIONS. In the sphere of social organization, the transition from a kingdom to a republic had left control in the hands of the patricians. But their power was soon challenged from two sides: by rich plebeians who had gained their wealth as traders and demanded a share in the government; and by poor agriculturists and workers who needed relief and threatened revolt. During the long times of struggles for Rome's survival, they had carried a steadily growing burden: because of the inadequacy of agricultural lands, grain was often scarce; prices had risen as a result of the speculations of rich grain importers; military expenses and services weighed heavily; and debts mounted because of high taxes and excessive interest rates. Enslavement for debt was rigorously enforced, and many small farms, once belonging to independent owners, passed into the hands of patricians and bankers who used slaves and grew crops for trade rather than for local daily bread. The former peasants moved to the city and added their numbers to the hungry mass of the unemployed.

POLITICAL EVOLUTION. Social differences led to political changes. Early in the fifth century, desperation drove the plebeians to leave their work and even to withdraw altogether from Rome in order to establish a new city with better living conditions. This, and other subsequent rebellious moves, led in the course of some fifty years to substantial political concessions by the patricians. They admitted rich plebeians to the Senate; they allowed the election of two (later four, and then ten) new officials, "tribunes," whose task it became to protect the plebeians against injustices; and they agreed to the institution of a new Assembly, the *Comitia Tributa,* in which voting took place not according to property qualifications but according to the geographical distribution of the population. This Assembly of Tribes, whose importance grew slowly, shared in lawmaking and in appointing magistrates. Another step was taken when, toward the middle of the century, the tribunes were admitted to the deliberations of the Senate. Later, they received the right to veto legislation; and eventually, aides were assigned to them, called "aediles" (two of patrician and two of plebeian origin) whose tasks consisted in supervising building projects, temples, and local business activities, and in caring for public property.

Further concessions followed in the second half of the fifth century. After the introduction of the *Comitia Tributa* and the Tribunate, the patricians still monopolized the consulship and thereby the executive. They even secured for themselves two new offices, that of "quaestor" in 447 B.C. and that of "censor" in 443 B.C. To the quaestor fell the task of administering military finances; the censor was charged with the supervision of public morals and with the financial administration of the city. Since the duties of the censor included assessment of the population by censuses every fifth year, he wielded great power, for upon the assessment depended the tax burden and the military rights, and therewith the political standing, of the individual citizen. Even eligibility to senatorship depended upon assessment, since a minimum estate was prescribed for admission. However, the patrician monopoly on these two offices was quickly impaired by new moves: in 445 B.C., intermarriage between patricians and plebeians, long forbidden, was allowed; in 420 B.C., the quaestorship was opened to plebeians; and in 410 B.C., enslavement for debt was prohibited.

The Fourth Century. The fourth century brought a continuation of the trends of the preceding one insofar as it witnessed further equalization of civil rights—even if the distinctions between the social strata of the population remained essentially unaltered. In external affairs, the new century brought, however, a sharp change. It was then that Rome started on her road to conquest of all of Italy and that we can first trace in the thoughts and actions of the Romans a consciousness of Rome's "manifest destiny," which led to the building of a world empire.

EXPANSION. Success, which the capture of Veii at the beginning of the century had brought, was followed by reversals. The conquest of the town had caused the desired weakening of Rome's Etruscan neighbors, but it had also conjured up new dangers; for the crippling of the Etruscans, who had acted as a buffer, opened the way to invasion by Gauls, who lived in northern Italy. These Gauls attacked, defeated the Romans in the battle on the Allia, and in 390 B.C. took the city and sacked it. Only the capitol was saved—by, it is said, the cackling of geese which awakened the defenders. At enormous expense, the enemy was bought off. New invasions by the Gauls followed, and only after the lapse of another forty years could Rome begin with counter moves. These were aimed northward at the remnants of the Etruscans, who had often supported the Gauls, and southward at Samnites and Latins. The resulting wars span half a century and did not end until 290 B.C. They brought bitter defeats, such as that of 321 B.C. when during the Second Samnite War a whole Roman army had to surrender at the Caudine Forks; yet, Rome finally subdued the Etruscans as well as the peoples of Latium and Campania and established her domination northward to the Rubicon River and southward down to and beyond the Bay of Naples.

FOREIGN ADMINISTRATION AND COLONIZATION. Rome's conquest had a multiple effect: it brought booty into Rome's treasury, gave relief to needy Roman citizens who could settle on conquered land, and provided profits for wealthy landowners and speculators. It also created new problems, connected with the organization and colonization of the newly gained land; for, together with land, people were acquired and their relationship with Rome needed regulation. A few received citizenship rights; many were enslaved; a large part was, by treaty, accepted as "allies." These allies were exempted from taxation and granted local autonomy, but they had to render auxiliary military service. Again others, who lived in towns of special strategic or economic importance, were subjected to "colonial" status; on them fell a major part of the tax burden. Romans, to the extent to which they were resettled, always retained their former citizenship rights.

Once incorporation had been completed, a considerate Roman administration tried to bind all elements permanently to Rome. Roads such as the Via Appia connecting Rome and Capua were built; and a revitalized commerce, resulting from an economy supplementing the needs of city and hinterland as in Etruscan times, served to weld the commonwealth together.

INTERNAL REFORMS. Foreign enterprises and resulting needs for unity within contributed to a speeding up of the process of internal reform. A number of further changes in favor of the plebeians took place. In 367 B.C., it was decreed that one of the two consuls had to be selected from the class of the plebeians. Pay was provided for military service and battle formations were changed in line with tactical needs rather than social rank. Laws were passed providing for reduction of debts and limiting the size of estates any individual was allowed to acquire out of the public land. Although these laws were only lamely enforced, they made it possible to resettle small farmers and temporarily to stop the trend toward converting agricultural land into grazing land, which had rendered Rome increasingly dependent upon food imports. The concessions served not only the poor but the wealthy by reducing revolutionary pressures.

The development initiated by these laws led to a logical conclusion. Although the patricians had tried in 367 B.C. to counterbalance their political losses by the introduction of a new, exclusively patrician office charged with high judicial functions, the office of "praetor," this post, too, had to be opened to plebeians before the end of the century. Likewise, the dictatorship and, finally, even priestly functions were made accessible to them. Perhaps these concessions would have meant more had they come earlier; reform issues often lose their meaning in the course of time, and what seems important to one generation may seem of little value to another. In Rome, too, the significance of the reform work should not be overestimated; for the plebeian class was no longer what it had been and many of its wealthy and influential members had come to share patrician interests.

Rome at the Beginning of the Third Century. The Rome which we encounter on the threshold of the third century thus appears as a very different one from that which had existed at the time of the foundation of the Republic, and different also from the one that existed at the beginning of the fourth century. No longer just a town but a large state embracing almost half of the peninsula, Rome constituted a power which had to deal with problems befitting a powerful state.

Social Structure. By the beginning of the third century, the patricians had lost most of their prerogatives. Yet, besides social position they retained many of those manifold advantages which birth, connections, education, and wealth in land and slaves could secure. They also preserved a large share of political control since they continued to dominate the Senate and to provide the men for most of the high offices. The plebeian class had split in fact if not in form. Provincial aristocracy, bankers, and wealthy businessmen formed one group, and they were the ones who benefited most from the rights which the political reforms of the preceding age had brought to plebeians. The other, more numerous group consisted of the small farmers, the artisans, and the poor city proletariat; they had gained little—so little, indeed, that in 287 B.C., driven to desperation by debt and misery, the plebs once more seceded from the city and thus forced through a law putting final legislation entirely into the hands of the Assembly of Tribes. The lowest group of the population, that of the slaves, had likewise split. Some of the slaves, having been freed, had become "freedmen." These possessed limited civil rights; many of them had become "clients" of their former owners and, working on their former masters' lands or in their households, enjoyed, despite continued dependence, a large measure of economic security and personal influence. In exchange, they contributed through their work and political support to the financial and social standing and power of their masters. The other sector of the slave population had also changed in character; for the influx into their thinning ranks of new slaves, drawn from the increasing number of prisoners of war, altered their ethnical and labor patterns.

Naturally, bitter antagonisms divided the various layers of the population, and these class antagonisms were supplemented by new jealousies, arising between Roman citizens and non-citizens.

GOVERNMENT. Notwithstanding divergent tendencies, an elaborate governmental structure succeeded in holding the state together.

Senate. The chief influence in the state was exercised by the Senate. It had changed less than other institutions. To be sure, its members were drawn from all classes, but they were always appointed out of the number of propertied citizens and they retained their membership for life. The Senate's legislative functions were narrowly restricted after 287 B.C., but through control of taxes, advice to the consuls, conduct of foreign affairs, and personal authority of many of its members, it continued to exercise decisive power. Rome owed most of its progress to the Senate's conservative yet wise administration and counsel.

Executive Officers. The executive power rested with consuls, praetors, censors, aediles, and quaestors—in addition to tribunes. Those aspiring to the highest ranks had to run in a fixed order through the ladder of these offices (*cursus honorum*). With the expansion of Rome and the need for executive functionaries in the provinces and armies, additional offices, such as those of proconsul and propraetor, were created. These gave an opportunity to past consuls and praetors to remain in the state service and to employ their accumulated knowledge in positions of importance. Significantly, while occasionally an able "new man" joined the ranks of the highest magistrates, it was essentially a small circle of four or five old, often rivaling families, like the Fabii and Scipios, who again and again occupied the leading offices and, together with their friends and clients, almost monopolized the executive.

Assemblies. By 300 B.C., the Assembly of Centuries still existed side by side with the Assembly of Tribes. But the judicial and legislative powers it had possessed in early republican times had passed into the hands of the Tribes, where the preponderance of the higher classes was minimized. This Assembly of Tribes had become between 338 B.C. and 287 B.C., the final instrument for lawmaking but it had lost some of its "democratic" character. Its presidents, who generally belonged to the wealthy, exercised undue influence, and its most important elected officers, the tribunes, catered increasingly to the wishes of senators and fulfilled less and less their original tasks as defenders of the interests of the common people.

LAW. Roman law constitutes one of the greatest legacies of Ancient Rome. In early times, it had been designed strictly to serve the interests of the patricians. It had been extremely severe, providing for retributive justice and for the death penalty in numerous cases. It was handed down from generation to generation through oral tradition, and only around 450 B.C. had it been codified and engraved on "Twelve Tables." With the introduction of praetors almost a hundred years later and their assumption of many legal functions, a change had come, however; and this change was speeded up when the position of praetor (and subsequently that of priest or pontiff, who had also legal functions) was opened to plebeians. Thereafter law was no longer dispensed exclusively by patricians, and praetors gradually assumed the habit of preparing opinions which judges could follow. In assuming his office, a praetor would inform the population about the principles which would guide his opinions, and these principles, influenced by changing times and keyed to changing moods of the population, served to modify the existing legal traditions, to prevent stifling conservatism, and to lay the basis for a steadily developing law concept. The resulting *jus civile* set standards for the rights and property relationships of individuals and for legal procedures guaranteeing these rights. It was supplemented, in view of Rome's growing world position, by such legal principles as would apply in intercourse with foreigners—foreign traders or foreign allies—whose native concepts of justice had to be taken into consideration and reconciled with those of Rome. Thus, a *jus gentium,* an international law, was also evolved.

COMMERCE. The beginnings of a Roman *jus gentium* indicate the growing importance of Rome as an international center. By 300 B.C., this position was still insignificant in comparison with that of various contemporary Eastern trading cities. Conquest included no more than close Italian neighbors, trade was limited, and quite a share of it was still in the hands of foreigners. Agriculture predominated in Rome's economy, industrial enterprises were slight, and—except for some pottery, textiles, metal objects, and arms—not much was produced that could be exported. Coins as an exchange medium were introduced no earlier than 330 B.C., and even then they were only of copper and were minted abroad—in Capua. Not before 269 B.C. did Rome coin its own silver pieces. Nevertheless, Rome's position must not be underestimated. To be sure, the trade of the Phoenician town of Carthage was foremost in the western Mediterranean; a strong fleet guaranteed Carthage's safety; her colonies on Sicily and other islands contributed to her resources and wealth. But various trade treaties between Carthage and Rome, of which that of 348 B.C. is indirectly known to us, bear witness to the growing commercial importance of Rome and foreshadowed conflicts that were to redirect the path of Rome's history in the third century.

CHAPTER VIII

THE FLOURISHING
OF THE ROMAN REPUBLIC

THE INTERNAL POLITICAL and social struggle in Rome subsided somewhat after the plebeian gains of 287 B.C. Foreign issues took precedence; attention was focused on military efforts. Between 287 B.C. and 83 B.C., Rome gained enormously in territory, booty, and population and was enabled to solve internal problems, to satisfy demands of poor farmers and veterans for land, and to ease debts and taxation. Indeed, the sacrifices necessitated by continuous wars seemed worth the effort—at least for the survivors in victorious Rome. Even the arts began to flourish. But success brought also a transformation of institutions, economy, and society, which raised new problems and demanded new settlements. For this, the Republic was not prepared. The structure, which had helped Rome survive the struggles of the third and the second centuries, was by the beginning of the first century in the process of a complete breakdown.

THE THIRD CENTURY

The most famous and dramatic struggle in Roman history falls into the third century. It was the wars against Carthage. These wars brought, with the defeat of Carthage, Roman hegemony in all of Italy and Sicily and in parts of Spain, and Roman domination of the western Mediterranean Sea. Victory had, however, wider consequences than mere acquisition of new power and territory.

Rome gained a hitherto unknown feeling of her strength; she adapted herself to thinking in terms of a naval as well as a land power; she proceeded more resolutely on the path of democratization, which had proved useful during the wars; and through contact with Hellenistic civilization she changed her daily life and aspirations.

Conquest of Southern Italy. The wars against Carthage (the so-called "Punic" wars) began in 264 b.c. When the Samnite Wars had been concluded, the remnants of Etruscan power crushed, the alliance of the various Italian tribes against Rome shattered, and central Italy at a radius of about 150 miles around Rome annexed, the Romans found themselves faced with new dangers. For their advance frightened some of the new neighbors; particularly, Greek trading cities in southern Italy such as Tarentum saw their economy and wealth threatened by Roman competition and came to fear for their independence. Around 282 b.c., they therefore incited Pyrrhus, king of Epirus, to cross the Adriatic Sea with his troops and attack Rome. Joined by some of the subjected Italian tribes, Pyrrhus twice inflicted terrible defeats on Rome. But being far from his base of reinforcements and supplies, his costly victories, inasmuch as they failed to decide the war, only served to weaken his own position. In a third battle, at Beneventum in 275 b.c., he was defeated and forced to give up. His retreat made it possible for Rome to seize, by 265 b.c., the entire territory southward to the end of the peninsula, down to the Strait of Messina.

Conquest of Sicily. The next step consisted in crossing the Strait "for the protection of the mainland." Thus one war led to another; as long as there were neighbors, there were "threats and dangers." Crossing over into Sicily meant a struggle with Carthage.

FIRST PUNIC WAR. Friendly relations had existed between Rome and Carthage as long as they were far apart; during the Pyrrhic War, they had even been allies. But with Rome moving close to Sicily, the Carthaginians saw their commercial interests menaced. When, in addition, a rebellion of some mercenaries broke out in Sicily, they decided to station more troops on the island. This caused some Greek cities on Sicily to enter into negotiations with Rome, and in 264 b.c. the "First Punic War" ensued. Rome first turned against Carthage's friend Hiero, tyrant of Syracuse, who was forced by the Romans' superior might to submit and join them. Then, their disciplined legions, equipped with new arms to take advantage of ever-changing tactical needs, defeated Carthage's unreliable mercenary armies, led by the brilliant General Hamilcar. Even at sea Rome proved often superior. Despite reverses at the outset of the war and despite the failure of an invasion of Africa, her infant navy proved a match for Carthage's navy.

PEACE. The war dragged on for more than twenty years. Finally, in 241 B.C., lack of money for her mercenaries forced Carthage (which suffered more than Rome because she depended on unimpeded commerce) to seek peace. She had to surrender her Sicilian possessions—a loss augmented a few years later by that of the islands of Sardinia and Corsica—and to pay a large indemnity. With the acquisition of these islands, Rome gained control of the Sicilian grain production and the Corsican mining resources. Sicily became for the time being the foremost supplier of grain and helped to make up for the lack of foodstuffs which was caused in Rome by concentration of Italian farmers on the production of fruits, such as grapes and olives, and the raising of cattle. Moreover, Rome freed herself from trade restrictions which earlier treaties with Carthage had imposed upon her.

Conquest of the Po Valley. After the conclusion of the First Punic War, peace was kept for no more than ten years; then Rome engaged in a war with pirates in the Adriatic, who were destroyed, and thereafter with Gauls in the Po Valley. Like the Carthaginians in the south, the Gauls in the north feared that Rome with her land hunger would encroach upon their territories. Their opposition was in vain, though, and in 222 B.C. the major part of the Po Valley was incorporated by Rome into the now rapidly growing empire. By 219 B.C., Illyria on the eastern side of the Adriatic was also seized.

Rivalry in Spain. Next, Rome's covetousness was attracted by Spain, rich in mineral wealth and manpower. After the loss of Sicily, Carthage had concentrated on building and extending her Spanish holdings, and a treaty had provided for abstention of Rome from interfering in affairs south of the Ebro River. But difficulties arose in connection with the city of Saguntum, which was allied with Rome and which Rome sought to make into a base for the expansion of her power. In order to forestall this attempt, the young Carthaginian general Hannibal, son of Hamilcar, besieged and conquered the city (in 219 B.C.), and his act led to the Second Punic War.

Second Punic War. Through one of the most celebrated military feats in history, Hannibal, who again acted with alacrity, brought his army—infantry, cavalry, and elephants—across the Alps. Despite great losses on the way, he twice defeated in 218 B.C. Roman armies opposing him in the Po Valley.

HANNIBAL'S TRIUMPH. Marching south in the following year, Hannibal for a third time vanquished the Roman legions (at Lake Trasimene), and only the delaying tactics of the cautious Fabius Maximus Cunctator, chosen dictator by a desperate Rome, saved the city from possible ruin. But after the expiration of Cunctator's term, Hannibal crowned his career by his most brilliant triumph: at Cannae, he destroyed (in 216 B.C.) the legions which Rome, exerting herself to the utmost, had just succeeded in raising. Perhaps he should have marched thereupon on Rome as his generals advised; but as he was far from his base and ill-supported by his home government, he refused to attack the strongly fortified city, which showed astounding firmness. Rome congratulated her blundering and utterly defeated consul for having risked a stand against the mighty enemy and for not having despaired of Rome.

HANNIBAL'S DEFEAT. Thereafter, joined by some Italian towns including Capua, by Syracuse, and by Macedonia under the leadership of King Philip V (First Macedonian War), Hannibal made no further progress and found himself unable to force a final decision. For over ten years he had to be satisfied with living off the conquered land. During this time, Rome regained her strength, raised new armies, and chose new and more capable leaders. Eventually, she could seize the initiative and counterattack. In 212 B.C., Syracuse was retaken, in 211 B.C. Capua, in 209 B.C. Tarentum; in 207 B.C.. Hannibal's brother, Hasdrubal, was defeated in Spain and parts of this country regained. In 206 B.C., Philip V gave up his action and Rome's armies were ready to invade Africa. Hannibal was forced to return. At Zama, in 202 B.C., the decisive battle was fought. Under the command of Scipio (the Elder), the Roman legions, with the help of an old enemy of Carthage, King Masinissa of Numidia, defeated Hannibal and broke Carthage's resistance. Carthage had to surrender her navy, abandon most of her overseas possessions, pay another war indemnity, and forego the right to an independent foreign policy. The territories of her Italian allies were incorporated by Rome.

CONSEQUENCES OF ROME'S VICTORY. This time, Rome had bought her victory at the price of much suffering on the part of the

ITALY

peasants and city proletariat and at the cost of the lives of many nobles. Considerable concessions by the old patrician leaders to the war-profiteering class of traders, bankers, and new landowners, whose capital had made possible Rome's perseverance, had become necessary. Rome had also to pay for victory with an increase of those tendencies which made for more wars. For although it is said that Rome was not eager to engage in further conquests, it would be more correct to speak of a large party which tried to preserve, together with a homogeneous and limited dominion, the old Roman way of life. But another party, influenced by aristocratic families such as the Scipios and by numbers of war profiteers, worked for further expansion.

THE SECOND CENTURY

Within two years of Zama, Rome found herself involved in three new wars: in the north against Gauls; in the west against revolting Spanish peoples; and in the east against Macedonia. These wars, a logical consequence of the position Rome had gained in the third century, were all concluded victoriously. Of greater importance, however, than the military successes, which were followed by additional wars between 197 B.C. and 146 B.C., was the gradual change in Roman civilization, which took place during that same period. For the first time do we encounter men of peace—scholars and artists—who were to contribute to the lasting greatness of Rome.

Roman Expansion. The defeat of Carthage opened the way for further action. The first step the Romans undertook was the punishment of the Gauls in the Po Valley, who had used Hannibal's invasion to rise and to join the Carthaginians. As soon as the campaign against them had been successfully concluded, the Romans sent an army to Spain in order to hold down the inhabitants there, who were likewise rebelling. The Spanish war turned out to be an extremely difficult undertaking, starting anew each time the Romans thought they had won it, and lasting for more than half a century. The main forces of Rome were, however, directed eastward—against Macedonia, Greece, and Syria. Before the campaigns against these countries were concluded, Rome also turned once more on Carthage and destroyed the city altogether.

Second Macedonian War. The first undertaking in the East was a new war against Philip. After a decisive victory at Cynoscephalae in 197 B.C., the Consul Flaminius brought it to a successful conclusion. The Macedonians had to pay an indemnity, reduce their army, and give up their century-and-a-half-old dominion over the Greek city-states. To the enthusiastic joy of all Greeks, Flaminius declared Greece "free."

SYRIAN WAR. Victory over Macedonia led to the next war, this one being directed against Antiochus III. Antiochus ruled Syria and large parts of Asia Minor. Fearful that further Roman expansion would endanger his rule, and incited by Hannibal who, chased from Carthage, had sought refuge with him, he decided to engage in a preventive war. He invaded European territory, but his efforts were in vain. Not only had he to withdraw, but, in 190 B.C., Rome's legions for the first time crossed over into Asia. Antiochus was defeated, his kingdom severely reduced in size, and parts of his lands were put under the rule of Rome's ally, the king of Pergamum.

However, none of these settlements brought peace. The Macedonians refused to reconcile themselves to the loss of Greece; the Greeks rebelled when the Romans, notwithstanding their promises of independence, continued to interfere in Greek affairs; and the inhabitants of Asia Minor resented rapacious Roman officials and businessmen who, abetted by Pergamum, took the place of Macedonian and Greek exploiters. Thus, between 171 B.C. and 146 B.C. more wars had to be fought.

THIRD MACEDONIAN AND ACHAEAN WARS. Again Roman legions marched, devastating prosperous regions. In 171 B.C., they attacked Macedonia anew and finished by dividing the country; in 146 B.C., they made it a Roman province. In the same year, they broke up the Achaean League which the Greek states had formed to protect themselves, fearfully destroyed the city of Corinth, leader of the League, and imposed a heavy tribute. They also broke by force all resistance in Asia Minor and eventually incorporated most of the lands as provinces of the empire. In 133 B.C., they acquired by inheritance the formerly allied Pergamum.

THIRD PUNIC WAR. But before these enterprises could be concluded, a final settlement was sought also with Carthage. Under the pretext that Carthage had broken the existing peace when, without Roman consent, she took up arms against the provocations of Rome's ally Masinissa, Rome precipitated the Third Punic War. With Scipio Africanus (the Younger) in command, the Romans

conquered Carthage after an arduous siege in 146 B.C.; and lest
she ever rise again, they followed the advice of Cato the Elder, an
inveterate foe of Carthage, and razed to the ground the once so
mighty and prosperous town. The North African coastlands were
organized as another province.

SPANISH REVOLT. The destruction of Carthage was followed by
a new long-drawn-out campaign in Spain. After subduing previous
rebellions there, Rome had divided Spain into two provincial areas;
but she continued to be bitterly opposed by the native populations.
Even when Viriathus, the rebels' devoted and capable leader, was
assassinated, the fight went on. Not until 133 B.C., after Scipio the
Younger had been put in charge, did the Romans succeed in taking
the center of resistance, the town of Numantia. The conquest of
Spain necessitated yet another campaign; for in order to protect
communication lines, southern Gaul (*Gallia Narbonensis*) had to
be gained, too. This was achieved by 121 B.C.

Second Century Economic and Social Problems. Owing to
the wars, considerable changes had taken place in the economic
and social structure of Rome. The patricians and the Senate
(*Optimates*) had, in spite of the laws of 287 B.C., reasserted their
authority. Using their power cautiously, they had found themselves supported by the new capitalists, the wealthy bourgeoisie or
"Equestrian class" (*Equites*), and often also by the party of the
poorer sections (*Populares*). As the treasury could be filled by
tribute and booty, taxes at home could be kept low; moreover,
work projects, including the building of temples, homes, roads, and
aqueducts, helped the unemployed. Land in conquered territories
could be made available for settlement by veterans; Equestrians
were given chances to make profits either as tax collectors at home
or as traders in conquered provinces; and a young generation of
ambitious politicians could find positions of influence in a widening bureaucracy. Those who had exhausted the ladder of available
offices at home could continue in the service by securing newly
created posts in the provinces. But these opportunities did not solve
all the problems whose settlement had been postponed during the
periods of war. The conversion of individual farms in central Italy
into large estates had deprived numbers of citizens not only of their
livelihood, but also of their independent status and had violated
their pride. Many of them moved to the city and filled it with
displaced and dissatisfied elements. Indebted as they were when

they lost their farms, they had to be supported at public expense, while the estates (*latifundia*) were peopled with slave workers who were imported in increasing numbers. They were often badly abused and came to constitute another unruly element, whose desperate local uprisings frightened the upper classes. Even when freed, as many ultimately were, they constituted a source of unrest.

Civilization in the Second Century. The more than a century-long period of warfare and pillaging no less than the later periods of civil war and fearful murders, combined with the inclination shown by the Romans for bloody sports and gladiator fights, have earned Rome the reputation of having been "immoral, greedy, insatiable of blood and rule." Indeed, if we compare Roman history with that of the Greeks, we find Greece's history introduced by the majestic work of Homer; even before the Greek states were organized, we hear the voices of Sappho, Alcaeus, and Anacreon; we witness a Thales and a Pythagoras, a Hesiod and an Aesop; we stand in wonder before Doric temples and theaters; and we admire Greek festivals centering around sports, music, games, and religion. Nothing comparable is to be found in almost five hundred years of early Roman history. Wars, social upheavals, and questions of administration and organization fill its pages. It is only between 200 B.C. and 150 B.C., after the conquest of Sicily and Greece, that we find a gentle note introduced.

LITERATURE AND ART. Around 200 B.C., Rome began, under the influence of the Hellenic spirit, to promote the arts. In the preceding century, only a few books seem to have been written. Thereafter, however, Rome undertook to translate Homer, to enact Greek tragedies, to imitate Greek authors and artists, and to create original works of lasting merit. A history of Rome was composed in epic form by Ennius; another, in prose, was written by Cato, the Carthage hater (who, however, in his old-fashioned admiration of Roman achievements, despised Greek civilization). Satirical, humorous, and gay comedies dealing with love and wine were published by Plautus and Terence. The beginnings of philosophical speculation can be noted. Greek prisoners (often enslaved) were hired as teachers; and homes and temples were built in accordance with Greek models.

RELIGION. We perceive also the stirring of a more elevating religious belief. Narrow and primitive religious traditions connected with state, locality, and family began to broaden under the influence of Greece's rationalism and Epicureanism, and new ethical standards were introduced. Despite protests of virtuous old Romans like Cato, even emotional oriental cults and ecstatic and immoral celebrations of Cybele and Bacchus appeared in Rome and stimulated new trends in arts, thought, and daily life. Religious festivals in imitation of those of the Greeks were celebrated.

LAW. Despite such stirrings, the chief cultural achievements of second-century Rome lie elsewhere. This becomes apparent when we read the history of Rome written at that time by a Greek prisoner, Polybius. In describing the conquest of Greece, Polybius, notwithstanding Rome's wars against his homeland and his own status as a prisoner, makes us sense the relief which Greeks and Orientals felt when the legions of Rome invaded their lands. Despite all her greed and lust for blood, her pillaging soldiers, exploiting and rapacious officials and businessmen, imposition of harsh taxes, and confiscation of land for the benefit of Roman citizens, Rome had a great deal to offer. She brought what had been missing for centuries: a measure of peace, of order, and of law. Order and law, organization and administration, were indeed the great accomplishments of second-century Rome. They were based on the rapid and penetrating development of legal thought. Not only did the edicts of praetors and the opinions of jurisconsults, interpreting law and advising the layman, find a permanent place in the Roman system, but concepts of a higher justice and of inviolable individual rights were evolved. They were based on a *jus naturale* which could embrace the entire conquered world.

THE END OF REPUBLICAN INSTITUTIONS

If the Romans brought peace and order to the world they had conquered, they failed to gain them for themselves. The social gap between, on the one side, Rome's Optimates and Equites and, on the other, the Populares led to violent jealousies, and these were accentuated by extremes of luxury which sapped the health and vigor of the upper classes. Likewise, the populations of the Italian countryside, excluded as they were from Roman citizenship, became increasingly restive. Graft and corruption widely permeated officialdom, laws to check them proved ineffectual, and demagoguery of the politicians led Rome into ever new dangerous and bloody ventures. In the provinces, wealth and independence often allowed a governor to disregard Rome's laws and use mercenary legions to exploit the conquered.

Social Upheavals. Toward the end of the period of incessant foreign warfare, accumulated dissatisfaction released events at home which constituted a decisive break in Roman history. The beginning of this sequence of events was marked by the activities of two brothers, Tiberius and Gaius Gracchus, grandsons of Scipio Africanus, who served as tribunes of the people in 133 and 123 B.C., respectively; the end came with Sulla in 83 B.C.

THE GRACCHI. To all appearances, the brothers Gracchus merely proposed a number of reforms in line with Roman tradition. They demanded a limitation of the size of landholdings in order to resettle dispossessed farmers; they advocated the establishment of new colonies for veterans, an improvement of the financial administration, various measures against corruption, and the increase of public works. Gaius Gracchus added to these demands others for stabilization of prices and for abolition of the monopoly which the Optimates held on jury duty. But what gave special significance to these proposals, and especially to those of Gaius, was the fact that they were coupled with numerous demagogic demands, such as those to extend citizenship rights to all Latin allies, to distribute grain gratis to the city proletariat, to pay the poor out of public funds, and to shorten military service. These measures, and others which would have squandered public funds, were proposed not only for their intrinsic merits, but also in order to win a personal following for the Gracchi. Perhaps Tiberius and Gaius believed that the establishment of unprecedented personal power in their own hands was necessary to carry out desired reforms. But in attempting the task, they both infringed upon existing laws. Thus, Tiberius removed by force his colleague in the tribunate; and both he and his brother sought to retain office after it had legally expired. Eventually, Tiberius and Gaius were both murdered, the elder brother in 133 B.C., the younger twelve years later; and together with them, hundreds and thousands of followers perished. Of the measures which they had advocated, only few survived; but the example they set had permanent significance. It is debatable whether or not those historians are right who maintain that a democratization and leveling process (such as occurred in Roman history) is bound to lead to demagoguery and, ultimately, to the end of democracy and to dictatorship. In any case, Tiberius and, especially,

Gaius Gracchus stood at the threshold of the period which in quick succession brought forth a rush of pretenders to dictatorial power until the republic perished and a monarchy was born.

MARIUS. The first in the line of aspirants to personal rule—after Gaius Gracchus—was a man named Marius. With him began the age when the political fortunes of Rome merged with those of a few individuals. Offspring of a lowly family, Marius rose in the military service. He participated in a war against King Jugurtha of Numidia, who, as Rome feared, was building in North Africa a dominion capable of reviving the threat Carthage had meant for Rome. It was owing to the ability of Marius, elected consul in 107 B.C., that the difficult campaign was brought to a successful conclusion and that Jugurtha was captured—to be starved to death in prison. A second opportunity to gather military laurels and reputation offered itself to Marius when two Germanic tribes, the Cimbri and Teutons, invaded Helvetia, the Po Valley, and Roman Gaul and defeated one Roman army after another. The terror they spread influenced the Romans to choose Marius again as consul in 104 B.C.; against law and tradition he was re-elected during each of the succeeding four years.

The hopes which Rome put in Marius for delivering the Empire from the Germanic danger were justified. He restored discipline in the army, improved its training and equipment, imbued it with confidence in its leader, and then, in 102 B.C. and 101 B.C., completely annihilated the two Germanic tribes in the two battles of Aquae Sextiae and Vercellae. Once triumphant as military chief, Marius attacked the political problems of the day. He lacked the honesty, devotion, and political skill of the Gracchi; but he possessed what they had not had—an army. Backed by well-trained soldiers and veterans who gave him their personal loyalty in exchange for bonuses of land or money, he embraced the popular cause and allied himself with political opportunists and the mob. Resorting to violence, he undertook to overthrow the existing order. But, faced by powerful forces still devoted to republican tradition, he failed. He had proved himself unreliable, and an united anti-Popular front, chiefly composed of partisans of the wealthy classes, succeeded in driving him out and in killing many of his adherents.

DRUSUS AND THE SOCIAL WAR. There followed a short period when the senatorial families reasserted their leadership. Using a demagogue, Livius Drusus, they assumed the role of advocate of reform.

They declared their readiness to increase their own ranks by admitting Equites to the Senate (thereby allowing these to sit on juries) and they proposed to redivide the land, lower the price of grain for the poor, and accord full citizenship to Italian allies. In the general atmosphere of corruption, party hatreds, and violence, most of these proposals came to naught. Drusus was murdered, and in 90 B.C. a terrible rising of the disappointed Italian allies occurred. It is known as the "Social War." The danger threatening Rome temporarily united all parties, and eventually the rebellion was suppressed. However, citizenship rights were now extended, first to those allies who had remained faithful and, toward the end of the war in 89 B.C., to all free men from the Po River to the Strait of Messina. This measure meant little, though, since, owing to distances and to tactical political arrangements, the voices of the Italians did not count in proportion to their numbers.

SULLA AND THE FIRST MITHRADATIC WAR. After victory in the Social War was achieved, the Senate meant to resume its control of the state. A skillful politician was, however, already on hand who was to break the republican institutions. He was an officer who had served under Marius in the Jugurthine War, and later in the Social War—L. Cornelius Sulla, an Optimate and a member of the senatorial party. In 88 B.C., Sulla was made consul and secured the command against a new enemy, King Mithradates of Pontus, a kingdom on the Black Sea. Before marching against him, Sulla undertook, however, to crush the popular party, for the Populares had wanted the command conferred on Marius (who had returned from exile) and a bitter fight for power had resulted. In the course of the struggle, the Populares were defeated and Marius was forced to flee to Africa. Having thus eliminated the competition of the popular party and its leader Marius, Sulla curtailed the voting rights of the Assembly and re-established senatorial rule for the time of his absence. He then proceeded to the East. There, Mithradates had made rapid progress, finding ready co-operation from the subjected peoples of Asia Minor. Long outraged at the exploitation by Italian administrators and settlers, these peoples had at his behest slaughtered tens of thousands of Italians. Even Greek cities in Europe, foremost among them Athens, had joined Mithradates, and Rome was threatened with the loss of her eastern sources of wealth and her needed supplies in grain and in slaves. But after a four-year-long difficult and bitter campaign, which was marked by ferocious pillaging by Roman armies, Sulla defeated Mithradates, deprived him of his conquests, and forced him and his Greek allies to pay an immense indemnity. In 83 B.C., Sulla returned to Italy.

Dictatorship and Reconstruction. During Sulla's absence, the popular party had resumed its fight under the leadership of Lucius Cornelius Cinna.[1] Cinna was helped by dissatisfied Italians and revolting slaves, and in 86 B.C., while Sulla was abroad, his arrangements for Italy were undone. Marius was recalled and elected consul for a seventh time, but he died within a few weeks. Fearful violence was committed against the senatorial party, decimating the ranks of the Optimates; thousands of slaves were given their freedom, and all limitations on the suffrage of the Italians were abolished.

Sulla's Dictatorship. Despite these events, Sulla upon his return found the situation not unfavorable to his own plans. Brutalities and disorder had alienated the sympathies of all moderate elements for the popular party; the Senate needed help; and he, himself, returned, as once had Marius, backed by an army and in the luster of recent victory. Allying himself with his old friends, the Optimates, and winning over many of the Equites and even some of the Populares through promises and bribes, he precipitated a new civil war and after ruinous fighting took the city of Rome. He had himself declared dictator and issued long lists of proscription, by which his opponents were condemned to death without trial. Almost five thousand of them perished, and their confiscated property filled Sulla's treasury and the pockets of his adherents.

Reorganization. As dictator, Sulla then reorganized the government. Arbitrarily he increased the number of senators and had men of his own choice appointed. He cancelled the citizenship rights of former insurrectionists, reduced the authority of the consuls by restricting their powers mainly to Italy, and curtailed the powers of the people's tribunes. Moreover, he put the provinces, through the appointment of proconsuls and propraetors, under senatorial control, and he improved the judicial system. He settled his veterans on land and sought to gain the good will of the populace by festivals, bribes, and works embellishing Rome.

After three years of dictatorship, Sulla resigned in favor of the Senate. Soon thereafter, in 78 B.C., he died.

[1] Cinna was the father of Julius Caesar's wife Cornelia and of L. Cornelius Cinna who joined the conspirators plotting to assassinate Caesar.

CHAPTER IX

THE ESTABLISHMENT OF THE EMPIRE

Although Sulla had espoused the cause of the Optimates, he probably had no illusion as to the survival chances of his reorganization attempts and the ability of the Senate to resume its former position. Gone were the times of the Republic. Not that necessarily, according to a predetermined, unavoidable evolution or intrinsic historical logic, republican institutions had to fall. But the order in Rome at that particular moment of her history was undermined by tensions resulting from overly rapid expansion, by extreme economic and social inequalities, and by the ambitions of men of genius who happened to live at the time. In rapid succession, the powers of the constitutional officers, of consuls, praetors, tribunes, and senators, passed into the hands of individual dictators; and not until the age of Augustus was a new order created that could give stability to the commonwealth.

THE AGE OF JULIUS CAESAR

The period between 78 B.C., the year of Sulla's death, and 44 B.C., the year of Caesar's assassination, is one of almost uninterrupted civil wars. However, despite grave social issues which prompted the wars, it would be difficult to draw clear lines of distinction between the interests for which the opposing parties stood. Public interests were mixed with personal aims of outstanding individuals, and the masses followed individuals rather than ideas. Yet, during these times of turmoil, many works of lasting value were achieved.

Rome's borders were expanded more rapidly than ever before, Roman and Hellenic civilization was introduced in barbarian areas where it was to become the foundation of new civilizations, and taste and learning were promoted along with political and military aims. The city itself was adorned with works of art that have remained its pride through two thousand years.

The Struggle for Power. Promptly after the death of Sulla, the popular party sought to destroy the work of the former dictator. It engaged in a new civil war in order to reduce the power of the Senate; and while the population suffered, politicians and generals found unequalled opportunities for furthering their personal aims. Among the leaders were Sertorius, champion of the popular cause; Pompey, a former aid of Sulla; Crassus, immensely wealthy Optimate; Lucullus, Caesar, Catiline, Clodius, and others. Gradually the struggle for power narrowed down to one between Pompey and Caesar, and finally the latter emerged victorious from it.

RISE OF POMPEY. Pompey's career had started in the army under Sulla. With Sulla, Pompey had fought the Marian forces in Sicily and Africa, and, after Sulla's death, he made himself defender of Sulla's legacy. His first opponent was the new leader of the Populares, Sertorius, a man of ability and considerable honesty, an aspirant to dictatorship like his rivals, but perhaps more in the tradition of the Gracchi than that of Marius. After a six-year struggle, which was fought in Italy and in Spain, Sertorius was assassinated in 72 B.C., and the senatorial party with Pompey triumphed.

THE SPARTACUS REVOLT AND CRASSUS. The defeat of the popular party released another revolt. During Marius' reign, the Populares had espoused the cause of the slaves, and these now armed themselves and rose under the leadership of a Thracian slave by the name of Spartacus. A new, almost unequalled danger menaced Rome, and a desperate Senate raised a fresh army, put it under the command of another adherent of Sulla, Crassus, and sent it against the slaves. Only after bitter fighting did Crassus succeed in destroying the slave troops in 71 B.C. Having achieved his purpose, he, however, did not disband his legions; instead, he marched upon Rome, fearful lest Pompey, who had likewise retained command of his forces and also moved on Rome, might seize complete power.

POMPEY AND CRASSUS. Before a clash occurred, though, Crassus and Pompey came to an arrangement—at the expense of the very Senate which had charged them with its defense. Together, they forced the Senate, under the threat of arms, to allow their election as consuls for the coming year. As consuls they continued to speak in terms of earlier party slogans, to follow precedent and formally uphold existing institutions; but in reality, they established personal rule. They abolished many of Sulla's reforms and saw to a redistribution of power. Pompey in particular built up a private following among the Equestrians (for whom he secured the right of jury service) and among the masses (whom he won over by free distribution of grain).

THE RISE OF CAESAR. The carefully laid plans of Pompey and Crassus were soon challenged by new aspirants to dictatorship: by Julius Caesar, by the ambitious lieutenant of Sulla, Catiline, by the eminent general Lucullus, and by Lucullus' brother-in-law, Clodius. Caesar soon proved the most gifted. At the beginning of his career, he had married into the Marian party and had assumed its leadership; later, he had taken Sulla's granddaughter as his second wife and had sought the friendship of the Equestrian order. Although his reputation, owing to his debts, dissipations, and ruthlessness in politics, was low, he had built up a large following. The moment was, however, not yet in his favor, for not only did he lack an army to back him, but he was also bitterly opposed by the comparatively few, yet influential politicians who were still devoted to republican ways, Roman traditions, and the existing order. Among them was the orator and writer Cicero, a "homo novus" or newcomer, who won fame in a trial against an extortionist official, Verres, and who worked for a compromise to salvage some of the former institutions. Another member of this group was Cato the Younger, stern and uncompromising heir of the ideals of Cato the Elder.

POMPEY AND THE SECOND MITHRADATIC WAR. A decision between the various aspirants was postponed because the needs of the empire demanded that attention be directed elsewhere—to foreign issues. It is remarkable that internal disruption in Rome did not make impossible the survival of the empire nor even block its growth. Perhaps the fact that all aspirants to dictatorship had to have behind them a victorious army and the glory which only conquest could give accounts for the continued vigorous pursuit of an expansionist foreign policy. In any case, first Lucullus, yet another rising star, and then Pompey were called away from the Italian scene. For Mithradates, having recovered from the defeats inflicted on him by Sulla, had in 74 B.C. once more invaded various parts of Rome's Asiatic territories; and in addition, pirates endangered Roman trade and communication lines. The Senate charged Lucullus with the campaign against Mithradates, and subsequently Pompey with that against the pirates. Lucullus achieved great military success, defeated Mithradates at Tigranocerta in 69 B.C., and conquered the lands up to the Tigris and Euphrates rivers; Pompey concluded the war against the pirates victoriously in 67 B.C. But Lucullus could not turn his victories into political assets; he was recalled from the East at the insistence of Roman businessmen and provincial administrators who resented his honest and firm rule; and he thus lost his chance. Posterity knows him mainly for his connoisseurship of food, to which he devoted himself thereafter. His place as commander was taken by Pompey. Within another four years, Pompey had conquered the kingdom of Pontus, old Mithradates committed suicide, and all lands extending from the banks of the Black Sea to the Tigris River, including Armenia, Syria, and Judaea, were reorganized as new Roman provinces or dependent kingdoms.

UPRISING OF CATILINE. For a second time, Pompey returned to Italy at the head of a victorious army (61 B.C.). He found the situation much changed. In his absence, Catiline, descendant of an aristocratic family, after having failed to secure the consulship, had tried to organize a mob-rising in order to gain what he could not achieve lawfully. But Cicero, chosen consul instead of Catiline for the year 63 B.C., had discovered the plot, had denounced the demagogic nature of the laws proposed by Catiline, and, through a number of impassioned speeches, had aroused the Senate. Catiline was forced to flee, and in the following year he perished in combat. Pompey thus found the Senate greatly strengthened, and even Caesar, who had been involved in Catiline's projects, had to lie low.

The First Triumvirate. Under these circumstances, Pompey decided to demonstratively disband his army and to announce his return to private life. His action did not win him, however, the expected applause of the Senate, and he therefore approached Caesar, who on his part saw a chance of recovering lost ground by allying himself to a man of Pompey's standing. In 60 B.C., a secret agreement was concluded between the two and joined by Crassus, whose wealth and connections recommended him to the others. The "First Triumvirate" came into being. The three men pledged each other help in securing the most influential offices; they determined which one each should seek, which opponents should be eliminated, and which provinces should be given to whom. Their plan worked: defenders of the Senate like Cato and Cicero found themselves, one after the other, removed from the local scene; and Pompey, Caesar, and Crassus gained first the offices and then the provinces each one wanted.

CONQUEST OF GAUL. As it turned out later, the distribution of the provinces among the three triumvirs was of great consequence. For southern Gaul fell to Caesar, who went there in 59 B.C. and immediately set out to conquer the whole of Gaul. With determination and ability, he defeated Gauls, Helvetians, and Belgians; suppressed a mighty uprising of the Gauls under Vercingetorix; and crossed the Rhine into Germany and the Channel into Britain. He opened new opportunities to Roman business interests, tax collectors, and administrators, won wealth and reputation for himself, and gained, as envisaged, the support of a personally loyal army. The significance of his work is difficult to overestimate: through the Romanization of Gaul, which he initiated (and by refraining from a large-scale conquest of Germany, which thus was not Romanized), he deeply influenced the future of Western civilization. In 50 B.C., he returned to Rome.

END OF TRIUMVIRATE. During Caesar's absence, the senatorial party had regained considerable influence. Both Cicero and Cato had returned from exile or assignment in the provinces, and by 56 B.C., the Senate had succeeded in reasserting its supreme position. This had induced Pompey, Caesar, and Crassus to renew their triumvirate at a conference held at Luca. But three years later, their co-operation came to an end when Crassus was killed in the Battle of Carrhae against the Parthians. Thereafter, Pompey once more drew close to the senatorial party, and soon strife broke out between his adherents and those of Caesar, culminating in open and bloody street fighting. The Senate supported Pompey by creating him sole consul.

THE END OF POMPEY. In this situation, Caesar, who had once more gravitated to the equestrian and popular orders, offered upon his return to disband his troops, provided that Pompey do likewise and that he, Caesar, receive the consulship for the following year. Pompey and the Senate refused. This decided the issue. In January, 49 B.C., Caesar at the head of one of his legions crossed the Rubicon River, which constituted the limit of his province, and entered Italy proper. The die was cast. The Senate declared him a public enemy, and the leaders among his supporters were expelled from Rome. But Caesar could not be stopped, for lacking troops Pompey was forced to flee; and Caesar occupied Rome. Having seized the treasury, he promptly left again; set sail for Spain, where he destroyed the forces assembled under one of Pompey's sons; returned to Rome to make himself consul again; and left once more to attack Pompey himself, who had gone to Greece and had assembled an army there. In 48 B.C., at Pharsalus, Pompey was defeated. He fled to Egypt where he was murdered before Caesar arrived.

Caesar's Rule. Caesar spent the ensuing year with Egypt's Queen Cleopatra. He subdued an uprising in Egypt and through the queen secured a political alliance which brought Egypt virtually under Roman control. Finally escaping Cleopatra's enchantments, he left Egypt, annexed additional lands for Rome, gained new laurels for himself by attacking and defeating the Parthians, and reconquered the Pontus, then ruled by Mithradates' son, Pharnaces.

CAESAR'S ADMINISTRATION. In 47 B.C., Caesar returned to Rome. During his absence, his enemies had tried to rally. A republican army had been formed, but Caesar quickly destroyed it and drove Cato the Younger, the defender of the republic, to suicide. He likewise crushed a rising which the sons of Pompey staged in Spain; and he added yet another conquest—Numidia—which was incorporated as a province into the empire. Having then distributed lands and gold among his veterans, Caesar set to the task of reshaping Rome's institutions. With his power guaranteed by control of the army, he had himself appointed dictator, first for ten years, later for life, and united in his own hands the powers of a proconsul, army commander, censor, tribune, and also pontifex maximus. He named to administrative and senatorial positions men responsible to himself, disposed of foreign spoils to improve conditions at home, had new money coined, and reduced the debts of ruined farmers and the dole of the needy city population by resettling many dispossessed citizens on confiscated or conquered lands. He adorned Rome with majestic buildings. The system of farming out taxes was curbed, the administration of the provinces improved, and steps were taken to reduce slavery. Caesar also ordered the introduction of a new, more scientific, calendar.

CAESAR'S ACHIEVEMENTS AND DEATH. If the greatness of Caesar as a general and augmenter of the empire is generally recognized, his internal reforms—keyed to concentration of power in his own hands—are not unanimously accepted as proof of real statesmanship. Caesar knew how to please the commercial classes, the poorer sections of the population, and those non-Italians to whom he granted citizenship rights; but he did not solve fundamental problems in a way fruitful beyond the term of his own life. Although his government was "fair and mild," he did not, owing to his ambition and arbitrariness, reconcile the patricians and republicans. Senate and Assemblies were used by him in no more than advisory capacity and often served merely as a front. Within three years, the senatorial party revenged itself on him. Under the leadership of Brutus and Cassius, they assassinated Caesar in March, 44 B.C.

Social Scene. The assassination of Caesar did not aid the cause of the Senate. The Senate could not reverse a trend that resulted from the gradual evolution of the nature of the Roman republic and that was mirrored in the economic, intellectual, and moral climate of the age. No longer could the parochial views, domestic virtue, and revered traditions of Old Rome inspire. Wars, revolutions, proscriptions, and expansion had dissolved family ties, given women wide freedom, spread the habit of divorce, and promoted promiscuity among both sexes. They had decimated the ranks of the senatorial group and diminished the social usefulness of existing institutions; and they had increased the influence of those who, whether of equestrian or of senatorial or even of freedman origin, owed their position to political shrewdness or to wealth derived not from agriculture or industry but from financial and real-estate transactions. "Conspicuous consumption" marked the lives of the upper sectors of the population, not only in the capital, but also in leading provincial cities. It sharply contrasted with the poverty of the many who lived in the slums of the cities (foremost those of Rome) or eked out a meager existence on steadily diminishing peasant farms.

Cultural Scene. The picture of the crudity and brutality evinced in the political and social arena was somewhat relieved, however, by that of the cultural endeavors of Rome in Caesar's time. The closer Rome's contact came to be with the East, the stronger was the East's civilizing impact felt—despite certain depraving influences, which also came from the Orient.

FINE ARTS. Architecture, sculpture, and painting were developed under Greek influence. Original creations were rare, but many

Roman imitations of Hellenistic models were of great beauty. The Romans excelled also in large utilitarian projects, such as city planning, the laying out of networks of streets, the building of squares (such as fora in Rome and in provincial towns), and the construction of aqueducts and sewerage systems (cloaca). Many public buildings, streets, and parks were adorned with excellent statuary.

PHILOSOPHY, LITERATURE, AND RHETORIC. Writing and philosophy in Rome were likewise indebted to Greek examples. The predominant world view among the intellectuals of Rome was Epicureanism, advocating a rational life unconcerned with transcendental aspirations and with immortality and gods, and exhorting man to quiet enjoyment of what is within reach. This view was presented in poetic form in the work of Lucretius, *De rerum natura*. Lighter poetry was created by Catullus, who celebrated love and nature, and who, in equally elegant style, dealt also with political issues. Many prose works were written. Interest in the shaking events of the day inspired historical work. Diodorus and Nicholas of Damascus, Posidonius the philosopher, Cornelius Nepos the biographer, Sallust, and Caesar himself composed histories of artistic as well as factual value. Whatever their ulterior motives may have been, they evinced a historical sense which indicated a maturing spirit.

The most influential writer—if not in his own time then at least for posterity—was the great orator, Cicero. With integrity and courage, Cicero, child of a corrupt age, published political speeches, letters on art and philosophy, and works on government and law. He was a master of style, and even if, as an eclectic philosopher and transmitter of Greece's heritage, he formulated no great new ideas, he possessed wide influence owing to his genius for expressing thoughts with great clarity; and he left, through the elegance of his presentation, a deep impression for over two thousand years.

EDUCATION AND LAW. The times of disruption contributed also to Rome's growth in the fields of education and law. Many who were to give distinction to Roman civilization in the subsequent Augustan Age were brought up during the civil wars. Despite the troubles, private schools flourished under Greek preceptors. Law (though disregarded on the political stage) was developed further; magistrates and lawyers, whether of high or plebeian origin, attended with care, often with genius, to judicial functions. Even while serving the interests of the propertied classes (and thereby the cause of private property), the Roman bureaucracy enriched the treasure of legal ideas and of international concepts of justice.

THE AUGUSTAN AGE

If the murderers of Caesar had hoped that upon the death of the dictator the Republic could be revived, they found themselves quickly disappointed. The aims of Brutus and Cassius, leaders of the republican party, reflected neither popular wishes nor general trends. Both ran in the direction of personal rule by an efficient administrator who would put an end to internal strife and reorganize the empire. This man emerged in the person of Octavius, eighteen-year-old relative, and heir-designate, of Caesar. It was he who gave peace to the commonwealth and stimulated the latent forces to new cultural achievements.

Struggle for Caesar's Heritage. Immediately upon Caesar's assassination, three pretenders to supreme power arose: Antony, friend of Caesar and consul at the time of the assassination; Lepidus, a commander of Caesar's army in Italy; and Octavius. Since Antony and Lepidus joined forces, a triangular struggle followed. On the one side were the republicans under Brutus and Cassius, who drew their strength from the rich eastern provinces that had been assigned to them; on another were Antony and Lepidus, who were backed by the Populares and the political friends of Caesar; and then there was young Octavius. From the first, the latter showed unusual political acumen. He started out by putting himself at the disposal of the Senate and even convinced Cicero that he was the man least likely to overthrow republican institutions; then, he secured the support of Caesar's veterans through lavish gifts; then, he gained the consulship for the year 43 B.C. and took up arms against Antony; and, finally, he reversed his course and threw in his lot with Caesar's friends.

THE SECOND TRIUMVIRATE. Before the year 43 B.C. was over, Octavius formed, together with Antony and Lepidus, a "Second Triumvirate." Combining their resources, the three immediately turned against Caesar's murderers. They issued new proscription lists, had thousands of people killed (at Antony's insistence, including Cicero), confiscated their property, and then sailed to attack Brutus and Cassius. In 42 B.C., in a decisive battle at Philippi in

Greece, the two leaders of the conspiracy against Caesar were defeated; both committed suicide.

TRIUMPH OF OCTAVIUS. After the victory, Antony stayed in the East. He reorganized Rome's unruly Oriental provinces and undertook a campaign against the still unconquered Parthians. Then he proceeded to Egypt where, falling under the spell of Queen Cleopatra, he remained. Octavius returned to Rome. With outstanding statesmanship he managed to appease many of his enemies; at the same time, he used his veterans, whom he bound through further gifts closer to his banners, to suppress any opposition of the Senate. Shrewdly, he also countered the intrigues of Antony's friends, who feared for their absent leader's position. In 40 B.C., he even concluded a new agreement with the two other triumvirs, married his sister to Antony, and had Italy and the West assigned to himself; the East was given to Antony, and Africa to Lepidus. This arrangement lasted until 36 B.C., when Lepidus was removed; he had proved inefficient and of questionable loyalty during a war to which Pompey's ambitious and capable son Sextus challenged the triumvirs. Since Sextus perished in the course of the war, the fate of the empire was now left in the hands of Octavius and Antony. Their rivalry came to a head when Antony, who had continued his affair with Cleopatra, conspired with the queen in the building of an independent empire for themselves and their children. With the consent of the Senate, Octavius attacked his former colleague. In the Battle of Actium (31 B.C.), he defeated the combined forces of Antony and Cleopatra. The two escaped to Egypt, where they ended their lives and love by a double suicide—leaving Octavius in possession of Egypt and the East, as well as the West.

Reorganization of Roman Institutions. In 29 B.C., Octavius returned to Rome. Rid of fear, he could from then on cultivate the better facets of his character which he had had little opportunity to demonstrate while the struggle for power lasted. His earlier experiences had already presaged the statesman, but he now appears as a changed man.

EMPERORSHIP AND INTERNAL POLICIES. Without abolishing republican forms and ways dear to the Romans, Octavius assumed, with the rank of princeps and the title of "Augustus," the functions of consul, proconsul, tribune, and *pontifex maximus*. He preserved the Senate, but used it mainly for advice and for judicial decisions. Its membership was limited to six hundred—most of them coming from the old families and all of them required to possess a large fortune. He retained the two assemblies, but reduced their share in the government to a mere formality. He reserved for himself the right to nominate consuls and other magistrates, and he created two new offices which in due time were to become perhaps the most influential: Prefect of the City, and Prefect of the Praetorian (or Imperial) Bodyguard. In his hands were placed the rights to convoke the Senate and preside over it, to conduct foreign affairs and make war and peace, to sponsor legislation and exercise a veto, and—most important—to command the armies. As an imperial prerogative, he reserved for himself the control of strategically important provinces and of Egypt (of which he had made himself pharaoh), and he governed these domains through his own lieutenants. The rest of the provinces were left to senatorial direction. Thus, the income from large parts of the Empire went into his personal treasury, and gave him enormous wealth plus additional power. In the meantime, the state apparatus, dependent upon the Senate, decreased in size, resources, and importance. Most of the taxes were drawn from the provinces; those for Roman citizens remained light—consisting chiefly of land, sales, and inheritance taxes.

MILITARY AND EXTERNAL POLICIES. Augustus was to rule for forty-three years after his return to Rome. It was a time of restored order, law, and prosperity rather than of brilliant exploits. Military forces were kept at a minimum. They consisted of three parts: legions composed of Roman citizens who served for a long term, at the end of which they received bonuses and land; auxiliary troops of provincials; and the praetorian guard. Since peace reigned, their chief task consisted in securing the borders and helping with the pacification and Romanization of the provincial populations. Romanization meant infiltration of the Latin language and of Roman law and administration; it gradually expressed itself in the daily habits of the provincials, in their urbanized life, in their cultural interests, their styles of architecture. The mineral resources of Spain were developed; Carthage was rebuilt and became anew a center of the grain trade; Egypt was secured against invaders from the south; and Gaul's borders were defended. An expansion into Germany miscarried, though; Augustus suffered there the most shattering defeat (Battle of the Teutoburg Forest): in A.D. 9, his legions were destroyed by Cheruskans under Hermann (Arminius), and the

Germanic lands beyond the Rhine and Main rivers were never incorporated into the Empire. In the East, peace was fairly well maintained; the Parthians were held back, and Judaea was quieted after an uprising which followed the death of Rome's friend Herod. Existing local autonomy and Hellenistic patterns of civilization were left unchanged.

PAX ROMANA. Thus, the beginnings of a *pax romana* are traceable under Augustus' rule. Large-scale commerce revived and prosperity returned. Roads were built, connecting the capital with the provinces and the provinces with one another; seaways were made secure against pirates; and some daring highways were laid across Alpine passes. Roman administration was considerate and Roman citizenship was extended to many regions and many individuals. Corruption was reduced. Law schools were founded, the process of law was improved, and legal procedures were introduced in the various distant provinces of the Empire, protecting their populations. Some progress in the codification of the law was made. Although the trend toward large estates worked by slaves and producing crops for exchange for Oriental luxury goods could not be reversed, the interests of small landowners were better guarded.

Economic and Societal Structure. Economically, the Empire under Augustus became a more closely knit unit, but, owing to the lack of progress in science and technology, industrial production hardly improved. It continued to be based on small-scale home industries run with the help of slaves. Nor did agricultural production in Italy itself improve. The city of Rome remained dependent upon imports, upon the productive resources of the Empire, upon tribute and spoils, and upon speculators in needed commodities. Many of these speculators were foreigners—Orientals of Syrian, Armenian, Jewish, and Greek origin.

Socially, trends evinced before the times of Augustus persisted. The real winner of the civil wars was the equestrian class which had long been in the ascendancy. Membership in this class required considerable wealth (amounting to at least one-half of the fortune prescribed for a senator), and wealth gave not only decisive economic influence to the equestrian banker and financier, tax collector and businessman; it also secured him preference for positions in the civil service. From among the Equestrians were chosen the captain of the praetorian guard and other officers close to the person of the emperor. Artisans, also, found their lot improved, owing to peace, revival of trade, and public works; combining in guilds, they gained a measure of security. But the senatorial group, decimated, impoverished, and distrusted as it was, gained little. While retaining rank and prestige, it saw its political influence fade. Nor was the situation of the Roman proletariat much improved. Many continued to live in poverty and want, dependent upon gifts from the public or from Augustus' private treasury, and eager to be amused by spectacles and games. Likewise, the status of the peasant masses and that of the slaves showed few signs of change. However, the number of slaves who were freed steadily increased, and throughout the Empire freedmen played an important role as clerical workers or as supervisors and agents for state, private business, and landed estates.

Cultural Progress. In such an atmosphere, a new generation grew up. Cultural interests evinced in the stormy period of civil war were broadened; and wealthy men, uncreative themselves but attracted by peaceful arts, found satisfaction in sponsoring artists and scholars. Augustus himself and his friends Agrippa and, especially, Maecenas assumed the role of patrons of cultural endeavors.

Fine Arts. During Augustus' reign, public and private buildings of great splendor were erected. A new forum, theaters, temples, and fountains, inspired by Hellenistic tradition, were built. Sculptures were produced to decorate homes, streets, and halls; numerous imposing busts were created. The famous *Ara pacis* with its lovely reliefs was erected, made of marble as were so many Augustan structures.

Literature. Poets and writers composed surpassingly fine prose works and verse, even when they imitated Greek models. Horace's *Odes,* Ovid's *Metamorphoses,* and Vergil's *Aeneid* mark the zenith in Roman creative literature. Although many of the works were written in a patriotic vein, glorifying Rome, praising her ancient virtue, extolling present times, and advocating her mission, their real merit lies in the beauty of form in which great thoughts meaningful throughout the ages were expressed. Livy wrote a famous history of Rome from its beginnings, which has at least in parts survived. In the field of geography, the main contribution came from a Greek, Strabo.

Philosophy and Religion. The inner uncertainty of the age is, however, evinced by the state of philosophy and religion. A pessimistic trend, whether going back to Epicureanism or to Stoicism, can be increasingly noted. Faith in the traditional gods, which Augustus tried to revitalize, was lacking; and an appeal was made by the thinkers to bear with dignity whatever fate brought, to try to keep aloof from vulgar passions, and, if possible, to enjoy what each day offered. Virtue and lofty moral standards were seldom manifested; in the very family of Augustus, who did his best to further such values, they remained conspicuously absent; a similar atmosphere prevailed in Roman society throughout the Empire. Mystery cults connected with excesses such as Egypt, Persia, and Greece knew, continued to spread. But Jesus had been born in Judaea, and His teachings were to seal the doom of all the beliefs and cults nurtured by Roman philosophers and the emperor.

Augustus died in A.D. 14.

CHAPTER X

IMPERIAL ROME

IN THE AUGUSTAN PERIOD Rome had found a solution for her political problems. Under a monarchy instead of a democratic system, order was re-established; civil wars came to an end; dispensation of justice was improved; and the burdens of government and taxation were more equitably distributed. The Empire began to prosper under a system of government which had logically developed out of, yet was in contrast to, Rome's earlier institutions. This new system did not change during the first century A.D.; and in the second century, it brought the Empire to its climax. Rome's commonwealth reached its largest extent; its populations could live under a system of law which, even though favoring Roman citizens and among these the wealthy classes, made it possible for all to gain a measure of security, share in the advantages of a world-wide trade, and attain a considerable amount of self-expression; and while art and scholarship did not reach the heights they had attained in Athens at the time of Pericles, they, too, bore rich fruits. Only after more than two hundred years—in the third century—did reverse trends set in that foreshadowed the collapse of the Empire.

THE FIRST CENTURY A.D.

Upon the passing of Augustus, Rome's monarchical structure, which seemed so dependent upon the character and ability of the great emperor, did not break down. To the contrary, during the first century, monarchy was firmly implanted. Every ruler contributed a share to the steadily rising authority of the emperors—whether he was raised to his dignity by birth, or, as it generally happened, by army or praetorian guard, and whether he lived until a natural death or, as in the case of seven out of ten emperors, death by assassination or suicide claimed him. Therefore, neither the vicious stories of palace intrigues, murder, and debauchery in the imperial households, nor even the accounts of the excesses of the Roman rabble crying for bread and entertainment (*panem et circenses*) should be taken as the real story of the Empire. It survived and grew because its new institutions served the needs of the times and because sufficiently large sectors of the population derived profit from its existence and maintenance.

The Emperors. The rulers of the Empire caught the imagination of generation after generation; their colorful personalities left a strong impact upon history. Augustus' successor was his stepson Tiberius (A.D. 14–37), a conscientious and capable administrator and excellent general, whose later years were envenomed by his own suspicious nature and marred by acts of cruelty inflicted chiefly on those suspected of the slightest disloyalty. He was followed by Caligula (A.D. 37–41), cruel and half-mad, Claudius (A.D. 41–54), incompetent, yet attractive and cultured, and Nero (A.D. 54–68), half-insane and cruel like Caligula. Dignity was restored to the imperial office by Vespasian (A.D. 69–79), who followed three short-lived rulers, and who again brought order into the administrative and military services. The short reign of his generous and peaceable son Titus (A.D. 79–81) was an unfortunate one because of plagues, fires, and a disastrous eruption of Mount Vesuvius. Finally, there came Domitian, a despot who knew how to rule efficiently. Under him, the deification of the emperor, initiated by Caesar and Augustus and advanced by Caligula and Claudius, was furthered. Assemblies and Senate, which Vespasian had still respected, were stripped of almost all their prestige and power.

Under several of the emperors—Claudius, Nero, and Domitian—women, whether wives, daughters, or mistresses of the rulers, wielded considerable influence. They took a hand even in the making and unmaking of various emperors.

Imperial Administration. The emperors ruled with the help of the bureaucracy, in which Equestrians and freedmen played the chief role. The former filled most of the important official posts, and the latter, dependent as they were upon the personal favor of the emperor, could be trusted with his personal service and with high offices in the palace. Many proved to be able administrators, who merited credit for holding the Empire together and providing efficient and honest government.

EXTERNAL POLICIES. The Empire continued to grow. Revolts in Palestine, Britain, and Gaul were suppressed, and new provinces like Cappadocia, Judaica, and Britain were organized. Britain, the major part of which was conquered under Claudius, was protected by a wall (*limes*) against possible inroads from Scotland; and under Domitian, Rome's borders were expanded into Wales. Some conquests were also made in eastern Europe along the course of the lower Danube. Only Germany withstood Roman pressure. Attempts at conquest were halted under Tiberius, and the frontiers were stabilized along the Rhine and the upper Danube.

INTERNAL POLICIES. Foreign expansion was matched by internal improvements. Tiberius, Vespasian, and Domitian successfully built up the treasury; the administration of public and imperial funds, left to competing agencies by Augustus, was considerably centralized. Citizenship rights were given to Spaniards and other non-Italians. Domitian attempted a number of agricultural reforms to improve the situation of the poor farmers. New large public works were undertaken; building activities flourished. Additional aqueducts were constructed during Claudius' reign; and if Augustus had taken pride in the creation of marble palaces, temples, and theaters, great architectural undertakings were carried on likewise by his successors. Soon the pattern set by Rome was imitated in the smaller cities of Italy, in southern Germany and Gaul, and in Greece, Egypt, and Asia Minor.

Cultural Scene. Arts and literature flourished in first-century Rome, even if we cannot trace many decisive departures or innovations in style. Innovations we do find, however, in the religious scene; for there we come to notice an interest in transcendental beliefs unknown in most periods of antiquity, and we also witness a new approach to ethical concepts and human conduct.

FINE ARTS. Building activities were vigorous. Numerous villas and palaces were erected in and around Rome—among them the gigantic *domus aurea* of Nero. Other building projects were carried out in the provinces. Beautiful mosaics and frescoes were designed to adorn these buildings, whether public or private. Some have been preserved owing to the eruption of Mount Vesuvius in A.D. 79, which by burying the towns of Pompeii and Herculaneum claimed them for posterity. Fine statues were sculptured, most of them still imitating Greek style or copying Greek models outright, but some showing original Roman concepts and excelling through a straightforward realism.

LITERATURE, PHILOSOPHY, SCIENCE. Literature, philosophy, and the sciences were consistently enriched by contacts with lands conquered by Rome. Lucan excelled in poetry, and a later much-cherished figure, Petronius, contributed satirical stories mirroring life in Roman society. Flavius Josephus, a Romanized Jew, wrote a history of the Jews; Celsus and others made scientific contributions in medicine, law, and agriculture; and Pliny the Elder composed a natural history comprising a summary of the knowledge of his time. Outstanding among philosophers was Seneca, teacher and adviser of Nero during the emperor's better early days, and later his victim. This statesman, philosopher, and tragedian carried on the Stoic tradition. In the midst of a society craving the vulgar entertainment afforded by races, circuses, and gladiatorial contests, he emphasized the fact that a virtuous life and an ethical attitude in the pursuit of public obligations and personal relations constitute the aim of the wise. While abstaining from broad transcendental speculations, he sought a solution for overcoming the inescapable evils of this world.

RELIGION. It is significant that in some respects Seneca's thoughts contained seeds found also in Christian ethics. Actually, the official religious beliefs as well as the philosophy of the time were as incapable as ever of attracting the sophisticated minds of the learned and of satisfying the yearnings of those in search of a meaningful faith or the emotional needs of the masses.

Paganism. Worship of traditional Roman gods and of the emperor was required of everybody as a matter of devotion and service to the state. This not very demanding worship failed, of course, to meet the longings of the many who were searching for a more meaningful faith and for a guide to an ethical life. Some of them resorted, therefore, to teachings which reflected no more than crude superstitions; others sought satisfaction through mystical cults aiming at purification from sin and a blessed immortal life. Widespread among the religions thus adopted was Mithraism which, following the teachings of Zoroaster, explained the world in terms of an eternal struggle between light and darkness, good and evil. Other faiths which became popular in Rome were the imported religions of Isis and of Cybele; like the rites of Dionysus, they were often connected with orgies condemned by state authorities (which were anxious, as in Vespasian's or Domitian's times, to improve morals), but they appealed to a profligate, cynical, and superstitious society.

Judaism. More consequential than paganism was Judaism. Owing to their exclusiveness, their segregation ethnically as well as religiously, the Jews played a twofold—a secular and a religious—role. In the secular sphere, Judaism was important because, as traders and financiers, the Jews exercised considerable influence on the economy of Rome, and because, as members of a kingdom of their own, they offered bitter political resistance to their integration into the Roman Empire. Though they had been subjected, after their return from Babylon, to Persians, Macedonians, Syrians, and Egyptians, they had never reconciled themselves to foreign rule. In the second century B.C., under the leadership of the house of Maccabaeus, they had gained independence and preserved it for approximately a century. But in the time of Pompey, they had become Roman vassals. For a time, the wily policies of Herod the Great and his successors prevented new struggles for independence; but in the reign of Caligula, a revolt shook the country again—only to be followed, after its suppression, by another in Nero's time. This second revolt was not crushed until, in A.D. 70, under Vespasian, Jerusalem was destroyed by Vespasian's son Titus and the Jewish religious treasures were brought to Rome. The other aspect of opposition of Judaism to Rome—the religious aspect—persisted, however, also thereafter. At no time could the monotheistic creed of the Jews be reconciled with Rome's religious tenets or with the Hellenistic spirit that permeated Rome's society. Even after being deprived of their state, the Jews set themselves, through their religion, apart from other nations. Moreover, they held fast to a hope for a Messiah, who would fulfill their religious longings as well as liberate them from political domination. Under the circumstances, Judaism failed to provide that element for religious renewal for which the Roman world seemed ripe. It was the teachings of Jesus of Nazareth, whose public career fell into the reign of Tiberius, which were to initiate a new age in the religious development of the Romans.

Christianity. In contrast to the parochial views of the Jews and their concomitant connection with the Jewish state and traditional

Jewish law, the Christians early adopted cosmopolitan tendencies, and this made it possible for their faith to spread widely. In men like Paul of Tarsus, they found capable and devoted missionaries, in others like St. Sebastian (an early martyr) witnesses in life and death, and again in others (unnamed) humble and loyal workers. Christian teaching flourished particularly in the eastern provinces of the Empire, and it was there that in the second half of the first century A.D., through the writing of the Gospels and through the institution of rituals such as baptism, a historical tradition was established.

Despite Roman tolerance, the relationship of the young Christian sect and the Roman state suffered, however, from early times on. Christians were disliked because of their connection with the hated Jews and because of their refusal to perform such duties toward the state as emperor-worship and service in the army. A number of violent actions against them, which claimed many victims, were undertaken. Sometimes such "persecutions" were caused by spontaneous popular movements; sometimes they were sponsored by a government which sought to punish the sect for lack of devotion to the state. Most ill-famed among the persecutions was that in the time of Nero in A.D. 64, when the Christians were falsely held responsible for a devastating fire in Rome. A less spectacular, but more extensive, persecution occurred under Domitian.

THE SECOND CENTURY

The following century is known as that of the "good" emperors—although, to the historian, the personal influence of the ruler may appear as no more than one agent, and certainly not the decisive one, in Rome's evolution. It may be called an age of "benevolent despotism." During this time, the political as well as cultural trends initiated in the first century persisted; only toward the end of the century did they begin to show a new direction.

The Emperors. The most famous emperors during the second century, several of whom were of foreign origin, were Trajan (98–117), Hadrian (117–138), Antoninus Pius (138–161), and Marcus Aurelius (161–180). Except for Trajan, they were not, as earlier emperors, the creatures of revolting armies or of praetorian guards, nor of the Senate, which in any case had retained a formal right of confirmation; but each of them was appointed by his own predecessor. They were men devoted to their task and capable as generals and administrators. Hadrian was an untiring traveller, who personally supervised the execution of law; he and Marcus Aurelius were interested in art and philosophy.

Imperial Administration. The organization of the Empire had been so successfully fixed by the beginning of the second century that there was no need for major institutional changes. A peaceful, organic further evolution of existing patterns took place leading to greater centralization and, as a result, an increase in the imperial bureaucracy. The efficiency of the administration was improved. Perhaps the only important change lay in the direction of a more active foreign policy. This was to bring a further enlargement of Rome's boundaries.

EXTERNAL POLICIES. In the time of Trajan and Hadrian, the Empire reached its vastest extent. It expanded beyond the Danube into Dacia (modern Rumania), into the northern parts of England, and into Arabia, Mesopotamia, and Armenia. Revolts, such as still occurred in Judaea and in the Black Sea area, were quickly suppressed. Imperiled borders were provided with strong fortifications, walls, and castles; and Parthians and Germans were held in check. Additional roads were built and postal services were instituted connecting the new provinces with the capital. As a whole, *pax romana* reigned and remarkably few troops were needed to maintain it. Only under Marcus Aurelius did serious difficulties arise on the borders of Parthia and Dacia, and only in the time of his son Commodus (180–193 A.D.)—the first emperor to be assassinated after almost a century of peace in the imperial households—did a process of contraction begin. It was then that a few Danubian conquests had to be given up to invading German tribes.

INTERNAL POLICIES. In the newly included provinces as well as the older ones, Roman law, administration, language, and culture were vigorously supported. Benefiting from the many links, including common institutions, law, customs, commerce without barriers, and cultural connections, the Hellenizing and Romanizing process was speeded up and a feeling of unity developed throughout the Empire.

Organization. The provinces remained formally divided into senatorial and imperial domains, although in actuality they were all under the emperor's direction; and the emperor knew how to counterbalance the power of senatorial proconsuls and propraetors

ROMAN EMPIRE UNDER TRAJAN

AT ITS GREATEST EXTENT - ABOUT 117 A.D.

by the appointment of Equestrians as procurators and commanders of his legions. The legions were made up of volunteers who enlisted for long-term service; many of them were natives or colonists of border provinces who by enlisting became Roman citizens. Cities sprang up in the areas of northern Europe which Rome had occupied. Local autonomy was, however, more and more restricted and eventually was found only in the towns.

Law. In legal affairs, as elsewhere, centralization progressed. The will of the emperor alone was law; neither the ancient nor those newly risen families which the emperor appointed to the Senate exercised effective influence, and executive power rested with the magistrates responsible to the emperor. Among them were men of all ranks: senators, Equestrians, freedmen, and slaves. This efficient bureaucracy was strengthened by a steadily refined legal system. Specially qualified jurists collected and codified the existing body of judicial decisions and worked out important additions; an imperial court of appeal was created. Ideas of a supreme "unwritten" law applicable to all men (*jus naturale*) became more widely accepted; they had a humanizing effect—for example, by reducing the use of torture, easing the burdens of slavery, and advancing concepts of the fundamental inviolable rights of the individual.

Finance. Finances were handled with greater care than in earlier periods. However, a consolidated treasury system, such as modern times have found indispensable, was never worked out. Imperial and state treasuries derived income from tributes, from sale of monopolies, from special levies, and from taxes. Taxation became more universal; land, sales, and inheritance taxes, and tithes were levied not only upon conquered nations but also on Roman citizens. Yet, despite a decline in income from booty, the burden remained moderate. The system of collecting taxes through tax farmers was continued to the detriment of the treasury, and a decrease in corruption could only partly make up for the costs of the bureaucracy and the inefficiency of the system.

Commerce. Under a firm rule and within the wide and diversified area covered by the Empire, commerce could develop rapidly, even though modern forms such as corporations and joint-stock companies were little developed in Ancient Rome. Throughout the age of the good emperors, the currency in gold coins remained stable, and not until Commodus' reign did debasement start. Mining of iron and coal was encouraged in Spain and Britain as well as in

Danubian regions; production of building materials and handicrafts flourished in many regions. Oriental products were imported from India and even China; textiles, jewels, and spices were brought to the less-developed West; amber from the Baltic and furs from Russia became coveted luxury items for Rome's wealthy citizens. Construction of houses, roads, and bridges contributed to creating work, trade, and prosperity. Yet, in the second century, as in preceding centuries, large-scale industrial production failed to develop; technological improvements remained few, and especially in the Empire's western regions, industries provided for no more than bare necessities. Indeed, economic activities remained parochial, out of key with the fact that the Empire had created an universal market, and their weakness had an adverse effect even on the political administration.

Society. In contrast to the fact that social conditions under the "bad" emperors of the first century had ushered in an age of greatness and peace in the second, certain undercurrents during the reign of the "good" emperors—discernible to the historian in retrospect—augured less well for the third. Ephemeral disasters like the plague, which struck the West during the reign of Marcus Aurelius and again under Commodus, were perhaps less ominous than persistent adverse changes in societal structure.

UPPER CLASSES. The trend toward greater social and economic inequality continued. Extreme poverty, which was widespread, contrasted with the extreme luxury of the few. Among the upper classes, family life, already undermined in late republican times and the Augustan age by a high rate of divorce and immorality, continued to disintegrate. Women like Augustus' daughter Julia, his granddaughter Agrippina, and Nero's mistress Poppaea had set bad examples that were widely imitated in the second century. The population increased and urbanization took place, yet a middle class with stern morals and a concept of duty did not develop, as has happened in parallel situations in other ages and regions. More and more, the upper classes allowed political responsibilities to be absorbed by the imperial court, put up with whims and intrigues of the government, and contented themselves with the fulfillment of lucrative bureaucratic functions.

LOWER CLASSES. Among the lower classes, both in town and in country, conditions deteriorated. Independent farmers decreased in proportion to the total number of the peasantry. Though some of them improved their lot, the majority of the country population, as well as the city proletariat, hard though they labored, suffered gravely. Not enough grain was produced to feed their increasing numbers—partly because of soil exhaustion and continued trends toward large luxury estates. More free gifts had to be distributed to humor them, more feasts and circuses sponsored. Slaves, who had carried part of the economic burdens, became scarce as soon as the Empire ceased to expand. In their place, there grew a class of tenant farmers who held an intermediate position between the free peasant, who owned his plot, and the slave. Tenant farmers cultivated, as personally free workers, the large estates or *latifundia* of the rich, but here and there we can trace as early as the second century, the imposition upon them of certain restrictions on their freedom of movement, which foreshadowed the later evolution of serfdom.

Cultural Scene. Looking backward, it has appeared to many investigators of the rise and decline of civilizations as if Roman literature and art in the second century also bear witness to growingly ominous undercurrents. Instead of new creative endeavors, the practice of merely collecting and cataloging data prevailed; interest in historical records and in the sciences increased; and tendencies toward imitation of traditional patterns and styles dominated in the arts, consciously encouraged by partisans of Hellenism such as Emperor Hadrian. Yet, some works were created, particularly in literature and in architecture, which do show an independent spirit and an original approach to problems of artistic expression.

FINE ARTS. Since too little has been preserved of Roman paintings, our judgment of Rome's creative artistic endeavors is derived mainly from the numerous works of sculpture and architecture which have been preserved. They followed, as earlier, the tradition of the Hellenistic era, but in architecture we also find a measure of emancipation from Greek models. The Colosseum, the Circus Maximus, the Tomb of Hadrian, and numerous villas bear witness to the ability of the Romans to combine daring engineering techniques, evinced by the application of broad and high arches and mighty roof constructions, with a sense of proportion and a beauty that defied the temptations of mere size and utility. Most of the emperors paid attention to the beautification of their cities, especially in Rome, where—in addition to traditional public buildings—triumphal arches, victory columns, and baths were erected that belong to the outstanding monuments of ancient times.

LITERATURE AND SCIENCE. The literature of the second century, written in both Latin and Greek, was comparatively rich and still excelled through purity of style. Works of poetry and phantasy were less outstanding than those written in prose and concerned with rational and scientific investigation. Tacitus composed his *Annals* and his *Germania,* which provided not only information on facts, conditions, and characters of the past, but also thought and judgment about the affairs of man in general. Plutarch wrote his *Lives* with their sharp character studies, and Suetonius, almost a generation later, his *Lives of the Twelve Caesars.* Among the poets, the outstanding figures were Juvenal, Apuleius, and Lucian, famous for their satirical descriptions of contemporary society. In the sciences, the works of two men were unequalled in importance and remained basic texts for more than one thousand years: those of Galen, who wrote medical treatises and who, a sober student of anatomy and physiology, laid down principles of therapy and evolved a "system of medicine"; and those of Ptolemy, a mathematician and astronomer, who described the geography of the earth and drew a picture of the cosmos. Ptolemy's writings also included treatises dealing with cartography, musical harmony, and optics. Works of other authors included discussions of agriculture, engineering, and other scientific topics.

PHILOSOPHY. Epicureanism and Stoicism remained the chief philosophical schools of the age. Toward the end of the second century, however, a certain disintegration of both these schools of thought becomes noticeable. Some of their adherents, especially among the intellectuals, turned increasingly to Cynicism; others embraced Neo-Pythagoreanism and Neo-Platonism, which combined concepts of virtue and Stoic forbearance with transcendental and mystic views about the soul and the supernatural; still others became increasingly receptive to the new Christian cult. The best-known philosopher of the second century was the Emperor Marcus Aurelius. His *Meditations* (composed in Greek) not only commend Stoic virtue and resignation to help man to overcome his fate, but demand also an active humanitarian attitude which expresses itself in deeds of commiseration and helpfulness for the unfortunate, the weak, and all who suffer.

RELIGION. Most important for the future of Western civilization was the evolution of the Christian Church, which took place during the second century A.D. The Gospels and other sacred writings were put into final form, a Christian moral code was evolved, and some of the early church fathers—among them Polycarp of Smyrna—appeared. Necessitated by the increasing numbers of adherents, the building of a Church hierarchy was begun and bishops were appointed to enforce established rules. Rites such as communion were introduced, the principles of priesthood were established, and other traditions were initiated. Missionary activities were broadened; they became more successful as Greek and other philosophies began to affect Christian thinking and to make it acceptable to the educated upper classes of Rome. Essentially, the unity of the Empire, its well being and resultant tolerance, promoted the growth of the Christian Church. To be sure, Christianity was perhaps somewhat more suspect than other religious cults because of its own intolerance toward other creeds, its vigorous proselytism, and its social, rather communistic, tenets; yet, few impediments were put in its path so long as its members did not refuse to fulfill the obligations of the Roman citizen or subject. Nevertheless, some persecutions occurred. Those under Trajan and Marcus Aurelius were of local origin and resulted from personal grievances; a more widespread persecution took place under Hadrian—brought about by a new revolt of the Jews, with whom the Christian sects were often still identified. While the Jewish uprisings, led by Bar Cocheba, were crushed and through the dispersion of the Jews an end was put to the remnants of their state, the Christians found themselves exposed to vigorous, apparently centrally directed attacks.

THE THIRD CENTURY

With the end of the second century A.D. began the period of decay of the Roman Empire. Decay was evinced, in the internal structure, by the debasement of the office of the emperor, the weakening of the economy, the deterioration of morals, and the failure of justice. Externally, it was evinced by a shrinking of the Empire. However, it would probably be incorrect to maintain that this process was extensive and that it was irrevocable. As at all times, there existed manifold divergent forces; and even in a period of pronounced retrogression, many achievements were accomplished which were not inferior to those in the age of Rome's greatness, and many individuals demonstrated creative ability, did their duty, and led irreproachable lives. Actually, the Empire displayed a remarkable power of resistance.

The Emperors. The reign of Marcus Aurelius' tyrannical and dissipated son Commodus marked the transition period from an age of peaceful and conscientious emperors to one of licentious and incompetent men. The authority of the ruler was steadily weakened under Commodus' successors. The Senate, the wealthy, and the educated suffered under their arbitrariness and jealousy, while the masses increased their demands for circuses and free distribution of grain. Most of the emperors gained their offices through bribery or were again, as in the first century, creatures of the legions or the praetorian guards. They demanded godlike treatment, yet they were deposed and murdered by the very same schemers who chose or elected them. They followed each other in quick succession, sometimes ruling less than a year. Several of them came from Asia and Africa and governed the Empire not from Rome but from the provinces. Their withdrawal from Rome, as well as their provincial origin, emphasized a change in the political balance. The prestige of the city and the influence of Romans were lessened, emperors of barbarian origin appointed other barbarians to highest positions, and, furthermore, the Senate came to include numerous non-Italian members.

Imperial Administration. Third-century Rome was unable to deal successfully with administrative problems. The situation was worsened when, under the vicious Emperor Caracalla, citizenship rights were extended to every subject of the Empire. This step was the ultimate logical consequence of the mixing process which marked the path of the Roman Empire since the days of Julius Caesar. Far from strengthening cohesion and unity, it only served to weaken Rome in the face of internal and foreign dangers.

External Affairs. The defense of the Empire turned out to be increasingly difficult. Parthian inroads ceased when the Persians conquered Parthia in the second quarter of the century, but the Persians themselves became a new menace. They revived their empire, imbued it with a remarkable new culture, pushed Roman legions back and reduced Rome's status in the East. Small states, such as that of Palmyra in Asia Minor, made themselves virtually independent. German and Dacian invasions in Britain and Gaul and in Helvetia and the Danubian lands also brought losses of territory. Not until the reign of Aurelian (270–275), who reduced Palmyra to obedience and established a safe boundary in the Danubian region, was the process of decay stopped so that revival seemed possible. Still, the third century ended with net losses of territory.

INTERNAL CONDITIONS. More serious than the external problems were the internal ones. Law and order were no longer maintained; piracy and highway robbery increased. Attempts at enforcing justice by comparatively responsible governments under Septimius Severus (193–211), Alexander Severus (222–235), and Aurelian (270–275) came to naught. Despite measures for collecting taxes more effectively and distributing the burden more justly, and despite steps to encourage industry and business, the decay of public life, morals, and order progressed. Debasement of currency and inflation ruined the treasury, and confiscations of property undertaken with almost every change of ruler could not restore the financial strength of the government. The military forces became undependable; foreign soldiers, settled on lands near the borders, could no longer be trusted, and attempts at reform, as under Septimius Severus, brought no lasting improvement. Birth control and plagues (a particularly severe one occurred in 251) contributed to depopulation; laborers became scarce and production fell. Metals needed for coinage and for industry were mined in decreasing quantities, while purchases of luxury goods from the East drained existing resources. The growth of cities and of urban civilization was checked. In agriculture, slave labor became too expensive and more and more slaves were freed; but this no longer meant the advantage which it had signified heretofore because the status of all free peasants deteriorated. Indeed, the number steadily increased of those who voluntarily gave up their independence and became tenants (*coloni*) on imperial or privately owned large estates. The trend toward serfdom was accelerated.

Civilization. Secular culture of the third century produced little that later generations have considered great treasures. Neither in building, art, science, and literature, nor in philosophy do we find works of supreme achievement or men reaching out for new horizons. Outstanding figures—men who combined thought and action—appeared essentially only in the field of religion.

EDUCATION, PHILOSOPHY, AND LAW. Education was spread through the establishment of a number of schools, but a basis for a new educated class was not laid; metaphysicians, Neo-Platonists, and Neo-Pythagoreans continued to dominate the scene with their teachings. But even the best among them, such as Plotinus, did not add substantially to earlier insights. History in traditional style was written by Dio Cassius and a few minor authors. Perhaps the jurists could lay claim to the merit of increasing Rome's great legacy. New schools of law were founded and practical and theoretical knowledge reconciled. Eminent jurists emerged with Papinian and Ulpian; both served as praetorian prefects, the former under Septimius Severus, the latter under Alexander Severus, and both were able to set an example in applying legal talent to practical political and administrative work.

RELIGION. It is often pointed out that a feeling of doom dominated the atmosphere of the third century A.D. However, it is impossible to say to what extent such a feeling actually pervaded the thinking of the masses, or even that of the educated classes. We can recognize, though, a relationship between the climate of opinion in the third century and the progress of Christianity. The more depraved the world and its politics appeared, the more insistently mystery-religions called on men to consider their immortal souls and turn away from the affairs of this world, and the stronger the desire became for purification and cleansing—the more effectively was the ground prepared for Christianity. The answers which Christianity offered to an apparently hopeless situation satisfied many of the longings of the day; persecutions, such as that under Emperor Decius (249–251), far from extirpating the Christians, only served to strengthen them both spiritually and politically. And the devotion of the members of the Church, many of whom accepted a martyr's death, won thousands of proselytes to their cause. Among the most famous churchmen of the time were Tertullian (d. *ca*. 220), who took a vigorous part in the developing struggles over Christian dogma and who left numerous pastoral writings; Origen (d. 252), a great teacher first in Alexandria, then in Caesarea, who continued the polemics of Tertullian, explained the Bible, and promoted biblical scholarship; and Cyprian (d. 258), who occupied himself with doctrinal questions (such as baptism) and with institutional problems.

Simultaneously with the interpretation and propagation of their faith, the Christians carried on the building of their worldly organization. They strengthened discipline among the members of their Church by conferring larger powers on the bishops and by enforcing a more formal training of the priests. They also extended their organization to remote regions—to Abyssinia and Britain, Nubia and Gaul, Persia and Spain.

CHAPTER XI

THE END OF THE ANCIENT WORLD

IN MANY RESPECTS, the Ancient World lives today. As a historical period, however, it came to an end in the fourth century A.D. with the dissolution of the Ancient Roman Empire. As a social phenomenon, this "decline and fall" has received so much thought and so many interpretations that no single view will satisfy. Certainly, the traditional concept that Rome, owing to inner decay, loss of faith, of "virtue," of creative genius, was doomed to death seems as little acceptable today as the concept that the Roman world and population had reached a point of biological exhaustion. With equal justification one can argue that Rome was doomed in the first century B.C.—a century of economic disruption, population decline, social anarchy, corruption and debauchery, when a foreign, Hellenistic, spirit inundated it. Yet, the first century B.C. was followed by an unequaled flowering of Rome, while nothing similar occurred in the fourth century A.D. No more than a temporary revival materialized, which began with the reign of Emperor Diocletian.

THE POLITICAL AND ECONOMIC SCENE

During the last phase of the Roman Empire, while it still embraced both East and West, the Ancient World produced again remarkable personalities. Several rulers of great ability occupied the throne, such as Diocletian, Constantine, and the short-lived Julian the Apostate; and a number of excellent ministers, advisers, and other officials, often of barbarian origin, were available. But human genius did not suffice to counterbalance the forces of disintegration which pervaded the social and economic scenes; nor was Roman strength sufficient to stem the flood of external attacks which vigorous and fresh peoples just emerging from barbarism launched upon the very Rome which they themselves considered and cherished as their teacher. The glory of the city of Rome itself faded; it ceased to be the seat of the emperors, and the Senate became a mere municipal office. Magnificent buildings, with which the emperors still embellished the city, reflected no more than past grandeur.

The Reign of Diocletian. Diocletian (284–305) was the first of the great emperors during the last stages of the Empire. An Illyrian by birth, he was a man of energy and vision, who restored order and brought about a recovery of trade and an improvement of agriculture. He abandoned Rome as capital and seat of government.

DIOCLETIAN'S ADMINISTRATION. Diocletian surrounded himself with capable advisers and governors, promoted men on the basis of merit, and—though at the price of an oversized bureaucracy—reorganized the administration of the Empire. He divided the provinces into smaller units which could be supervised by special officers appointed from four new central seats of government, and he saw to it that, as much as possible, uniform laws superseded the many existing local privileges. Notwithstanding well-meant but unduly strict and often stifling government interference (evinced, for example, by abortive maximum-price laws), a measure of prosperity and confidence returned.

MILITARY AND EXTERNAL POLICIES. During Diocletian's reign, revolts broke out in many outlying provinces—in England and Gaul, in Egypt and Libya. Great efforts had to be expended to subdue them. Frontier defenses were subsequently strengthened, and soldiers ready for action were settled along the borders. Strict discipline was kept among them and new self-respect and authority were given to the officer corps. Yet, power among the officers was divided and they were carefully supervised by civilian officials so as to preclude such military influence in the central government as praetorian prefects and generals had exercised earlier.

DIVISION OF THE EMPIRE. Diocletian's most important decision concerned a division of the supreme power in the Empire. Two emperors with the title "Augustus" were instituted to rule jointly, one in the West and the other in the East; as one of them, Diocletian chose for himself the Eastern division. Each Augustus was given a "Caesar" as his deputy and successor and the rule of two subdivisions was assigned to them. Each Augustus and each Caesar chose a capital of his own. All four assumed a halo of divinity; nobody could approach Diocletian personally without prostrating himself.

The Reign of Constantine. Having made these reforms and having ruled for twenty years, Diocletian, old and tired, together with his co-Augustus, abdicated in 305; the Caesars succeeded them. But when within a few years Diocletian died, new civil wars broke out between the new Augusti and their Caesars. They lasted for ten years and did not end until one of the successors, Constantine, had defeated all others. Constantine eventually reunited the four parts and made himself emperor of the entire realm.

CONSTANTINE's ADMINISTRATION. Son of one of Diocletian's Caesars, Constantine had risen to the command of the legions in Britain and Gaul. Having gained the Caesarship with their backing, he defeated various rivals and, in 312, met his most powerful adversary in battle near Rome (Battle of the Milvian Bridge). Victory gave him the city and the rule of the West. A few years later, he attacked the Eastern Augustus, defeated him, too, and by 324 had achieved his ambition to become sole ruler. As such he continued many policies of Diocletian. He encouraged economic growth by protecting trade, but he raised the taxes and further enlarged the bureaucracy. In order to strengthen his sole and absolute rule, he reserved for himself command of all military forces and revised the provincial divisions, introducing still smaller units than had been instituted under Diocletian. As seat of government, he chose a new capital, which he founded in the eastern parts of the Empire on the site of ancient Byzantium, and which was named "Constantinople." Like Rome he had it adorned with mighty buildings; and he made it the center of cultural life.

CONSTANTINE's RELIGIOUS POLICIES. Aside from political reunification, Constantine also reversed another of Diocletian's most important policies—that toward the Christians. Diocletian had staged one of the most cruel persecutions against them; Constantine decided to win them over to his side. It would be erroneous, though, to see in his decision no more than political calculation; in an age of uncertainty, religious motives and fear of the wrath of an unknown god played perhaps as decisive a role as diplomacy. In 313, soon after the Battle of the Milvian Bridge, through the Milan Decree, Constantine granted toleration to the Christians. Subsequently, he restored their confiscated property, accorded them tax advantages, permitted Church jurisdiction, and even made them grants and paid them subsidies. It is unknown at what time, if at all, he himself became a Christian and was baptized.

COUNCIL OF NICAEA. Regardless of personal religious convictions, Constantine laid claim to supreme overlordship of the Church, as of every other institution in the Empire. For this reason, he presided in 325 at one of the greatest events in the history of the Christian Church: the Council of Nicaea. Ever since a Christian dogma had been worked out, there had been "heretical" groups within the Christian community which declined to accept one or another article of faith. Among them had been Ebionites and Gnostics, Manichaeans, Nestorians, and Donatists. In Constantine's time, a controversy arose over the question whether God and Christ were identical or similar. The two contending parties were led by Bishop Athanasius and Bishop Arius, respectively. Anxious to see unity preserved everywhere within the Empire, Constantine called a general council, and (although the West was represented by only six churchmen, the old and weak bishop of Rome not being among them) some three hundred bishops and churchmen assembled. A number of questions were discussed, including the marriage of priests, the finances of the Church, and the feast days; but the main decision concerned the acceptance of Athanasius' views and the condemnation of the Arian position. Thus was established the Nicaean Creed, which has remained to this day the accepted creed of almost all branches of the Christian Church.

Final Division of Empire. Constantine died in 337. Immediately, new struggles arose. Economic and political interests as well as differences in customs, language, and attitudes increasingly alienated the Western part of the Empire, with its tradition of sternness and law, from the Eastern, where Oriental pomp and despotism reigned. Although some emperors still succeeded in asserting their over-all power, a division into an Eastern and a Western Roman Empire became final with the death of Emperor Theodosius in 395.

Economic Disintegration. In the meantime, the Empire's economic position disintegrated further. Diocletian's reforms had borne no fruit: price regulations had been ineffective in restoring production; tax collection remained unsatisfactory owing to continuing corruption; social divisions were not diminished. Nor did Diocletian's successors succeed in restoring a balanced economy. Rich landholders and bankers grew even richer in times of disaster; the middle class could not recover under the burden of heavy taxation and inflation; and the farmers and tenants continued to suffer. Constantine contributed to worsening their situation when in order to raise agricultural production he promulgated laws which required a peasant not to leave his land. Thereby, a formal step in the direction of the introduction of serfdom was undertaken. Outlying provinces, weighed down by the financial demands imposed on them to alleviate the bankruptcy of the government, no longer derived benefits from being subject to a central authority. Centrifugal forces increased; every part tried to achieve greater economic self-sufficiency, and small-scale industrial and agricultural production for local use helped not only to diminish trade but also to reduce interchange of ideas and lessen common interests. They led to a more primitive organization of life. Towns declined and cultural achievements became fewer.

THE CULTURAL SCENE: TRIUMPH OF THE CHRISTIAN CHURCH

When Constantine promulgated in 313 his toleration edict of Milan, perhaps no more than one out of every ten inhabitants of the Roman Empire had been a Christian. By the end of the century, whether for the sake of faith or of material advantage, a vast majority belonged to the Christian Church. It is, therefore, perhaps not surprising that during the last phases of the Ancient Roman Empire most of the creative cultural forces came to center around the Christian Church. Hellenism and pagan arts, literature, rhetorics, and law became imbued with a Christian spirit, and the absorption of Neo-Platonist trends by Christian thinkers helped to increase the impact of Christian views. Although the Church was disestablished during a brief interlude in the time of Julian the Apostate (361–363), Christianity soon recovered its privileged status and continued to dominate the cultural scene in the Empire.

Problems of Church Organization. With official recognition of the Christian religion and with the mass of the people turning to it, the Church was faced with the necessity of integrating millions of neophytes. For this purpose, new bishoprics were founded and the training of the clergy was broadened. Moreover, since the possibilities for proselytizing abroad were vastly enhanced, missionary activities were intensified. But inner and outer expansion brought numerous difficulties. In an organization increasingly concerned with institutional arrangements and other worldly affairs, rivalries came to the fore; and, occasionally, bloodshed occurred. The Western Christian Church with its see of Rome—the only apostolic see in the West, with a bishop claiming primacy over all others—was gradually alienated from the great old Eastern centers of Christianity with sees including Jerusalem, Alexandria, Antioch, Constantinople, and Ephesus. The split between the two parts was sharpened by economic jealousies and by the conflict of opposing attitudes: the mystical leanings and asceticism of the East and the rationalism and emphasis on discipline in the West. Moreover, not only did the teachings of Arius, condemned at Nicaea, continue to be propagated and Arianism continue to spread, but also new "heresies" appeared. Therefore, a second great ecumenical Council was held in 381 at Constantinople. It settled some problems, successfully stemmed pagan Oriental influences, and brought a statement on a disputed dogma of the procession of the Holy Ghost; but peace was not established and divisions within the Church organization persisted.

Christian Culture. In the face of growing tensions, or perhaps stimulated by them, a considerable number of great thinkers emerged, both in East and West. Most were churchmen; among those who were not stands out Ammianus, who served under Julian the Apostate and who wrote a history of Rome which brought Tacitus' account up to the fourth century. Among the churchmen, the most notable members belonged to the Alexandrine school of Christianity. In the preceding century, this school had become the distinguished heir of the classical tradition cultivated so long in Alexandria.

SCHOLARSHIP AND ART. Many of the great scholars of the fourth century belonged to the Alexandrine school. Foremost among them were: Eusebius of Caesarea, adviser of Constantine, who became famous for his interpretations of dogma and for his Church history; Gregory of Nyassa, fighter against Julian's anti-Christian, Neo-Platonic policies, who excelled as an orator and a priest; and John

Chrysostom, for a while patriarch of Constantinople, likewise one of the great preachers and Bible scholars.

Together with early Christian learning flourished early Christian art. It, too, continued the style of classical times, and it, too, used classical models for new purposes. Christian artists transformed established artistic patterns to fit the needs of Christian architecture, of the basilica for Christian worship; they employed the existing marvellous technique in the art of making mosaics and painting frescoes to represent Christian motifs and express Christian thought. They bent the realism of late pagan representations to suit their own transcendental views, and out of what they found they created new symbols. Their impact was such that they began to influence also secular art. Indeed, during the fourth century were created many beautiful palaces, villas, triumphal arches, and tombs—in Constantinople as well as in Rome and other cities.

MONASTICISM. The growing involvement of the Church in worldly tasks strengthened, as a reaction, a movement which was to become one of the most important forces in the Church: monasticism. Whether it was for the sake of leading unblemished lives that people sought to retire from the rush and temptations of the world, or whether they simply sought refuge from the material dangers threatening them in a state of disorder, or whether they tried to forget disappointments which had shattered their private lives— many men and women, lay people rather than regular clergy, embraced the monastic ideal. To be sure, solitary preparation for a life in the Hereafter was not unknown to other religions, and the ascetic ideal had attracted Christians as early as the first century; in the third century, it had inspired men such as the famous hermit St. Paul of Thebes. But it was only in the fourth century that asceticism came to full flourishing with St. Anthony (d. 356). In order to avoid excesses, Church authorities, however, toward the end of the fourth century took a stronger hand in regard to those who were fleeing worldly responsibilities. They demanded greater discipline among those given to the ascetic ideal and came to view the life of a monk within a monastic community as preferable to the solitary life of a hermit. Therefore, St. Basil from Caesarea established definite rules for monastic life, and these have survived in the East. In the West, too, regular cloisters were erected and eminent churchmen like St. Ambrose supervised their organization and supported their growth.

COLLAPSE OF THE EMPIRE

Despite the spread of a new faith, despite the appearance of great men of thought and action, and despite the gradual adaptation to new economic patterns, the collapse of Rome occurred. It came with the breakdown of the defense system. In the East, the Persians attacked with success, and Emperor Julian the Apostate, who rushed to the aid of the Eastern provinces, died during a campaign against them. In the North, inroads came from the side of Germanic tribes. For five hundred years, attacks had been launched by them, but it was only in the fourth century A.D. that they succeeded in pushing into the heart of the Empire. Hard necessity impelled them: an Asiatic tribe, called "Huns," had crossed into Europe in 375 and had invaded their territories, depriving them of their means of sustenance. Under the impact of the Hunnish attack, Germanic Goths living in southern Russia on the northern shores of the Black Sea had left their domiciles. The western group of these Goths, the Visigoths, had seen no other possibility of escape than by crossing the borders into the Roman Empire. In vain did Roman legions, commanded by the Emperor Valens, try to stem the tide. In the Battle of Adrianople, in 378, he was defeated and killed; and while the Huns pushed deep into central Europe, the Goths occupied Roman lands. Soon, other tribes were forced to move in turn. People after people were uprooted, and finally the complexion of the entire European world was changed. What happened has later been called the "Migration of the Peoples," and rightly can this migration be considered as the decisive event which ushered in a new age—the Middle Ages.

CHAPTER XII

BARBARIANS, CHRISTIANS, AND MOSLEMS
(375–741)

THE MIDDLE AGES (375–1492) were for a long time regarded as "Dark" Ages—a thousand years of superstition and intellectual stagnation. This long era of world history was so regarded at least during the eighteenth century when the leading thinkers in that age of the so-called "enlightenment" held the view that only in their time had the "light" of reason begun to shine again. Modern research has, however, revealed that the "darkness" which appeared to have reigned in the Middle Ages must be credited to the ignorance and conceit on the part of the observing eighteenth-century "rational" philosopher and historian rather than to any real lack of cultural contribution. As knowledge about medieval times has increased, the period of darkness has shrunk. If at first the Age of Darkness encompassed the full span from 375 to 1492, soon a century and a half of early Renaissance (from 1350 to 1492) had to be subtracted. Then, the thirteenth century had to be eliminated, the "greatest of centuries," as J. J. Walsh has called it in a book of the same title, and then the twelfth century, another "Renaissance," as C. H. Haskins has shown. The period of darkness receded further in the light of a tenth-century "Ottonian" and a ninth-century "Carolingian" Renaissance. Finally, no more was left in darkness than the era from 375 to 800. Yet, the fifth and part of the sixth centuries have also been found so replete with significant events and meaningful thought enriching Western civilization that today at the most the period from 550 to 750 remains to be characterized with some justification as the "Dark Ages." Perhaps even this period can be so termed only because of our meager knowledge or our different attitudes, and not because of a lack of cultural achievement.

THE BARBARIANS

The Age of Darkness was supposed to have been ushered in with the disintegration of the Roman world when barbarian Germanic tribes attacked the effete Empire. Yet no definite borderline can be drawn between the Roman and barbarian worlds. For centuries, Germans had been trained in, and assimilated by, the Roman Empire. By the fourth century, some had gained the highest posts in Rome. Others, having adopted Roman ways, had rejoined their tribes to spread Roman customs and culture among them. Thus, Rome's disintegration was in reality a slow process of fusion; justly has it been said that "Rome plus barbarians constituted a happy union." The Germans brought with them ideas of freedom, of human worth, of individual independence, of free elective government, and of democratic law, unlike those of Oriental autocracies, and they added these traditions to the cultural heritage of Rome.

Migration of the Germans. The migration of the Germanic peoples, which began around 375 and was brought on by the invasion of the Asiatic Huns, accelerated the fusion process. As the Huns advanced and devastated one region after another, tribe after tribe was put to flight and sought refuge within the confines of the Roman Empire.

THE GOTHS. The first of the migrants who pierced the Roman defenses had been the Visigoths. After defeating Emperor Valens at Adrianople in 378, they were ceded territory within the Empire's borders. They settled, but remained satisfied for a short time only; after a few decades they sought richer lands and, led by their able King Alaric, attacked Italy. West Rome was at that time ruled by the indolent Emperor Honorius, and actual control of Italy rested with Honorius' minister and adviser Stilicho, a German, who successfully defended the country against the invading Visigoths. In 408 Stilicho, a victim of palace intrigues, was however executed, and disunity and inefficiency after his death paved the way for the Visigoths. They conquered Italy, sacking Rome in the year 410,[1] and they might have established in that country the first Germanic kingdom if death had not claimed Alaric. Deprived of his leadership, they were compelled to withdraw into southern Gaul where, in accordance with the terms of a treaty with the West Roman Empire, they settled in Aquitaine as *foederati* (allies) of the Romans. There they founded a kingdom of their own.

VANDALS, BURGUNDIANS, ANGLES, AND SAXONS. Next among the Germanic invaders of the West Roman Empire came the Vandals. Accompanied part of the way by the Suevi, the Vandals migrated through France and Spain into North Africa and settled there in 439. From North Africa they sailed into the Mediterranean, pillaging Sicily and Rome (455). Burgundians moved into southeastern Gaul (later France), Alamanni into southern Germany and Switzerland, and Angles and Saxons from the North Sea coasts into Flanders and (expelling Celts and Scots) into England (449). Unable to withstand their assaults, the Roman defenses crumbled.

ATTILA AND THE END OF THE HUNS. In the meantime, the Huns, led by Attila, the "Scourge of God," plundered and then collected tribute from the northern provinces of East Rome. Having pushed through partly vacated Germanic lands they reached the center of Gaul in 451. There, their advance was finally stopped by a combined West Roman and German army under Aëtius, which defeated them in a terrible battle on the Catalaunian Fields. The Huns retreated to their base in Hungary, whence in 452 they invaded Italy; but eventually they returned to their Asiatic homeland or were assimilated by indigenous East European populations.

End of the Western Empire. A century of Hun inroads and Germanic migrations brought an end to the West Roman Empire. Deprived of much of its territory outside Italy and unable to repel the invaders or to maintain law, order, and prosperity, the government of the Empire in the West collapsed. In 476, the German leader Odoacer put an end to pretenses by deposing the last emperor, Romulus Augustulus, and making himself Italy's ruler. Thus the once-glorious empire with its capital at Rome ceased to exist.

The Ostrogoths. Odoacer ruled for thirteen years. But in 488, at the behest of the East Roman emperor, the Ostrogoths attacked Italy in order to reconquer it for East Rome. The Ostrogoths, who

---

[1] The emperor no longer resided in Rome. Honorius had taken up his seat in Ravenna—a city on the Adriatic Sea, which could be easily defended.

at the time of the Hunnic invasion had evicted the Visigoths from their homes, had later themselves been forced to leave the Black Sea shores. In 451, they had settled for a time in the Danubian and Dalmatian parts of the Eastern Empire. It was from there, led by their King Theodoric, that they invaded Italy. Odoacer had to retreat into the fortress of Ravenna, where during negotiations Theodoric had him assassinated. Once victorious, the Ostrogoths established their own virtually independent rule. They were Christians, for Bishop Ulfilas (d. 383) had converted them to the Christian faith (in its Arian form) while they lived in the South Russian steppe. They used a Bible translated into Gothic, and a manuscript of their Bible is still preserved in Upsala, Sweden.

The Germanic peoples and the Romans differed in creed, race, and tradition. Nevertheless, Theodoric, residing in Ravenna as did Honorius and Odoacer before him, built a model kingdom in Italy. He maintained law and order, displayed tolerance toward the Catholics, protected property rights, and saw to it that Goths and Romans, each group following its own traditions, could live peacefully side by side and even intermarry. He preserved intact Rome's legal institutions, built monuments after Roman and Byzantine models, and took an interest in Roman philosophy. He encouraged trade, skilled crafts, and agriculture; and he entered into alliances with neighboring kingdoms.

The Franks. At the same time, another Romanized Germanic kingdom was built in Gaul. Early in the fifth century Northern Gaul had been conquered by the Franks who had defeated a Roman army at Soissons in 486, and then under their king, Clovis, (a brutal but efficient leader—d. 511) had extended their rule over the entire country. Clovis became a Catholic Christian like most people in the Roman Empire instead of adhering to the Arian creed which various Germanic tribes had adopted, and thus he avoided religious tensions in the newly conquered land. Shrewdly he secured political backing from the Gallic clergy. Like Theodoric he adopted many features of the Roman administrative system; but he used his own Germanic counts (*comites* or "companions") as advisers and military officers, and he published a code of German laws. Since ample land was available for agriculture, the settlement of the Franks was easier than that of the Goths in Italy. A fusion of Germanic and Roman ways of living, marked by frequent intermarriage, occurred in Clovis' realms to a greater extent than in Ostrogothic Italy. The

Roman heritage remained stronger in the south, whereas Germanic influences prevailed in the north and east.

Extinction and Survival of Germanic Kingdoms. Of all the Germanic states created within the borders of the old Roman Empire, only the Frankish kingdom was able to consolidate itself; each of the others disappeared after a brief existence. In the course of the sixth century, the Vandals were defeated and extirpated by the armies of East Rome (534–553). The Ostrogothic state suffered a like fate under Theodoric's successors, who had failed to maintain the peace, prosperity, and tolerance established by the great king. After adversity and hardship had spread throughout the country, a Byzantine army, sent to reconquer Italy, attacked and after twenty years of war defeated them and drove out the survivors (555–562). The Visigoths, expelled from southern Gaul by the Franks (507), migrated to Spain, and though they maintained themselves there for about two centuries, their state, too, found a violent end when conquered by Moslems. Various other Germanic tribes were assimilated by native populations. The Angles and Saxons remained in isolated Britain but created no cohesive state or unit; instead, petty kingdoms incessantly warring upon each other arose. Only the Franks survived. As Catholics they had strong support from the Church, which they repaid with grants of land, privileges, and rights of jurisdiction. Thus, notwithstanding incompetence and disunity of Clovis' descendants—known as the "Merovingian dynasty"—and the political division of the land into nearly autonomous entities such as Austrasia and Neustria, the Frankish kingdom not only survived but even expanded to the east and south.

Economic and Social Life. The creation of a political foundation for a new Roman-Germanic civilization was in itself an event of major significance; but its immediate effect on economic and social conditions was limited. Only in a few areas was the landowning nobility replaced by Germanic conquerors. In most areas, property rights were respected and the Roman system for the cultivation of land was preserved without change. The old system of taxation was seldom disturbed although, with the coming of the Germans, there was perhaps more emphasis on local administration of financial affairs. Most of the Roman laws were kept in force and were only gradually influenced or supplemented by Germanic laws and customs. These latter emphasized personal loyalties and kinship instead of abstract legal concepts, written codes, and courtroom procedures, such as those which had been worked out by Rome through the centuries.

Literary and Artistic Life. Literature and art of the late fourth, fifth, and sixth centuries bear witness to the strength and persistence of the Roman heritage and to the comparative weakness of early Germanic contributions. One of the most prominent writers of the age was the Roman Boethius, (onetime friend of Theodoric and well versed in classical scholarship) who is most famous for his *Consolation of Philosophy* which he wrote in prison after falling into disgrace. Others were the historians Cassiodorus, who had also served Theodoric and who wrote on political and educational developments; the East Roman Procopius, who described the Gothic wars; and Gregory of Tours, who composed a *History of the Franks*. Boethius, Cassiodorus, and others like them pursued in addition to their philosophical interests the study of languages. Influenced by the literary accomplishments of the Eastern Empire and the Roman Church, they translated classical literature, and some of them used classical writings as a means of promoting Christianity. They compiled Christian legends and *Lives* of Saints. Poets of merit were, however, few.

From the Eastern Empire and the Church, the West drew inspiration also in the field of Fine Arts. Many of the chief contributions in art were made in church architecture; famous basilicas were built, their interiors adorned with beautiful mosaics, and some of the finest which survived may be seen today in Ravenna.

EASTERN EMPIRE AND CHRISTIAN CHURCH

The invading barbarians left many traces, especially upon the political organization of Europe, but they were not so destructive as had been feared by those who had anxiously witnessed their coming. In many localities, old ways persisted and existing institutions were only slowly modified through a process of gradual evolution. The Byzantine Empire and the Christian Church were especially potent factors preventing too radical innovations.

The Byzantine Empire. After the final division of the Roman Empire toward the end of the fourth century, its eastern regions, in contrast to West Rome, regained their importance. When, in 476, Odoacer deposed Romulus Augustulus in Ravenna, he did not hesitate to recognize the formal suzerainty of the East Roman emperor. Subsequent Germanic kings, as well as Roman bishops, followed his example. Nevertheless, despite its imperial authority, its comparative wealth, and its vigorous intellectual life, the East did not attempt to control the West's political and cultural affairs until the reign of Emperor Justinian (d. 565). It was he who led the Byzantine Empire to new greatness. With the help of his wife, the shrewd and brutal Theodora (who had been a circus actress), and that of able generals such as Belisarius and Narses, Justinian succeeded in defending the Empire's borders in the east and north; and he reincorporated the African and Italian territories seized by the Vandals and Ostrogoths, respectively, and even a part of Visigothic Spain. Thus he restored that unity of the Mediterranean world which was necessary both for the expansion of trade and the survival of culture. Moreover, by establishing a firm personal regime and reasserting the emperor's political authority over the Church, he laid the basis for that absolute dominion of the Byzantine rulers over political and ecclesiastical affairs of the East which became known as "Caesaropapism."

The most lasting contributions of Justinian's age were made in the fields of art and law. The Byzantine style, heir to classical tradition and influenced by the Orient, was brought to perfection. Representative of the Byzantine style was the Christian "basilica," a church building of simple, severe exterior, consisting generally of three naves with the central one larger and higher, and lighted by clerestory windows; an apse was soon added to give the interior the form of the cross, and the roof was often crowned by a dome. One of the great examples of Byzantine architecture is the church of Santa Sophia in Constantinople, built in Justinian's time.

In the decorative arts, the Byzantine style excelled through its mosaics depicting mainly religious topics. Representations appeared on a golden background, the human figure was realistically presented, but seldom with individualistic features. In the course of subsequent centuries, icons, ivories, enamels, miniatures, and book illustrations of unusual perfection were created in the same Byzantine style.

A code of law, the *Corpus Juris Civilis,* was created. It derived from collections of imperial edicts and the precedents established through the ages by jurists' opinions. This code, along with its *Digest,* became not only the foundation of Justinian's own legislation but also a basic part of modern law.

Christian Church. The fifth and sixth centuries witnessed outstanding achievements in the Christian Church. Much of the dogma had been formulated earlier, and standards of scholarship had been established—generally by men who had lived in the eastern parts of the Empire and belonged spiritually to the East. Around the turn of the fifth century, however, some of the greatest thinkers and workers of the Church appeared also in the West, and the organization of the Roman Church was perfected. Pope Leo the Great (440–461) stated the doctrine ("Petrine doctrine") that to the Roman bishop, as successor of the Apostle Peter, belonged supreme rights and final jurisdiction within the Church.

THE FOUR DOCTORS OF THE CHURCH. The West could take pride in Ambrose, archbishop of Milan (d. 397), one of its foremost statesmen. He was a devoted advocate of Church rights and supremacy, ard of tolerance and Christian forgiveness which he courageously demonstrated toward "heretics" in the face of imperial opposition. His contemporaries admired his vigorous sermons and his theological writings; his hymns became a permanent contribution to Church service. Jerome, another of the doctors of the Church, was a rather violent participant in numerous fundamental disputes on faith. He insisted on strict Orthodoxy and shaped Church dogma by means of the theological interpretations he promulgated in numerous letters and other writings. He had studied the classical authors and his scholarship enabled him eventually to produce the "Vulgate," a Latin translation of the Bible from the Hebrew and Greek, which is still in use as the basic text of the Roman Catholic Church. The third and most famous of the Church doctors was Augustine, bishop of Hippo, who had been a profligate youth but had reformed to become a militant supporter of the Church, seeking its purification and its expansion. He was influenced by Ambrose and, following Jerome's example, had also become fully conversant with the works of the great pagan writers. Augustine wrote three outstanding works: the *Confessions,* the *Retractions,* and the *City of God,* in which he defended papal supremacy, denounced heresies, warned against Nature the temptress, and described man's futile endeavors in his earthly city and his destination for the "other world," the City of God. He was a firm exponent of monasticism.

He aided missionary activities and under his influence St. Patrick went to Gaul and Ireland to convert the pagans there. The founding of monasteries in Ireland by St. Patrick initiated two centuries of such cultural eminence as Ireland would never again attain.

The fourth doctor of the Church, who lived more than a hundred years later, was Gregory the Great (d. 604). Like Augustine, he was converted to Christianity during his adult years and devoted himself to the strengthening of the Catholic Church and the papacy. He started as a monk, became pope in 590, and in that capacity showed himself to be one of the most able administrators in the history of the Church. He was widely respected for his firm leadership, and like Leo the Great he insisted on the supreme authority of the popes within the entire Christian Church. He is famous for his piety and his teachings and writings (*Dialogues, Pastoral Care, Homilies*). He contributed to the clarification of dogma, the composition of the liturgy (Gregorian Chant), the founding of hospitals and schools, and missionary activity. It was he who sent another "St. Augustine" (a monk) into England and missionaries into France and Germany.

MONASTICISM. Monasticism had developed rapidly after Augustine. Its foremost representative was Benedict of Nursia (d. 543). By the sixth century, monastic life was in need of reform. The longing to seek a retreat from the demands of the day and to find a place in which to live a pure life had often been perverted after the official acceptance of Christianity. A large number of men and women, including many wealthy persons, had embraced monastic ways simply to enjoy a quiet carefree life; others had done so to gain "merit" by indulging in various excesses of asceticism. An extreme case was that of the "pillar saint" Simeon the Stylite (*ca.* 450), who claimed to lead a life pleasing to Christ by sitting for many years on top of a column. As he observed these sterile practices, Benedict became aware of their danger to Christian standards (it was easy for a hermit to succumb to worldly temptations) and, on the basis of earlier precedents, he introduced in his monastery of Monte Cassino a general rule for communal monastic life. For each monk this rule prescribed celibacy, poverty, and obedience to the abbot; prayer and manual labor; and a vow of "stability" which forbade the monk ever to return to secular life. The rule spread to all parts of Christendom. Under the influence of Cassiodorus (d. 575), scholarly activities were soon added to a monk's tasks, and monasteries became the greatest cultural force. They maintained this position throughout much of the Middle Ages.

CHURCH-STATE RELATIONSHIP. During the fifth and sixth centuries, the Western Church increasingly emancipated itself from state influences. The Roman bishop steadily raised the position of his see. At the Council of Chalcaedon (451) Leo the Great had gained recognition for Rome's primacy within the whole Christian Church, and, since no emperor resided in Rome, none could claim the superiority of imperial power. Neither Alaric nor Clovis nor other powerful Germanic kings could effectively interfere with the pope's functions; only Theodoric among the Germans and only Justinian among the East Roman emperors kept a measure of control over the Roman administration. But after Justinian's death, the popes, through their temporal power over the city of Rome, built a foundation on which were based their future claims for complete independence and superior position in world affairs.

THE RISE OF ISLAM

By the end of the sixth century the great Germanic migrations were over. The Lombards were the last tribe to seek new homes. Under their King Alboin, they invaded northern Italy in 568. They confined the East Roman administration, which had functioned there since the expulsion of the Ostrogoths, to the so-called "Exarchate of Ravenna" and established in the Po Valley a kingdom of their own which prospered for over a hundred years. But new storms threatened the West—though from a different direction—when, with the birth of Islam, powerful new leaders and conquerors emerged in Asia.

Origins of Islam. Islam, "Submission to God," is the name of a new religion which originated with Mohammed (569–632). He was an Arabian who was inspired by the teachings of Persians, Jews, and Christians as well as by his own visions. He had come to profess one God and, as his prophet, to preach a life of righteousness on earth and to promise an eternal bliss for the pure after death. He combined this faith with belief in a predestined fate for man, whose life and death were completely in the hands of God. His thoughts were set forth in the *Koran,* a collection of pronouncements published posthumously which exhorted man to love his neighbor and to be helpful and devoted, and which included locally applicable rules for eating, drinking, marriage, political activity, and other aspects of social conduct.

Spreading of Islam. Coming as it did in a time of renewed religious agitation, Mohammed's work was taken up with enthusiasm and devotion and was carried on by such extremely capable disciples as Abu-Bekr, Oman, and Othman. They gained not only a religious following, but also political leadership among the roaming tribes of Arabia; and then, motivated by economic forces as well as religious enthusiasm, they started on a road of conquest abroad. Moslem armies took Syria in 636, Jerusalem in 638, Mesopotamia in 640, Alexandria in Egypt in 642, Cyprus in 649, and Persia and other countries later. The Islamic faith spread rapidly as far as India and China.

The Moslems and the Eastern Roman Empire. Islam offered a serious challenge to Christian Europe. After Justinian, the Byzantine Empire—Europe's eastern bulwark—had quickly lost its briefly regained strength. Internal disruptions had weakened the frontier defenses. Dangerous attacks on the empire were launched by the Mongols, the Slavs and, especially, the Persians. Only in 626 had Heraclius (d. 641), a capable emperor, succeeded in stemming the Persian tide and in repelling Mongolian and Slavic assaults. But his victorious efforts had exhausted the resources of the empire, nor could he reconquer all the lost territories. Consequently, ten years later when the Moslems in turn launched their attack, they were able to defeat the Byzantine armies, albeit, they were ultimately stopped before crossing into Europe. Constantinople held out, its strong strategic position and its wealth saving Europe from a new Eastern invasion. But the danger remained. Vicious, intriguing, and dissolute emperors did little to lessen it until, in 717, Leo III (the Isaurian) came to the throne. Leo strengthened imperial authority, augmented the ruler's autocratic, divine position, reorganized the government, and had the law codes revised. He emphasized his supreme rights even in clerical affairs, challenged the position of the Roman popes, and supported the so-called "iconoclastic movement" which condemned the use of religious images. His administration saw the revival of commerce, the expansion of the grain and textile trades, and the further development of the jewelry and other industries. Even though debauchery, despotism based on oriental models, and incompetence returned with his successors, a firm basis had been laid whereby it became possible for the Byzantine Empire to resume its place as Western civilization's eastern bastion.

The Moslems and Western Europe. No such bastion existed in the West. Western Europe was divided. Italy was split in many parts, populations in many formerly prosperous areas declined, and impoverishment increased in Rome as well as in numerous other towns. In Spain, Visigoth rule was effective in the northern and central regions, but there was no such firm control in the south. The Frankish kingdom was a battleground of competing lords and ambitious women; Clovis' successors became known for their immaturity, inefficiency, and laziness as *rois fainéants* (do-nothing kings) and assassinations bedeviled their regimes. The early Merovingians had possessed vast resources, including gold; their connections with Byzantium and the East had been close, and lively trade was still carried on in the Mediterranean Basin. But with the conquests of the Moslems and their domination of Mediterranean trade routes, large-scale commercial activity, and the coining and use of money, almost ceased in Western Europe. These economic difficulties helped to unsettle the social order and weaken the West militarily so that it was unable to stem the Moslem advance. The kings no longer enjoyed the prestige which had its roots in the traditional Germanic relationship between a leader and his followers—a relationship of trust; nor did they possess that unlimited authority which the emperors could claim in Rome and Byzantium. They had to rely on the increasingly independent group of nobles who gave them sustenance, advice, and support in war, but in return had to be accorded a role in the king's household and, in most cases, had to be given royal grants of land for their use. Though morally obligated to serve the king, they often rejected their end of the bargain.

Moslem Conquests in Africa, Spain, and France. Under the circumstances, the Moslems found little opposition when their armies reached the lands around the Western Mediterranean. Advancing along the North African coast, they seized Carthage in 698; thereafter from near-by Tunis, they dominated not only the eastern but also the western Mediterranean sea lanes. In 711, they crossed the Straits of Gibraltar. They conquered most of Spain, including Visigoth areas in the north and east. By 732, their advance forces had reached the center of France. Only then were they stopped. Long weakened by disunity, the Franks, too, would have been unable to offer much resistance had it not been for the fact that, in 687, Pepin of Heristal, who had been serving the Merovingian king as adviser and "Mayor of the Palace," had assumed virtual control of the kingdom. Pepin had reunited its various parts, checked the unruliness of the independent nobles, strengthened the bonds with the Church, and regained prestige and support. Pepin's illegitimate son, Charles Martel (714-741), who had succeeded his father in the office of Mayor of the Palace, defeated the Mohammedans. After a battle (in the area between Tours and Poitiers) in which the reorganized forces of the Franks, making effective use of their newly built-up cavalry, demonstrated their power, the Moslems retreated to the Pyrenees.

Soon thereafter the united stand of the Moslem realms was abandoned as competing rulers established independent regimes in Spain, Egypt, and Mesopotamia. Thus, the danger to Europe passed.

Cultural Decline in the West. During the period when the East witnessed the regeneration of political and religious life connected with the rise and conquests of Islam and the flourishing of Byzantine culture, the Western world made few lasting cultural achievements. Isidore of Seville's (d. 636) survey of the sciences and ethics of his age was an outstanding achievement of that era; yet, it can serve now as evidence of the remarkably low level of the contemporary state of knowledge. Some more significant contributions to Western civilization were made in religious thought and art. Irish monasteries and monastic schools flourished. The production of copies and translations of early Christian writings, often beautifully illuminated, raised the level of Christian scholarship. Inspiration flowed from Ireland to England, where Canterbury and Jarrow became notable centers of learning. A gifted writer emerged in the person of Bede (d. 735), who wrote numerous religious works, of which the best-known is his *Ecclesiastical History of the English People*. The Irish and the English carried on a brisk missionary activity, during the course of which Winfred (St. Boniface) became famous as Apostle of the Germans in Thuringia and Bavaria. (He was martyred in 754.) But not until the age of Charles Martel's successors did intellectual endeavors spread broadly and begin to reflect a genuine revival of civilization in the West.

CHAPTER XIII

THE EARLY FEUDAL AGE (741–1000)

THE PERIOD FROM 375 TO 741, described in the preceding chapter, is considered by some historians as a part of Ancient Times. Thus, the Belgian historian Pirenne has suggested that the Middle Ages did not "begin" until the eighth century. The contemporary student of history may accept Pirenne's suggestion; or he may prefer to date the start of the Middle Ages as early as 375; or he may choose another intermediate date, such as the year 476 which is often used since it marks the end of the West Roman Empire. In any case, Pirenne has correctly pointed out that during the period from 375 to about the middle of the eighth century Roman imperial concepts, classical scholarship, the spirit of early Christianity, and especially the commercial organization of the Roman Empire still prevailed widely; and it may be held that the new epoch in history began with the rise of Islam and Arab dominance in the eastern Mediterranean, rather than with the organization of the Germanic successor states on the soil of the old Roman Empire. By the time the advance of Islam and the Arabs occurred, the world of the Middle Ages had, however, clearly emerged.

FORMATION OF THE CAROLINGIAN EMPIRE

The region in which ancient cultural institutions of mankind had flourished differed geographically from that in which medieval cul-ture was to blossom. The Medieval world included central and northern European territories far beyond the limits of the Roman

Empire, but it did not comprise many of Rome's eastern and non-European possessions. This new world—"the West"—was not organized as a unit ruled from a center like Rome, even though the Church formed a universal link and the imperial idea was revived, first by Charlemagne in 800 and again by Otto the Great in 962. Instead, the new world was based on local, territorial units which slowly amalgamated to form larger political entities or nations. Most of the peoples showed some Germanic traits and ways of life modified by Christian views and standards and by Roman legal and cultural traditions. "Feudal" institutions flourished. They were founded not on despotic rule, circumscribed law, and economic power derived from extensive capitalistic undertakings, but on the vague authority of the heads of Christianity (the German emperor and the Roman pope), on the leadership of numerous kings and dukes, on a great variety of local legal customs, on honor as the link between ruler and follower, and on land as the basis of wealth and social status.

The Carolingians. After the death of Charles Martel, his son Pepin the Short became Mayor of the Palace. He put an end to the Merovingian dynasty and had himself anointed king by St. Boniface, who acted in the name of the pope. Pepin thus established the so-called "Carolingian" dynasty. His rule emancipated the Frankish kingdom from the old Roman system of government and marked the triumph of northern (Germanic) ways.

REIGN OF PEPIN. Pepin's main objective was to re-establish royal prestige and power. For this purpose he chose the Church as his ally. Profiting from religious and political rivalries which strained the relations between the pope and the East Roman Empire and which forced the pope to seek Pepin's support, he followed a policy of close co-operation with the Church. By means of the so-called "Donation of Pepin," he ceded to the pope the Exarchate of Ravenna, which he had conquered from the Lombards after the latter had driven out the last remnants of the Byzantine garrisons. In exchange, he secured through the pope not only the support of the Frankish clergy (which he was then able to use to counterbalance the influence of the Frankish nobility), but also far-reaching control of the clergy itself. Under Pepin, all classes had to make regular contributions to the military and administrative service. The borders of the Frankish kingdom were extended into the Lowlands, Lombardy, and the Pyrenees.

CHARLEMAGNE. Pepin's son, known to history as "Charlemagne" (768–814), continued his father's policies. A towering figure in history, an energetic leader, a wise politician, a clear-minded and enterprising though brutal and profligate ruler, he re-established a Western Empire.

External Policies. Charlemagne put an end to the Lombard kingdom and made himself its ruler, expanding it far into Italy. He repulsed the Avars (another Eastern invader) and gained control of Bavaria and the area which would later become Austria. He fought the Moslems beyond the Pyrenees, where he conquered Barcelona. After long and bloody wars he extended his realms deep into northern Germany by defeating the Saxons under Vidukind, then converting them or killing them off. Along the Elbe River, and elsewhere, he next established "marches" (frontier districts) under special "margraves," who were his local administrators and responsible directly to him. He maintained peaceful contacts with the Eastern Moslem world, arranging for embassies and exchanging gifts with the famous Caliph Haroun al Raschid (d. 809) in Bagdad, at whose court the sciences and arts flourished. Similar relationships were developed with the Byzantine Empire.

Relations with the Church. In 800, Charlemagne was crowned emperor by Pope Leo III—a new dignity for the Frankish king who eventually succeeded in having his new position recognized even by the Byzantine emperors. The act of coronation inaugurated, or at least evinced, a dubious relationship between emperor and pope; for later popes derived from this act a claim to spiritual superiority over future emperors, whereas Charlemagne's successors derived from their imperial position the emperor's traditional claim to sovereignty in Church as well as worldly affairs. This question of imperial-papal relations was to remain a key political issue throughout the entire medieval period. In Charlemagne's time, owing to the strength of his personality and the low state of the papacy, there was no doubt as to the emperor's final authority.

Internal Policies. In internal affairs, Charlemagne continued the policies of his father. He autocratically supervised the Church in the Frankish kingdom, appointed bishops and abbots, endowed the Church with lands, and used the clergy and its missionary work, especially in Germany, as instruments in the extension of his political authority. He held the nobles in line, but often called upon them as well as upon the clergy for advice in connection with state

CAROLINGIAN EMPIRE

— Charlemagne's empire about 814
--- Division of empire by Treaty of Verdun, 843

Farthest eastward extension of the Carolingian Empire (843)

BALTIC SEA

NORTH SEA

ATLANTIC OCEAN

ADRIATIC SEA

IRELAND

ENGLAND
Jarrow
York
London
Canterbury
Thames R.

DANES

WILZIANS

POLES
Vistula R.
Oder R.

SORBS

MORAVIA

BOHEMIA
Prague

SERBS

CROATS

NETHERLANDS
Utrecht

SAXONY
Hamburg
Bremen
Elbe R.
Hildesheim
Magdeburg

THURINGIA

AUSTRASIA
Cologne
Aachen
Meuse R.
Mersen
Rhine R.

LORRAINE
Verdun

FRANCONIA
Frankfort
Fulda
Würzburg
Mainz R.
Worms
Spires

SWABIA
Reichenau
St. Gall
Basel
Strassburg

BAVARIA
Ratisbon
Augsburg
Passau
Salzburg
Danube R.

CARINTHIA

ALPS MTS.

LOMBARDY
Milan
Po R.
Genoa
Pavia
Bologna
Ravenna
Florence
Pisa

Venice

Drave R.
Save R.
Danube R.

BURGUNDY
Geneva
Lyons
Rhone R.

NEUSTRIA
Rouen
Rheims
Paris
Seine R.

BRITTANY

AQUITAINE
Tours
Poitiers
Limoges
Bordeaux
Loire R.
Garonne R.

PYRENEES MTS.
Barcelona

Marseilles

CORSICA

Rome
Monte Cassino

KINGDOM OF ASTURIAS

CALIPHATE OF CORDOVA

policy. He dispensed justice with a firm hand, even though he did
not act as lawgiver—aside from issuing edicts (capitularies) for
specific purposes; general laws were based primarily upon the traditions of each locality. His domains were carefully administered. He
appointed counts and margraves to govern the various parts of his
realms, designated members of his household as civil servants, and
often sent royal messengers or *missi* (in pairs consisting of one
layman and one clergyman) to supervise the execution of the laws
and to report to him both orally and in writing about conditions
in his lands. Charlemagne reorganized the military forces, obtaining
recruits through the service of all free men in his realms. Like his
grandfather, he devoted special attention to the cavalry. He chose
Aachen, Germany, as the site of his chief residence, and at his
palace there he arranged for the organization of schools to supplement the educational institutions administered by the Church. In
contrast with these achievements, however, there was little progress
in commerce and finance. The feudal economy based on agriculture
and designed to meet the immediate everyday needs of each locality
was a principal obstacle. Money remained scarce; silver coins which
were minted had merely local, temporary value. No central tax
and treasury system could be introduced; without adequate sources
of income from taxes, even so powerful a ruler as Charlemagne had
to obtain necessary funds mainly from the income of his own
domains and to seek to supplement it by a few traditional general
levies, such as highway tolls.

DIVISION OF CHARLEMAGNE'S EMPIRE. Charlemagne's personality
left an indelible stamp on future generations but his empire failed
to survive and was divided among his three grandsons. In the treaty
of Verdun (843) they split it into three segments: (1) the region
comprising central and northern France and extending eastward
to about the Meuse River; (2) the region comprising most of central and southern Germany from the Rhine eastward; and (3) the
intermediate region, stretching northward into the Netherlands and
southward into Italy. Upon the death of the oldest of the grandsons,
a new treaty was drawn up (at Mersen, 870) whereby his lands,
consisting of the intermediate strip, were divided between the two
surviving brothers. These treaties were of fundamental importance;
for modern France and Germany, with their differing languages
and diverging customs, evolved from them. The center region,

partitioned at Mersen, has remained subject to influences from both sides and constituted for a long time an object of strife between the Germans and the French.

THE CAROLINGIAN RENAISSANCE. More lasting than Charlemagne's political work was the impact of learning and the arts in his time; it brought the "Carolingian Renaissance." In monasteries and palace schools, classical texts were once more studied, theological problems pondered, books collected, and manuscripts copied. This work was aided greatly by the development of a minuscule handwriting which made possible a new, faster, and more legible method of writing. Beautiful books and psalters, created in monastic centers such as St. Gall, Rheims, and Fulda, were illuminated and illustrated with exquisite miniatures, and they have been preserved to this day. The direction of the interests of the Carolingian scholars may account for a certain lack of originality, yet there was enormous progress in the intellectual life compared with preceding periods. This progress extended also to the field of education. The curriculum of the "seven arts"—the *trivium:* grammar, rhetoric, and logic; and the *quadrivium:* arithmetic, geometry, astronomy, and music— found its first practical application, and even though the traditional idea of strict disciplinary training of mind and body (including the practice of systematic floggings) remained an integral part of the medieval educational method, new patterns of instruction emerged. Scholarship was highly prized. Among the Christian scholars, teachers, and writers at Charlemagne's court were Paul the Deacon, who composed a *History of the Lombards;* Walafrid Strabo who wrote theological commentaries; Alcuin (d. 804); and Einhard (d. 840). Alcuin contributed, among other theological works, to an improved version of the Bible, and Einhard composed a *Life of Charlemagne.* Under the influence of the Byzantine style, architecture, painting, and handicrafts improved. Remarkable church buildings were erected in Italy, western Germany, and southern France; and in the Rhineland and Lorraine splendid gold, silver, ivory, and enamel works were created. Soon the Carolingian revival had repercussions in many parts of the Western world. Carolingian schools and arts and crafts were widely imitated and they stimulated cultural advances also in Anglo-Saxon regions, from which they once had drawn inspiration. The scholarly contributions of Johannes Scotus Erigena (*ca.* 850) are an example of the cultural progress achieved since the time of Isidore of Seville; they foreshadowed in some respects the major trends of theology and philosophy in the twelfth century.

VIKING INVASIONS AND THE REORGANIZATION OF EUROPE

During the ninth and tenth centuries, new invasions endangered the cultural progress of the Western countries. The assaults came from all sides: from the south, where Moslems began the conquest of Sicily (in 827) and a few years later plundered Rome; from the east, where a new power, the Magyars had arisen and had begun to threaten the West; and, most important, from Scandinavia in the north, whence a new great Germanic migration started—that of the Northmen or Vikings.

The Vikings. Hardy, bold, and restless, the pagan Vikings excelled as seafarers, traders, and warriors. Their pillaging expeditions—primarily along the coasts of the British Isles and Ireland, the Netherlands, France, Spain, and North Africa—extended as far as the shores of Greenland and America, and eastward into the lands of the Baltic, Finnish, and Slavic peoples. Since no defenses against seaborne invasions had been set up anywhere, the Vikings swept forward without difficulty. They sailed rivers into the interior of each region. Crossing Poland and Russia via the Vistula, Düna, Dnieper, and Volga, they reached the Black and Caspian seas; crossing the Frankish kingdom via the Seine and Meuse rivers, they reached as far as Burgundy. They plundered and destroyed everything in sight but eventually were tamed and absorbed by the higher civilizations with which they came into contact. Settling on lands ceded to them by the defeated peoples, they were soon converted to Christianity, and amalgamated with the native populations. In this way they settled in Normandy (911), within feudal France; in Anglo-Saxon England north of the Thames (870); and in Russia (862). Under the leadership of Rurik and his associates, they founded the first Russian state in recorded history.

France. Wherever the Vikings settled, they changed the political institutions of the country. In France, Charlemagne's successors were unable to drive them out, nor could they insure the safety of their realms by paying tribute. The Vikings occupied extensive areas far beyond the borders of Normandy. Their presence strengthened the tendencies toward feudal decentralization; the king's government was weakened and thus the nobles saw a chance for challenging royal prerogatives. Seeking widest autonomy, they did not even hesitate to engage, upon occasion, the support of the Viking enemy. In vain did the kings try to counter their efforts by buying the services of some of the nobles with the help of gifts of royal land (*demesne*) and then playing these nobles against others. The surrender of royal *demesne* only served to diminish still further the strength of central authority. Dissolution of the realm resulted and, especially, differences between northern and southern France in language, tradition, and law were accentuated. Trade and commerce again declined, individuals grew more and more insecure, and living standards remained at a low level. The fine arts and scholarship deteriorated. Only toward the end of the tenth century was a new period ushered in when the last of the inefficient Carolingian rulers was replaced as king of France by Hugh Capet (d. 996), count of Paris. Hugh initiated the Capetian line of kings. He stopped the alienation of royal *demesne* and introduced a measure of stability in government by establishing the tradition of primogeniture, i.e., the automatic right of the first-born to inherit the lands and position of his father instead of seeing the property divided between himself and his brothers. This procedure of inheritance eliminated the weakening effect which the nobles could often exercise by making recognition of a dead king's successor dependent upon his granting them broader privileges once in power. But even under Hugh Capet, effective royal authority remained limited to his own domains around Paris. Feudalism with its politically divisive and economically retarding influences reached its full development.

England. In England, the effect of the Viking invasions under Danish leadership proved more disruptive than in France. Despite its Christianization, the island had not become politically united. Indeed, Christianization had at first caused additional differences between the eastern (Anglo-Saxon) and the western (predominantly Celtic) parts, and these differences had not been settled until 664 when a Synod in Whitby established standards acceptable to both. But even then, political integration had not made much progress. Not until the ninth century brought closer commercial and religious connections with the continent was a strong regime created. This was done by the Saxon King Alfred the Great (d.

899), who succeeded in asserting his authority over the major part of the country and provided leadership for its cultural progress. His work had, however, no lasting effect, for, when the Northmen invaded the country, its newly gained unity was shattered; and after Alfred's death the Danes obtained control over most of Central England north of the Thames. To be sure, some of the Danish possessions (the "Danelaw") were reconquered by the Anglo-Saxons in the middle of the tenth century and royal control over the local nobility was restored, but this did not bring stable government. Shortly after the year 1000 the Danes, strengthened by reinforcements received from their homeland, regained the initiative and the struggle for power was resumed.

Spain. In Spain, too, the Norse invasions impeded Western civilization. Viking assaults put a stop to the progress of the Christians in their continued efforts to expel the Moslems from the peninsula. By 834, the Christians had nearly reached the center of Spain, had taken Burgos, and had begun the process of organizing monarchies based upon Western concepts. But the invasions compelled them to concentrate upon self-defense and prevented the recovery of further territories.

Russia. As in the West, so in the East, the Northmen shattered the old regimes and thus necessitated the creation of new political systems. Tribes with different racial backgrounds inhabited the plains and forests of what was later to become Russia; they possessed but primitive political institutions and were often the prey of invaders from the north or east. The Goths, Huns, Avars, Norwegians, and Swedes, had invaded the country; in the seventh and eighth centuries the Norwegians and Swedes had settled along the great waterway of the Volga and had begun trading with the Moslems. After the middle of the ninth century, Christianity infiltrated from the south as a result of the activities of St. Cyril and Methodius, the "Apostles of the Slavs," who had devised an alphabet for the Slavic language. From that time on, cultural relations, particularly those with the Byzantines, supplemented commercial relations with the Scandinavians and Moslems. But not until the Northmen, under Rurik, arrived in Novgorod in 862 and established their political sway along the great trade route connecting the Baltic and the Black seas by way of the Dnieper River, did a Russian state properly speaking seem to have come into being. Soon Kiev became its capital. By 988, one of the Norse rulers, Vladimir

I, accepted the Christian faith and enforced it throughout his realms.

Central Eastern Europe. During the tenth century, in addition to Russia, certain other Christian nations were formed in Eastern Europe. Poland, inhabited by Slavs and centering around the upper Vistula, emerged as a state under Miesco I. Hungary, where remnants of various eastern invaders (including the Huns and Magyars) had mixed with indigenous populations, also achieved statehood.

The German Empire. While the regions in the East and West of Europe were being transformed by the Norse invasions, the central area of the continent remained largely untouched by them. In Germany and Italy, the two main forces of the Middle Ages— Empire and Papacy—evolved.

RENEWAL OF THE EMPIRE. In Germany, the last Carolingian rulers proved to be as weak as those of France. They could hardly hold their own in wars against the nobles and clergy, who ruled powerful duchies such as Saxony, Franconia, and Swabia or large bishoprics such as Mainz and Cologne. But in Germany, even earlier than in France, the dynasty died out, and the great lords, following an old Germanic tradition, elected a new king from their midst. They chose Henry the Fowler (919–936), duke of Saxony, whose family was destined to retain the crown for a hundred years. He brought new authority and dignity to the royal office, achieved peace at home, continued the work of eastern colonization, and successfully defended the German frontiers. He left a well-ordered kingdom to his son Otto the Great (936–973), who became one of the great rulers of the nation. In 962 Otto, taking Charlemagne as his model, had himself crowned emperor and reinstituted the "Roman Empire" or, as it later came to be called, the "Holy Roman Empire." Thenceforth, for almost a thousand years, the office of emperor remained in the hands of German kings. It has been asserted that the desire to maintain the empire diverted their attention from domestic affairs and that national interests were sacrificed to international, imperial aims; for as emperors, Otto and his successors were drawn into preoccupation with Italian policies and problems. Yet the concept of an imperial authority (as a worldly sword) analogous to the spiritual authority of the papacy was in harmony with the religious feelings of the age and the climate of political opinion. Moreover, the close relationship between Germany and

Italy immensely fructified the cultural life of both areas and contributed to some of the outstanding achievements of Western civilization.

NATIONAL AFFAIRS. Otto the Great continued Charlemagne's work in other respects as well. He expanded his territories eastward, spreading thereby Western Christian civilization and at the same time protecting Europe from new assaults by Oriental invaders. In the decisive Battle on the Lechfeld, in 955, he defeated the Magyars, who had plagued Germany with their attacks since the times of Charlemagne. He occupied Bohemia, and extended his realms southward along the Rhone Valley. He maintained close relationships with the Byzantine Empire, even to the extent of arranging for his son and successor, Otto II, to marry a Byzantine princess. At the same time, in domestic affairs, he concentrated on building up the military and economic power of his hereditary duchy Saxony, thus increasing the resources at his command and making it possible for him to suppress numerous rebellions. He then redistributed the great fiefs, assigning many of them to relatives or to loyal princes of the Church, and he entrusted the supervision of the Empire to officials (counts, margraves, and *missi* as in the court of Charlemagne) appointed by himself. He retained control over the papacy, even deposing two of the popes, and firmly supervised all ecclesiastical affairs in Germany. Cultural endeavors were encouraged, and there began the "Ottonian Renaissance." Like Charlemagne, Otto the Great sponsored schools and promoted learning and scholarship. Beautiful manuscripts, jewelry, and book illustrations (reflecting the influence, as in earlier times, of Byzantine models) were produced by craftsmen in the Rhenish regions and in southern Germany.

The Church. During the period which saw the rebirth of the Empire and the restoration of its prestige, disorganization and iniquity were prevalent in the Church. In the tenth century the Church exercised an all-pervasive influence on daily life, doing much to shape the education and culture of the time; but in many regions, lack of discipline, of devotion, and of piety interfered with the fulfillment of her tasks. Among the higher clergy were many who primarily sought possession of land, economic power, and jurisdictional rights. Churches and church endowments were often handed over, as if they were fiefs and feudal rights, to laymen from the nobility, and these used them for ends which contradicted the proper ones of the Church. Monasteries again served as places of refuge where the wealthy lived in luxury and idleness instead of seeking salvation. It was in the face of such trends that in the course of the century a reform movement started within the ranks of the Church which became known as the Cluniac Reform Movement.

WEAKNESSES IN CHURCH ORGANIZATION. The decline in the affairs of the Church had manifold roots. Wealth corrupted the morals of many of her servants; popes and bishops paid more attention to political than to spiritual duties; simony (i.e., the purchase of clerical offices) affected the choice of many high ranking officials; high birth opened the way to such positions as bishoprics and abbacies, which could provide land, wealth, and prestige to those younger sons of the nobility who could not secure a fief. Intrigues among the nobility in Rome and at the Curia made good government in the Church impossible. Finances remained in constant disorder. The tithes, consisting of a tenth of the income of the common people and originally intended for the maintenance of the Church, were generally collected by the landed nobility who financed religious activities in their own territories and paid something to the bishop, but then kept the balance for themselves. Clergymen resorted to such means of bolstering Church power as forging documents (e.g., the "Donation of Constantine" and the "False Decretals") which purported to justify the popes' worldly authority in Rome and their dominion over all Church affairs and appointments. Popes enforced their worldly authority by threat of excommunication and other religious penalties. Moreover, the status of the Church was endangered by a rift between the Western and the Eastern hierarchy. It had begun in the course of the seventh and eighth centuries over the question of religious images which the "iconoclasts" wished to see banned, and had come to a first climax in the ninth century, when the East Roman Emperor Basil I (867–886) and his powerful patriarch Photius of Constantinople sought to bring about complete independence of Constantinople from the popes. Although this rift was temporarily healed after the death of Photius, tension persisted.

REFORM MOVEMENT. Christian devotion lived on, however, in spite of worldliness. It lived on in the hearts and deeds of innumerable individuals; and thus a mighty reform movement grew up. This reform movement centered around the cloister of Cluny, which was founded in 910, and which established daughter houses in many regions. The Cluniac monks, led by devoted abbots, adhered strictly to the Rule established by Benedict. They sought to purify the morals of churchmen and to improve the conduct of ecclesiastical affairs. In this they were aided by the emperors and a number of lesser princes who, out of conviction as well as for political reasons, favored reform. Notably Otto the Great's grandson, Otto III (d. 1002), who made his distinguished teacher Gerbert of Rheims pope (Sylvester II), led the way to a revival of a true Christian spirit. Inspired perhaps by the Caesaropapism in his mother's native Byzantium, he tried to conduct his imperial office in this spirit. Thus, owing to the efforts of practical-minded leaders and the influence of Cluny, a spiritual revival eventually occurred which brought the Church, during subsequent centuries, to the peak of her power.

Europe in 1000. By the beginning of the second millennium, Europe appeared to be quite different from what it had been in the age of Charlemagne. The Church was making progress toward reform and new prestige. States which were to become the nations of the modern world (France, Spain, Germany, England, the Scandinavian countries, Russia, Poland, and Hungary) began to emerge. European civilization was no longer on the defensive but in the beginning of an age of expansion. The foundations for a great intellectual and artistic development had been laid. Political conditions were gaining in stability, population was increasing, commerce was being revived, and economic activities were coming to embrace manifold industrial activities and no longer centered almost exclusively in agriculture. Craftsmanship was improving and industries, such as those making textiles, armor, and enamelware, were expanding. The tenth century witnessed the rise of Italian towns such as Milan, Venice, Genoa, and Pisa; and north of the Alps, German and French towns such as Cologne, Mainz, Verdun, and Lyons gained in importance.

FEUDALISM

Feudalism as a form of social organization reached maturity in the ninth and tenth centuries. Not unknown to other civilizations at a certain stage of their economic evolution, it assumed a special form in the West as a political system built on an economy involving land tenure and personal service. Some of its roots can be traced to late Roman times, when slaves were gradually acquiring a new status as tenants; others can be traced to the times of the great migrations when peasants, in order to achieve security, offered their personal services to a lord who would defend them. Certain characteristics of feudalism derived from Germanic traditions, as, for example, the custom of German kings, lords, or lesser nobles of taking into their households and supporting a number of friends who were obligated to serve them loyally in the government and in time of war. In this way a type of social organization emerged wherein one segment of the population assumed responsibility for government and military defense against external enemies, while the other segment provided a livelihood for all by tilling the soil.

Feudal "Pyramid." As time went on, the social organization developed in such a way that it resembled a pyramidal structure. At the top was the king and below him, as "vassals" and "subvassals," were the nobles (including the dukes, counts, barons, and knights). The base consisted of the peasants, who made up perhaps 90 per cent of the population. Inasmuch as a rigid hierarchical pyramid never developed, however, transition from one step of the pyramid to another was not uncommon, and the system allowed numerous exceptions for reasons of tradition, geography, fortuitous circumstances, and economic necessity. Yet, as a rule, every person had specific work to do in conformity with the class (or "estate") into which he was born. Since everyone was responsible only to the one immediately above him in the "pyramid," with whom a personal direct relationship connected him—a relationship strengthened in the case of the nobility by an oath of fidelity—general allegiance to the person at the top of the pyramid, to the "government" or the "nation," did not develop. Nor could a ruler dispose directly of the services of vassals (or peasants serving his own vassals), except within narrow, customary or specified bounds.

VASSALS. The duties of the nobles (the vassals) were manifold. A vassal was obligated to serve his overlord for a specified time during the year; to help him in case of war (e.g., to be on hand, fully armed, mounted, and accompanied by a stipulated number of men); to make certain payments upon special occasions (e.g., by presenting gifts on certain feast days); to give counsel when called upon; to act as judge; and to offer hospitality to his overlord and court for a given period each year. In exchange, he was given land, a "benefice" (later, a "fief"), which he could hold in trust if not by virtue of property rights. From about the tenth century on, a vassal could leave his land to his son—generally the first-born—but the heir had to assume the duties connected with the possession of the fief. If a family died out, the land "escheated" to the overlord who would either keep it or entrust it to another vassal as a reward for his services.

The obligations of each vassal to his overlord—and ever since the time of Charles Martel, military duties constituted the predominant obligation—were regulated by some kind of personal contract, which presupposed reciprocity. Personal and territorial rights were interwoven, for the use of land and the performance of service could not be separated. Often a vassal would hold lands or fiefs from several overlords, in which case he would owe service to each. Conflicting duties, especially in time of war among the lords, became so burdensome that ultimately the concept of a "liege lord" developed to whom primary service and allegiance were due. As a whole, mutual relationships rested upon a feeling of honor, which derived from early Germanic leader-companion relationship and emphasized rituals, such as performing homage, swearing fealty and being knighted. Not to live up to one's duties as a vassal to his lord was considered a disloyal act and, inasmuch as the whole system was based on personal relationships and mutual trust, disloyalty constituted the greatest dishonor, punished by forfeiture of the vassal's fief to his lord. Nevertheless, disloyalty was common. Kings and other overlords consistently increased their economic demands and attempted to enlarge their judicial and military rights, whereas vassals tried to gain privileges and "immunities," and to reduce the number of their obligations. Vassals especially desired lands (known as "alodial" lands) which they could fully own and control in their own right, free and clear of the service obligations usually involved in the use of feudal lands.

PEASANTS. Just as the estate of the noblemen had its rights and duties, so had the estate of the peasants. They did not own the soil they tilled, nor could they sell it any more than a vassal could sell his fief. But they enjoyed perpetual use of the land. Likewise they had a right to use common woods for fuel and building materials, pastures for their cows, oxen, sheep, and horses, and streams for fishing. They generally worked the land belonging to a fief collectively. A share of the harvest had to be surrendered to the lord. He was also entitled to a share of the working time of each peasant so that his own lands (his *demesne*) would be cultivated and so that roads and bridges would be kept in passable condition. On rare occasions, instead of contributing their personal services (*corvée*) the peasants were allowed to make payments in money or goods. Furthermore, the peasants or their wives had to help in the lord's household as servants and artisans and to accompany him in military campaigns. They had to pay various kinds of fees whenever certain events occurred (e.g., a marriage or death in the lord's castle or the peasant's household). The total burden imposed on a peasant varied with geographic conditions, fertility of the soil, regional customs, and the personal character of his lord. Generally, the lot of the average peasant was hard and the absence of other productive forces in the early medieval economy meant that the full weight of the economic burden rested almost completely upon his shoulders.

SERFS. Most of the peasants in Germanic lands had originally been free men, but during the great migrations they tended to sink down to a level similar to that of the Roman tenants. A leveling process took place, which was speeded up by the fact that the uncertainties of the times made the peasant prefer protection by a lord to complete freedom. Subsequently, the obligations placed on the peasants combined with their economic weakness plunged many of them in various parts of Europe—but especially in Western Europe —into deeper dependency. Eventually to compel them to fulfill their duties, their movements were more and more restricted by those who wielded the sword, and neither the peasant nor his children were then allowed to leave the land to which they belonged. They became "attached" to it in perpetuity; they became "serfs." As such, they gradually passed under the jurisdiction of their lord, so that even if obligations and fines were regulated by custom, or in some cases by a written law, the lack of legal recourse against a lord's decision left them subject largely to his whims. The lord's rights extended also to economic monopolies, such as milling and using common pastures, and might go as far as to include the imposition of capital punishment. Of course, not all peasants became serfs; until the twelfth century, and especially in Germany, many enjoyed a greater or lesser degree of freedom, and in regions like Scandinavia, serfdom hardly developed at all.

Church and Towns. Besides the two major segments of the population ("those who defend" and "those who labor with their hands") there were, of course, others, which were comparatively small in numbers. They included the clergy ("those who pray") and the craftsmen, traders, and unskilled servants, carriers, and other laborers. The Church adapted itself to feudalism by obtaining possession of lands and supplying the necessary services through its own vassals and serfs. Feudal towns, however, had little opportunity to develop under the restrictive social system; the towns which did expand often came into conflict with the controlling authorities.

Living Conditions. For lack of scientific, medical, and technological progress, which generally depends upon the growth of towns (and particularly a division of labor), life for knights and nobles, as well as for peasants, was hard and dangerous. Living conditions were primitive. Food was often scarce owing to the widespread use of the two-field system (one field under cultivation, the other pasture) which severely curtailed crop production; industrial output was insignificant. There were sharp distinctions between the classes, but differences in living standards were somewhat less pronounced than in other ages—in Roman or in modern times—when a variety of luxuries were available and people had money to pay for them. "Chivalry," the conventional way of behavior which gradually developed imposed burdens on the nobles. The honor of a knight required valor in tournaments (often quite dangerous affairs), generosity toward enemies (even if tempered in practice by a view toward economic gain through ransom and spoils), proficiency at hunting, and the like; it also required faithful service to the overlord, who could not otherwise have fulfilled his own duties as administrator of justice and protector of all persons under his jurisdiction. Castles were rarely to be seen before the late ninth or early tenth century. The "manorial system" was only slowly developing. Manors were fortified residences of nobles that became focal points around which workshops, churches, schools, and markets were built. They constituted centers for an advancing civilization. Often the lord, instead of supervising matters himself, appointed an official to whom he delegated administrative responsibilities. In many such instances, the lot of the peasant was harder than it would ordinarily have been on a small farm.

Feudal Fragmentation. The feudal system as a whole, varying as it did from region to region and from generation to generation, indicates the high degree of local independence which generally prevailed. Each domain of a lord, and even each manor, was designed to constitute, economically and politically, an almost autarchic unit. Since each vassal cherished his autonomy, conflicts of interest between his lord and overlords—especially kings—often developed; for the overlords were always eager to integrate the various individual domains into their own larger holdings. This endeavor led to a perpetual struggle between the forces of centralization and those of fragmentation. The conflict began as early as Carolingian times and continued as the noblemen tried to retain their independence against the attempts of emperors, kings, dukes and other great lords to impose their will. Charlemagne had used the *missi* system for enforcing his administrative orders; later German kings achieved a degree of centralization through the appointment of officials who in time became known as *ministeriales*—officials and clerks (including even some of "unfree" birth) who served only the king, upon whom they depended for their livelihood and from whom they derived their power and administrative authority. Basing their authority not on right by birth or on possession of a fief, they found themselves outside the customary feudal hierarchy and constituted an incipient bureaucracy. In other countries, a similar officialdom subsequently came into being, and thus adjustments were made which enabled the feudal system to serve the common needs of the people for centuries.

CHAPTER XIV

BEGINNING OF A NEW MILLENNIUM
(ELEVENTH CENTURY)

M ODERN CONCEPTS OF SCIENCE, of natural causes and laws, were alien to medieval men's way of thinking about nature and human destiny. No wonder then that many in the tenth century, living in an intellectual climate of superstition and ever fearful of wondrous events to come, seem to have taken the Scriptures literally and to have looked forward with trepidation to the close of the millennium since the birth of Jesus. But the year 1000 passed and still the world had not ended, the Last Judgment Day had not come, great catastrophes had not occurred—not even a new plunging comet had appeared or a widely devastating pestilence. The first century of the new millennium began uneventfully. It brought a continuation of old conditions as well as slow changes toward something new. The two great powers (the Empire centering around Germany and the Papacy centering around Rome) had jointly attained predominance, but now they began to drift apart and entered an age of conflict. The minor kingdoms in Western Europe, especially France and England, gained in stability, even though in England an equilibrium was achieved only after the island had been subdued by Norman conquerors. Christianity completed its victorious march into the border areas of Europe; it embraced Scandinavia and most of the Slavic East; it also made headway in Moslem Spain. Trade and commerce increased. Literary and artistic activities multiplied and, before the century was over, the first university had been founded. The restoration of its intellectual and economic strength made it possible for the West to spread its enriched culture not only into adjacent European territories, but also, through "Crusades," into Asiatic lands which had been lost to Christianity ever since the rise of Islam.

THE POLITICAL SCENE

In the course of the eleventh century, three spectacular events occurred which have retained a special hold on the imagination of posterity: the Battle of Hastings (1066), the dramatic incident of Canossa (1077), and the First Crusade (1096–99). Of more lasting significance than these isolated events, however, was the common trend, notwithstanding the crusade, toward political diversity. Despite the renewal of the Empire under Otto the Great and the regained authority of the Church under the impact of the Cluniac reforms, cohesion among the European peoples diminished steadily. Separate states were organized, and the historian concerned with the Middle Ages has to deal with them individually.

Empire and Papacy (1002–1056). Early in the eleventh century, the Saxon line of kings and emperors died out and, following established custom, the German nobility convened on an open field near Mainz to elect a new king. Their choice was Conrad, duke of Franconia (Emperor Conrad II). Like its Saxon predecessors, the Franconian house was destined to rule for about a century. During this period, the danger of foreign invasions lessened, but internal rivalries increased, and particularly a conflict between emperor and pope developed which constituted a serious peril to European civilization.

GERMANY. From the last Saxon emperor, pious and able Henry II, who founded the majestic cathedral at Bamberg, Conrad II (d. 1039) inherited amicable relationships with the clergy. He did his best to remain on good terms with them and followed Henry's practice of using clerics as his advisors and administrators. On his first expedition to Italy, he was crowned emperor by the pope, in the tradition of his Saxon predecessors. He reasserted those imperial prerogatives which under his weaker predecessors had lapsed and, in order to provide greater stability to the imperial status, promoted the system of primogeniture. This policy enabled his son, Henry III, to achieve prestige that was not to be surpassed by any monarch throughout the Middle Ages. Henry III's empire extended from the

Baltic Sea to Rome, from Flanders to Hungary; and his influence was felt throughout Europe. In the West, he dominated northern and central Italy and acquired important territories along the Rhone River; in the East, he became the overlord of Hungary, Poland, and Bohemia. He put up fortresses along the borders of the Empire to protect it from invasions. He held the feudal nobility in check by assigning many administrative duties to *ministeriales* solely responsible to himself. Deeply religious, he kept in close touch with the conduct of Church affairs and promoted reform measures in this field. The extent of his power and influence in religious matters is shown by the fact that at the Synod of Sutri (1046) he was able to depose three popes and choose a fourth one to replace them; within the short period of three years thereafter, he witnessed the elevation of a pope advocating the Cluniac reform, namely Leo IX, to the Roman See. But in 1056, in the midst of his manifold activities, the young emperor suddenly passed away, leaving a mere child as his heir and successor.

ITALY. During the reigns of Conrad II and Henry III, Italy gained new political importance. At the beginning of the eleventh century, the country consisted of many subdivisions subjected to a variety of rulers: Byzantine governors in the South (where they maintained themselves after being expelled from the Exarchate of Ravenna); popes in the center; emperors in the North; remnants of the Lombards in the mountains; and Moslems in Sicily. Further fragmentation occurred when, in the first quarter of the eleventh century, Vikings (or "Normans") also succeeded, after decades of pillaging raids, in gaining a foothold in Italy and in carving out a dominion of their own. But conditions changed in the second quarter of the century. As Arab power declined, some of the lands occupied by Moslems were reconquered; North Italian towns, owing to revived Mediterranean trade, gained in strength, independence, and prosperity; and order was brought to the affairs of Rome through the joint efforts of Cluniac reformers and emperors. The ambitious Roman nobility, which had long fought for supremacy in the city and for dominance over the papacy, was relegated to a lesser role, and competent, effective government was restored. Italy thus rejuvenated became an important asset in the struggle for international power and prestige. Its new significance in world affairs became apparent when Henry died and his young son Henry IV ascended the throne.

Empire vs. Papacy (1056–1106). The accession of Henry IV marks the beginning of a two-hundred-year struggle for supremacy between Empire and Papacy. From the outset of this contest, the popes held advantages such as they had not enjoyed for centuries. As workers for religious and social reform, they had regained spiritual authority; a purified Church meant enhanced prestige for them. They had succeeded in strengthening their ecclesiastical independence by enforcing the rule that popes should not be chosen by the emperor and other worldly powers, but canonically.[1] They had increased their political independence by means of an alliance with the Norman invaders, whom they no longer treated as enemies but as vassals and whom they used against the Roman nobility, the Byzantine armies, and, especially the emperors. Indeed, although Leo IX (whom Henry III had installed as pope) and his successors were German by origin, they turned against the emperors. The struggle reached its first climax during the regime of Gregory VII.

GREGORY VII. Gregory adhered to the Cluniac reform movement, and his program embodied that of the Cluniac reformers with regard to elimination of simony, strict observance of celibacy by all the clergy, and the abolition of "lay investiture."[2] In addition, Gregory demanded supreme authority in all Church affairs; to this end he appointed a group of "legates," who had to supervise the entire administration of the Church in the pope's name. This program led necessarily to conflict—the more so as Gregory VII was an intelligent, ambitious, and strong-willed man, whose policies envisaged worldly as well as spiritual power.

CANOSSA. As Henry IV grew to manhood, he developed an independent mind and showed himself to be just as ambitious as Gregory. Soon Gregory clashed with him over the question of investiture. Each insisted on his right to nominate and install bishops, and, after bitter recriminations, the emperor ordered the deposition of the pope. The pope's answer was to excommunicate the emperor. This act played into the hands of Henry's vassals, who

[1] Within a few years after Henry III's death, the authority to elect a pope was vested in a college of "cardinals." The right to confirm the elected pope, however, remained with the emperor; the Roman nobility, clergy, and people, who had also had a voice up to then, retained only a right of approval which was more or less of a formality.

[2] "Lay investiture" meant the right of lay lords to participate in the choice of bishops, abbots, and other churchmen whose functions included the rule over lands and estates, and to invest them not only with their secular but also their spiritual authority and demand homage, loyalty, and feudal dues from them.

had been awaiting an opportunity to take revenge for a severe defeat they had suffered in an earlier rebellion. Resenting his arbitrary rule they promptly deserted Henry, who in midwinter was forced to cross the Alps to Canossa (1077) and submissively seek absolution from the pope. The Canossa incident has remained famous in history as a symbol of extreme humiliation, but its practical effect was different from appearances. The act of submission turned into an eventual victory; freed of the ban of excommunication (the pope could not refuse pardon to a penitent Christian), Henry promptly gained control over the rebellious German princes and then resumed the struggle with Gregory. Again the pope used the weapon of excommunication, but this time to no avail. In vain also did he seek the help of the Normans under their able Duke Robert Guiscard; he was forced to flee while Henry took Rome and once more ordered the pope's deposition. Although the Normans eventually reconquered the city (and terribly pillaged it), Gregory did not return and in 1085 died in exile.

THE FINAL YEARS OF HENRY IV. The emperor survived Gregory by more than twenty years, continuing his unceasing struggle against the papacy and the feudal nobility. Soon, the rebellious nobility was joined by members of the emperor's own family: first, by his elder son, then by his second son and successor; and finally, after a disastrous second marriage, by his new young wife. By the end of the century Henry had to give up Italy, and even in Germany he found few supporters. Only the growing urban communities, which he had had the foresight to favor throughout his reign, remained loyal. But their support was not sufficient to maintain his position and in 1106 he was forced to flee the country. He was again excommunicated and died shortly thereafter without receiving a Christian burial—which was not arranged until weeks later.

France and England. France and England, having no imperial rights, aims, or pretensions, did not become involved in as serious conflicts with the popes as Henry IV. Since to them the issue of investiture was not so important, their rulers could focus their attention on internal questions.

FRANCE. No single political event stands out in French history during the eleventh century. The country remained divided into numerous duchies and counties such as Normandy, Aquitaine, Burgundy, and Flanders, each enjoying a large measure of independence. Central power and royal authority were restricted mainly to the king's *demesne*. Economic progress was a slow and gradual process.

ENGLAND. In England, however, many changes took place. Early in the century, recurring Danish invasions had given the Danes control over the major part of the country, and a measure of stability was restored to it—particularly during the regime of King Canute the Great (1016–35). Canute reorganized the administration, maintained peace, and allowed the Church to carry on its work without opposition.

Norman Conquest. This situation did not last. Seven years after Canute's death, Edward "the Confessor," who was reared in France and was a friend of the Normans, ascended the throne. When he died, leaving no heirs, a struggle over the right to inherit the throne of England followed. The chief contenders for the throne were Harold, a Dane, and William, a Norman. In 1066 William set out to enforce his rights and pretensions. From Normandy he crossed the Channel with a large fleet (depicted, along with subsequent events, in the famous Bayeux tapestry) and, in the battle of Hastings, defeated and killed his rival Harold. The Dane's forces had been exhausted by a campaign against Scandinavians, simultaneously invading from the North.

Norman Administration. The Norman conquest was of lasting significance. Once established as king, William distributed English lands as fiefs among his Norman nobles, built castles, reduced many peasants to serfdom, and spread the feudal customs of his native land. Yet, he preserved many English laws and traditions. Moreover, he endeavored to avoid feudal fragmentation and prevented the Anglo-Norman barons from gaining that independence which lords enjoyed on the Continent. In 1081, William ordered a survey and evaluation of the land and cattle, and this survey constituted, for the eleventh century, a rare instance of thorough royal supervision and economic statistical investigation. The results were incorporated in the "Domesday Book," which provided a basis for uniform tax levies. Relations with the Church were peaceful. The archbishop of Canterbury, Lanfranc, was a scholar of distinction, who displayed tact and wisdom and co-operated with the king. William did not challenge the Church's right to independent ecclesiastical courts. In fact, Gregory VII's investiture struggle had few repercussions in England, at least until the reign of the Conqueror's son, when Lanfranc's successor Anselm raised the issues of Church autonomy and lay investiture.

The relations between the Anglo-Saxon and Danish inhabitants and the Norman conquerors, especially the ruling class, were at first tense; but by the time Henry I came to the throne in 1100 an amalgamation of Danes and Normans, originally forbidden, was rapidly progressing.

Spain. On the Iberian peninsula, the struggle against the Moslems was resumed after the Norman invasions had ended. The progress of the Christians was slow, however, for their forces were divided; numerous principalities, often fighting each other, then existed, such as Aragon, Castile, Leon, Navarre, and Portugal. On the other hand, Moslem strength was also divided inasmuch as the Moslem rulers of Spain, residing in Cordova, had fallen out with the caliph in Bagdad, and their own lands were similarly disunited. Eventually, the Christians began to win the upper hand, especially after they had consolidated their holdings and after Castile and Leon had formed a union in 1037. By 1085, with the capture of Toledo, Christian rule had been extended beyond the center of the peninsula.

The Moslems made up for their decline in political power by means of a marked increase in their economic and cultural influence. Some of their agricultural methods, such as terracing, irrigation, and the cultivation of vegetables and flowers unknown in Europe, spread to Western countries. Their commercial, banking, and credit systems, their advances in the textile industry, as well as in making jewelry, cutlery, and glassware, and their knowledge of physics, chemistry, mathematics, and, particularly, of medicine,[3] began to give their remaining Spanish possessions an importance for Western civilization which their military and political exploits had never had. However, the example they set in tolerance—in permitting religious groups (Christian or Jewish) other than their own was not imitated by the West.

Northern Europe. In Scandinavia, the migrations of the Northmen ended during the eleventh century. In that century, too, after long resistance, the Christianization of Denmark, Sweden, and Norway was completed and the three countries were rapidly integrated with the European medieval world. Feudal institutions,

---

[3] Their outstanding contributor to medical science was Avicenna (d. 1037).

however, did not take root there to the same extent as in France, Germany, or England. In particular, serfdom never gained the same importance in the north which it had attained elsewhere.

Eastern Europe. The eleventh century saw the rule of three eminent men in Eastern Europe: King Stephen, King Boleslav I, and Yaroslav the Wise.

Stephen (d. 1038) was a king of Hungary. Famous for his piety—a quality for which he was later canonized—he established close collaboration with the Roman Church. He introduced feudal institutions, contributed to the Westernization of his country, and raised it to the status of an eminent power in Eastern European affairs.

Boleslav I, "the Brave," (d. 1025), king of Poland, started this country on the road to political importance and also tied her to the West. He, too, promoted Catholic influence. Although he was responsible for a long series of aggressive wars such as were to mar Polish history throughout, and although his attacks on one neighbor after the other—Russians, Czechs, Germans, Magyars—led, after his death, to a break-up of his kingdom and the subjection of Poland herself to imperial vassalage, it was largely due to the efforts made in his time that the country was established as an independent Slavic realm.

Yaroslav the Wise (d. 1054) was a ruler of the grand duchy of Kiev, which comprised early medieval Russia. In bitter fratricidal wars he won the throne of his father Vladimir and despite the fact that he was of Norse descent and relied largely on Scandinavian advisers and troops, he promoted Slavic national customs. Repulsing invading forces from east and west, he vigorously carried on the work of political stabilization at home. A code of laws was completed during his regime. Kiev became a prosperous center of lively commerce with Byzantium and the Orient. Commercial relationships and dynastic connections with Scandinavia, Germany, England, and France were also maintained. Yet, owing to distance, to differences in traditions, and to Byzantine influences, close ties with Central and Western Europe were not established; in fact, the gap widened when the tension between the Eastern and Western Christian churches (a tension dating back to controversies about icons and to the political rivalries during the reign of Patriarch Photius) led in 1054 to a new split and Russia adhered to the Eastern, or "Orthodox," Church.

ECONOMIC, SOCIAL AND CULTURAL CONDITIONS

The sequence of great invasions and depredations of Europe by Huns, Magyars, Moslems, and Northmen had contributed their share to a deep decline of economic conditions in Europe. In the eleventh century, the economy of the continent began to improve markedly in comparison with the low level of activity in the preceding eras. Similar progress was achieved in the creative arts. The Ottonian Renaissance was carried forward into the eleventh century as beautiful and increasingly appreciated art treasures were created. Architects and artisans did outstanding work. Exceptional skill was developed in jewelry and leather crafts, in book binding, and in book illustration and illumination of manuscripts. New beginnings were made in classical scholarship, philosophy, and literature.

Business Enterprise. As the political system of the Middle Ages approached maturity, the spirit of commercial enterprise began to spread. Towns increased in number and size. Some industries, especially those engaged in textile production, expanded. Aided by the central location of her harbors, the profits derived from her shipping industry, and the business sense of her merchants, Italy became a leader in a variety of business undertakings. Merchants in towns north of the Alps likewise improved their business methods and, instead of providing solely for local needs, sought wider markets. Iron, copper, silver, tin, salt, and wine, as well as manufactured goods such as armor, were shipped abroad. Silver was coined in increasing quantities. Important mining centers arose in Germany (the Harz region, Bohemia, and Tyrol), northern Sweden, England, and elsewhere. Feudal lords accorded better treatment to traders within their territories, promoting fairs and markets from which they derived profitable taxes and tolls.

Agricultural Enterprise. Not only trade and industry, but also agricultural production increased as a result of the growth in population, the practice of intensive cultivation, and an increase in the acreage of arable land through clearing of forests and colonization of Eastern European regions. Foodstuffs were in greater demand because brisk commerce had enriched the townspeople, and some of the money which became more freely available flowed into the hands of peasants as well as into the coffers of the landed nobility.

Social Organization. As early as the eleventh century changes in some aspects of the social system under feudalism began to occur. The interests of the nobility, formerly preoccupied with military and governmental functions, were broadened to include commercial activities. The people in the towns utilized in their trades a greater specialization and division of labor. Since goods could be produced in larger quantities, new wants and needs were created and a different type of urban society emerged. Economic changes also affected the social status of the peasants. In some regions these appear to have attained, despite maintenance of existing feudal relationships, higher standards of living or to have succeeded in reducing their burdens; in others, they found it possible to change the relationships to their lords and to lease land from them instead of working for them; and in still others, where improvements were too slow in coming, at least some of the peasants found ways of escaping bondage by illegal means and moved to newly colonized regions where they would be free.

Scholarship and Literature. The concentration of population in the towns and the diversified activities of the townspeople stimulated cultural endeavors. In the time of the Carolingian Renaissance, cultural work, aside from that of the palace schools, had centered mainly around monasteries and churches; and this trend continued. But more of the eleventh-century cultural achievements came from outside ecclesiastical institutions.

ECCLESIASTICAL CONTRIBUTIONS. The Cluniac reform movement had a stimulating effect on scholarship. The monks wrote many new Lives of Saints and a number of historical chronicles. A musical notation with the lines and spaces on which music is written was invented; it made possible a consistent musical tradition and served to improve standards of performance. In philosophy and classical learning, some famous teachers and scholars appeared. Among them were Gerbert of Rheims and, later in the eleventh century, Lanfranc and Anselm of Canterbury. Anselm, like Scotus Erigena, is often considered one of the forerunners of scholasticism, although he himself insisted that a Christian scholar cannot rely on logical thinking but must depend on faith and the teachings of the Church. The Latin works of Boethius and other classical writers were studied, and a beginning interest was shown in Arab achievements.

SECULAR CONTRIBUTIONS. The revival of sciences, literary activities, and arts, which took place outside the ecclesiastical field, is evinced by poetry on topics of love, epics dealing with heroic deeds, and

legal writings. In contrast with the slight evidence of achievements
in literature during the tenth century and earlier (among these
achievements was the epic of Beowulf, dating back to the eighth
century) we find numerous secular works dating from the eleventh
century. They include the famous early southern French *chansons
de geste,* composed in the vernacular. The *Chanson de Roland,*
though existing versions were written down somewhat later, was
also created in the eleventh century. From the same period date
parts of the *Anglo-Saxon Chronicle* and certain of the Arthurian
tales and other legends. Studies of Roman law, especially of Justinian's *Corpus juris civilis,* were revived. As these and other
"higher" studies were added to the traditional school work circumscribed by the seven arts (the *trivium* and the *quadrivium*), their
influence was gradually felt all over Europe. It was in connection
with the study of Roman law that one of the most significant
cultural developments occurred—the establishment of "universities."
The university provided a regular meeting place for outstanding
teachers and mature students, who organized themselves into a
closely knit community in order to be able to pursue their studies
in freedom and to be protected against disruptive outside interference. Bologna in Italy, which lays claim to having possessed,
around 1088, the "first" university, excelled in the teaching of law.

The Arts. The early eleventh century brought the "Ottonian
Renaissance" to full flowering. Germany under the Ottonian (or
Saxonian) emperors held the leading place in this artistic reawaken-
ing. "Schools of art" flourished in Trier, Fulda, Hildesheim,
Cologne, and, especially, the island of Reichenau in Lake Constance; they emphasized a Christian spirit rather than any secular
feudal or classical tradition. Notwithstanding the continuing influence of Byzantine culture, an original quality of aesthetic expression
developed in these centers. A transcendental element prevailed,
contrasting with the more lifelike, impressionistic trends of the
Carolingian Renaissance a hundred years earlier. This quality can
be traced in the illuminated manuscripts, in the elaborate book
covers, and even the handwritten state documents drawn at the
time. Later in the century, these art centers slowly declined.

ARCHITECTURE. In architecture, the eleventh century saw the
Romanesque style fully matured. During its early stages in the
ninth century, it had rivalled the Byzantine style, and the latter
persisted in Western Europe deep into the eleventh century, as

evinced by St. Mark's in Venice with its extraordinary mosaics. But by that time, the Romanesque had become the decisive, original expression of Western artistic trends. Romanesque churches, most of them the work of now unknown masters, represent some of the noblest achievements of man. These churches are beautiful in proportions, the exteriors are often severe, with plain and heavy walls, small doors and small, high windows; the arches are simple and rounded. A separate bell tower is often found next to the church. On the whole, the designs were appropriate to the way of life in southern countries, beckoning worshippers out of the hot, noisy, bright, busy marketplace into the serene, cool, peaceful atmosphere of another world. But the Romanesque style—somewhat modified to suit different climates (often requiring special provisions for air and light)—spread also to regions north of the Alps, notably northern France, Germany, Scandinavia, and England. Some of the Romanesque churches were adorned with frescoes; and beautiful sculptures or bas-reliefs can be found both on the outside and the inside walls. The Romanesque style was also employed for secular structures; stone castles, which appeared in increasing number, were built in this style. Simultaneously, its influence was reflected in the minor arts and crafts.

RELIGION AND THE FIRST CRUSADE

Perhaps owing to the reforms within the Church and the new devotion they engendered, a strong religious fervor became evident toward the end of the eleventh century. It showed itself in the building of numerous churches, in the appearance of great preachers, and in revived missionary zeal. It was expressed in literature, in the scholastic work of the monks, and in mystical writings evincing inwardness and warmth of faith. It can be traced in the arts, in the loving care with which sacred books were copied and adorned, and in the craftsmanship applied to objects of worship. It was reflected in the regained esteem and authority of the popes, as well as in the reforms effected among the old monastic orders and the establishment of new ones.

New Monasticism. The religious fervor which led to the founding of new monastic orders was akin to that which had inspired hermits in early Christian times. In contrast to the organizational concepts of the existing orders (which had been so often misused to serve secular purposes), the hermit's ideal of solitary devotion to God was one of the driving forces behind the establishment of new orders, such as those of the Carthusians and Cistercians. The Carthusian monks, named after their first house in Chartreuse, France, accepted the Benedictine rules in their strictest form; they abjured all worldly possessions (in which they recognized the greatest danger to the Christian Church), lived almost like hermits, restricted themselves to vegetarian fare, and devoted their lives to silent meditation, prayer, and physical work. The order of the Cistercians, or gray monks, was also founded in France—in Cîteaux in 1098. But the Cistercians moved to regions distant from cultural centers and, setting up numerous retreats, became famous as colonizers in Eastern Europe. Along with the Christian faith they disseminated knowledge about Western methods of cultivating the soil. Eventually they possessed no fewer than seven hundred monasteries. They, too, prescribed the habit of silence, manual work, simplicity, vegetarianism. They also sponsored missionary schools and encouraged teaching of arts and crafts.

Crusading Spirit. In a still more spectacular manner than through the founding of new monastic orders, the religious spirit of the age was evinced by a mighty enterprise, known as the First Crusade. To be sure, other motives, in addition to religious enthusiasm, inspired the Crusaders. Nobles were interested in conquests so that they could acquire lands for fiefs; knights hoped for adventure, glory, and spoils; popes hoped to extend the area subject to their authority and to gain the increased prestige that they needed for their struggle against the practice of lay investiture. People in the towns hoped the Crusade could bring them new trade connections, Oriental goods, and profits. To many individuals, the Crusade meant escape from pestilences, or from dangerous neighbors, or from personal problems. Yet, there was also a deep religious feeling. There was the hope of gaining forgiveness of sins, of securing salvation by means of an undertaking pleasing to God, of promoting Christianity and protecting pilgrims to the Holy Land against infidels (though their ill-treatment by Moslems was certainly exaggerated), and of converting the Moslems.

The Moslems and the West at the Time of the First Crusade. The time seemed favorable for a successful Crusade, for the Moslems were divided. In the course of the eleventh century, Seljuk Turks had gained domination over large parts of the Moslem world. They had conquered Bagdad, and in 1071 they had gained another great victory when, at Manzikert, they had defeated the Byzantine forces and seized large parts of the Eastern Roman Empire. But once established, the Seljuk emperors had begun to promote the arts of peace. Under Malik Shah (d. 1092) they had devoted themselves to city building, trade, scholarship, poetry, and science. His reign had been the age of the wise statesman Nizam-al-Mulk; of great geographers and historians following in the tradition of al-Masudi of the tenth century; of Hakim Omar Khayyám, the "Voltaire of the East," author of the *Rubáiyát* who won fame as scientist as well as poet. Commerce and industry flourished. The good prospects for a successful crusade which the temporarily peaceful orientation of the Moslems seemed to offer, were enhanced by new dissensions which occurred after Malik's death owing to the dissatisfaction among the Moslems with Seljuk rule.

East Rome and the West at the Time of the First Crusade. The time seemed favorable also in view of conditions in the Byzantine Empire. In 1094, its emperor, Alexius Comnenus, had suggested to the pope a joint campaign against the Turks. Although Byzantium could pride itself on its trade and commerce, on its arts and scholarship,[4] and although it possessed the most efficient governmental administration in Europe, its military power had long been declining. Even against a divided Moslem world, the forces of Constantinople alone seemed too weak. Alexius realized this, but he had good reason to expect help from the West. Not only did he know that the West was interested in preserving his empire as a buffer against the Moslem danger; he could also lure the Italian cities with promises of great trade advantages in Contantinople, and he could hold out hope to the popes for a reunion of the Eastern Orthodox and the Western Catholic Churches. This last issue was of special importance, for the break which had occurred only forty years earlier, in 1054, did not, at the time, seem final. To be sure, in 1054, at the height of the Cluniac reform movement, ambassadors of the pope had in their zeal once more excommunicated a Constantinople patriarch, the Greek Cerularius. Negotiations with him about controversial dogma regarding baptism, the provenience of the Holy Ghost, the use of leavened or unleavened

---

[4] One of the emperors, Constantine Porphyrogenitus (d. 959), himself wrote a distinguished book *On the Administration of the Empire*. He also excelled as a goldsmith.

bread at communion, the celibacy of the clergy, and, especially, the primacy of the popes, had broken down. But the popes had never given up hope of seeing the East return to the Catholic fold, and Alexius took advantage of their expectations.

First Crusade. The emperor's call released the accumulated fervor. In response to his pleas, Pope Urban II (1088–1099), at a Council at Clermont in southern France, addressed one of the most famous and eloquent orations to the throngs assembled there, exhorting them to take up the cross and deliver Christianity from the Turkish danger, and ordering a suspension of all feuds in Europe on pain of excommunication. His call was heeded by French, Germans, English, and Normans. The thousands participating in two abortive preliminary expeditions motivated by enthusiasm and desire for plunder were followed by a main body under Norman leadership, bent on conquest and salvation. Merchants from Genoa, Pisa, and elsewhere traveled in their wake. The Christian armies reached Constantinople, where a treaty with Alexius was negotiated. Since the Western host was unexpectedly overwhelming, the emperor was only too anxious to get rid of them, and he promised to make East Roman fiefs of all the lands the knights could conquer. The Crusaders then proceeded. In 1097, they took Nicaea and, advancing further, despite immense hardships and losses they successfully stormed Jerusalem in 1099. To the joy of Christendom, a Christian kingdom was founded. It became a fief of the pope, and the Norman Godfrey of Bouillon (soon followed by Baldwin I) was crowned king of this new Western feudal state. It was gravely endangered by internal jealousies, by attempts of the nobles to cut out independent principalities or fiefs for themselves, by the avariciousness of knights and traders and their brutality toward the Moslems; but it was to last almost one hundred years.

CHAPTER XV

FLOURISHING OF THE MIDDLE AGES
(TWELFTH CENTURY)

O NLY IN RECENT TIMES have studies revealed the complexities, and the breadth of achievement, of the twelfth century. In fact, a great deal of additional research, especially in economic history, will be required if we are to gain a valid picture of that age. To past historians, the century seemed to lead to the heights of feudal development but, in reality, there were many symptoms of feudal disintegration. Some of the patterns (indispensable in earlier times) of political organization, of kingship, and of knighthood had become largely ornamental by the twelfth century. Knightly ways were now merely praised as ideals instead of being practiced. As so often throughout history, theory and ideal were developed only when practice waned. The growing estate of the *bourgeoisie* (the burghers or townspeople) played a steadily expanding role. Although papal power rose and religious concepts permeated all endeavors of Western man—his scholarship, art and architecture, laws, politics, and everyday life—even attitudes toward religion changed as worldliness and wealth increased.

POLITICAL SCENE

The twelfth century witnessed a change in the political balance of power of Europe. Territorial lords—the kings of countries such as Sicily, France, England, or Denmark, and the dukes of large principalities in the German Empire or in Flanders and Aquitaine —gained strength in comparison with both the emperors and the popes. Likewise, the bureaucracies, which were developing rapidly everywhere, increased their influence; and, perhaps most important, growing towns which could defy lesser lords and even challenge the greater ones, were becoming significant factors in political affairs. Townspeople with their ambitious aspirations made their weight felt, redirecting the political evolution of Europe in regard to both internal and external issues. They speeded up the decline of the lower nobility, helped to strengthen the power of kings and central authorities, and promoted Western culture's eastward expansion deep into pagan and Moslem lands.

The Empire. During the twelfth century, the Franconian line of kings and emperors died out and the family of Hohenstaufen came to the throne. With it began, not only in Germany and Italy, but also in other countries, the most dramatic period in medieval history. It is marked by important events, great personalities, and astonishing cultural achievements.

CONCORDAT OF WORMS. After the death of Emperor Henry IV, the main problem facing his successor Henry V (d. 1125), last of the Franconians, was that of settling the issue of investiture. This was done in 1122 by means of the Concordat of Worms. It stipulated that the emperor would abandon the right of investing his bishops with the symbols of their spiritual office, i.e., the ring and crozier. The Concordat was a compromise which reflected a gain for the papacy, even though in effect the emperors still retained the possibility to determine the personnel of the episcopacy. It affected the imperial relationship to the German nobility, for it encouraged the nobles to persist in their opposition to central imperial power. Henry V was not the man to counter this trend successfully; in any case, he died soon after the Concordat had been concluded.

BEGINNINGS OF HOHENSTAUFEN RULE. Consequently Henry's successors Lothar of Supplinburg (d. 1137) and Conrad III, the first Hohenstaufen emperor (d. 1152), inherited extremely difficult problems. Neither of them could regain full authority over the German princes; but both at least maintained imperial rights in Italy more successfully than Henry, and both expanded the empire eastward. Lothar, in particular, encouraged colonization in the Slavic and pagan lands and promoted the extension of European culture. The advanced economic standards of the eastern German towns, their concepts of law, and their spirit of freedom were introduced in the less developed regions beyond the Elbe and the Oder.

REIGN OF BARBAROSSA. The second Hohenstaufen emperor was Frederick I Barbarossa (1152–1190). The Hohenstaufen family, which ruled for about a century, produced three outstanding emperors: Frederick Barbarossa himself, his son Henry VI (d. 1197), and (in the following century) Henry's grandson, Frederick II (d. 1250). Barbarossa was a man whose wisdom, energy, and ability deeply impressed his contemporaries. At least temporarily, he settled the struggle over supreme authority in Germany in favor of the imperial crown, emerging successful from a long and dramatic contest with his rival, Henry the Lion of the House of Guelph. Henry the Lion was one of the great Eastern colonizers and a farseeing statesman who founded and promoted towns and trade; but he was also a rebellious leader who fought bitterly for the independence and power of the territorial princes. Eventually, Barbarossa reduced him to obedience and restored firm imperial authority over all Germany. Barbarossa declared a general peace of the land, which he enforced with the help of *ministeriales,* upon whom he relied (like earlier strong rulers) instead of on nobility or Church. Laws were efficiently enforced, and infringements on imperial prerogatives were no longer tolerated. Barbarossa, moreover, continued the policy of extending German influence eastward into former Slavic lands, to which he invited prospective settlers. Towns were allowed free constitutions, and "Magdeburg Law," originally drafted for the great central German town and residence of the Magdeburg archbishops, was accorded to them. It provided for broad immunities and self-government, and it constituted one of the most important legal contributions of the Middle Ages.

Outside Germany, Barbarossa secured Burgundy as a fief. He was less successful in his Italian policies. Not only did he face the opposition of several popes who feared his power and resented his claims to a God-ordained worldly leadership of the emperors, but he also became involved in interminable conflicts with the growing towns or communes of northern Italy. When he attempted to enforce complete imperial authority in Lombardy, a number of wars resulted, and, after shifting fortunes had ended in his severe defeat at Legnano, he was compelled in 1183 to allow the towns a large measure of self-government. Only in southern Italy did his policy become profitable, for he succeeded in marrying his son Henry to the heiress of the kingdom of Sicily and southern Italy. This kingdom was governed by the Normans who, under Robert

Guiscard's brother Roger, had driven out the remnants of the Moslem forces as well as the Byzantine troops. A model feudal state, it had become under Roger II (d. 1154) the dominant Mediterranean power and a cultural center, which inherited much from the Byzantine and Moslem civilizations. By means of Henry's marriage, the German emperors gained not only control over southern Italy and large parts of the Mediterranean, but also a counterweight against papal power.

HENRY VI. Barbarossa drowned in 1190 while on a crusade; but his work was carried on. Henry VI, his son, diligently pursued his father's policies. By fully exploiting his power over Germany, northern Italy, and his wife's inherited kingdom in southern Italy and Sicily, he secured for the Empire a status superior to any it had held since the regime of the Franconian Henry III. But events after the premature death of Henry VI, comparable to those after the parallel early passing of Henry III, ended this era of accomplishment. The prestige and power of the emperorship were largely destroyed during the minority of Henry VI's son and eventual successor.

France. While the German kings in their role as emperors devoted their attention to great international tasks, the French kings concentrated on more modest objectives. Very painfully and slowly the processes of centralizing power in the hands of the royal court and checking feudal disintegration went on. With great difficulty, Louis VI (d. 1137) and his able adviser, Abbot Suger (d. 1151), held the lesser nobility in check and, ingeniously, even imposed their will occasionally upon the greater lords. Royal prestige and authority were based upon firm control and economically sound exploitation of the royal domain, and on a bureaucracy which was created along the lines of the German *ministeriales*. These officials were ordered to take over military command posts, to perform a variety of administrative duties, and to collect taxes.

During the second half of the century, Louis VII tried to continue this administrative system, and increase the royal authority, but he was so handicapped by internal rivalries and continuous wars with England that he could not even maintain the status quo. Moreover, in 1152 he made the mistake of having his marriage to Eleanor, heiress of Aquitaine, annulled for lack of male heirs, whereupon Eleanor married Henry II of England; and this added the military strength and economic resources of Aquitaine to those of England while France was weakened. Subsequent wars against England brought defeats, losses of considerable territories and, in the wake of defeats, rebellions of the nobility. Not until Louis' son Philip II Augustus came to the throne in 1180 did the political fortunes of France begin to improve.

England. For the future of Western civilization the political achievements of the French monarchy were less significant than the political ideas and institutions originating in England. The isolated position of this recently conquered country, the preoccupation of its rulers with their continental territories, its mixed populations and diversified traditions, and its economic needs—all these factors contributed to a unique political development.

HENRY I. With Henry I (d. 1135) the consolidation of a bureaucracy began. It counteracted feudal decentralization by strengthening the position of the royal court (*curia regis*) as the supervisor of law enforcement and the final tribunal for appeals. It administered the royal treasury through a new institution, called the "Exchequer." Henry restored peace with the Church, with which conflicts had developed late in the eleventh century when a struggle over the question of investiture had led to the expulsion of the Archbishop Anselm of Canterbury. Henry recalled Anselm; and a compromise on the investiture question (along the lines of the Concordat of Worms) was reached.

HENRY II. Years of anarchy followed upon the death of Henry I. But an unruly nobility with ambitions for local autonomy could not block the long-term trend toward consolidation and pacification. New advances in this direction were made under Henry II (d. 1189), who stands out as one of the most important of the English rulers. He required heavy financial contributions from the nobility as well as from the townspeople and vigorously enforced his will. By allowing individuals to substitute "scutage," or money payments, for their personal services, he enriched his treasury while relieving many nobles of tasks unwillingly and poorly performed. He rebuilt the bureaucracy organized by Henry I, revived the *curia regis* as the main agency of government (on which he could rely in his frequent absences during the wars against France), and while demonstrating his authority over local officials, he nevertheless promoted a measure of self-government and responsibility on the local level. The common law gained wide respect. A jury system for indictment in criminal cases came into general use along with assizes (county courts) to render decisions in disputes over landed property. In line with a precedent set by Henry I, final appeals to the king's judges were allowed so that legal procedures replaced resort to arms as a means of settling controversies. Thus, the twelfth century saw a rapid development of English concepts of law which were to influence the future development of legal systems far beyond the borders of England.

At first, Henry, seeking good relations with the Church, tried to secure the help of the clergy in his attempts at reorganizing the institutions of the country and his resultant struggles with the barons. But later he tried to bring the clergy as well as the barons under his sway; in 1164, he issued the "Constitutions of Clarendon" which reaffirmed royal authority over churchmen. When he also claimed jurisdiction over clergymen accused of crime, he became involved in a bitter controversy with his former chancellor, Thomas à Becket, then archbishop of Canterbury. The archbishop was murdered, an act which Henry (who was at least indirectly responsible) seems to have repented, although his repentance was not so deep as to stop him from enjoying the political advantages derived from this method of eliminating opposition.

Henry extended his realm into Wales, Ireland, and Scotland. Through his marriage with Eleanor of Aquitaine and through other marriage alliances in his family, he acquired extensive additional fiefs, especially in France, and he successfully defended them against the French and other enemies.

RICHARD THE LION-HEARTED. Misfortunes beset Henry II in his later years, and when the old king passed away, many of the achievements of his regime vanished with him. He had come to realize how frail were the foundations upon which he had built; for the barons, who had gained many privileges and immunities during the disorders prior to his accession, had revolted. Moreover, their example had been followed by his own sons, whose ambitions had been encouraged by their mother Eleanor and who, knowing too little about statecraft, had fought their father as well as one another. In the course of the wars, the eldest had perished, and thus the second son, Richard I (d. 1199), known to history by his surname the Lion-Hearted, ascended the throne when Henry died. Richard promptly began to waste England's military resources on crusades, reckless campaigns in France, personal luxuries, and gifts to friends. When his quarrelsome nature involved him in exploits which ended with his capture and imprisonment in Austria (on his way home from the Third Crusade) the country had to pay a huge ransom for his release. In fact, only after the city of London was pawned to the German emperor was Richard liberated. Meanwhile his absences had benefited the country, for at such times England was left undisturbed to develop the institutions which had been wisely created by his predecessors.

Spain and Portugal. In Spain during the twelfth century, the power of the Moslems declined and internal dissensions among them enabled the Christians to expand their holdings on the Iberian peninsula. Between 1139 and 1179, the area of Portugal was organized as an independent kingdom.

Eastern Europe. A number of grave developments occurred in eastern Europe. Of lasting significance among them was the steady eastward advance of Western civilization.

THE BALTIC REGIONS. The Germans and Scandinavians brought Christianity, feudal institutions, and economic development to the peoples around the Baltic Sea. Swedes conquered Finland, Danes invaded Estonia, and Germans advanced into Slavic territory beyond the Elbe and Oder rivers and also sailed across the Baltic to establish themselves in Livonia, south of the Finnish Gulf. Everywhere the Western peoples extended the areas under cultivation and founded cities—including Berlin. Thus, by the end of the twelfth century, Western civilization embraced the entire Continent (with the exception of Lithuania, which retained its independence and pagan worship) up to the borders of Russia and the Byzantine Empire.

RUSSIA. During the same century, drastic changes occurred in Russia. Under a wise and humane prince, Vladimir Monomachus (d. 1125), Russia had recovered from incessant strife within the ruling family; but after his death, civil wars broke out anew. These coincided with a number of other adverse developments, including invasions by neighboring countries from the east, rapid loss of the timber resources of the Kiev region through deforestation, and a steady reduction of trade—all of which undermined the strength of the state. In the second half of the twelfth century, the vigorous urban civilization of Kievan Russia began to decline, and more and more people emigrated, northeastward and southwestward. By the end of the century, Kiev had ceased to be the capital, and the once prosperous region, now depopulated, fell into decay and was partly absorbed by Western neighbors. The grand dukes moved from the Dnieper to the upper Volga Basin, i.e., from the Slavic center to a region largely inhabited by Finnish tribes. An almost entirely new, more primitive commonwealth was built there around Suzdal and, later, Moscow. This new state, being remotely situated, bore less resemblance than the preceding Kievan Rus to other European nations, with which it maintained but little contact. Only the town of Novgorod near the Baltic shores preserved through trade a significant link with the West.

The Papacy. Despite the gradual formation of individual nations with their own objectives and aspirations, the feeling of a community of interests among the Western peoples persisted. This sentiment was furthered by the common Church represented by Rome. To be sure, the popes, eager to preserve their independent status in Rome, had definite local interests, and these involved them in conflicts with the emperors, with the kings of the Western European countries, with factions among the Roman nobility and at times even with their own allies and vassals, the Normans in Sicily. But political considerations were always intertwined with broad religious aims and with the international tasks of the Church. At least during the second half of the century, popes such as Eugenius III, Adrian IV, and Alexander III understood how to maintain the dignity of the papal see, its position vis-à-vis the emperors, and its duties toward all of Western Christendom. They checked the renewed tendencies toward worldliness and corruption and, at the Third Lateran Council of 1179, took vigorous measures to improve the morals of the clergy. The system of electing popes was revised so as to avoid schisms. Though the leadership of Cluny came to an end with the death, in 1157, of Cluny's last great abbot, Peter the Venerable, the spirit of reform lived on and the monastic movement continued to show signs of strength. High standards in theological scholarship were maintained as outstanding and devoted churchmen set examples of a truly Christian life.

Second and Third Crusades. The twelfth century brought two new Crusades. The First Crusade having reached the goal of Jerusalem, a Second Crusade was precipitated because in 1144 the Turks conquered Edessa, a town in Asia Minor, and thereby cut the communication lines between the strife-ridden kingdom of Jerusalem and the European countries. Responding to the persuasive urging of St. Bernard of Clairvaux, the German emperor and the French king took up the cross and led their armies to the rescue. But in 1149 their enterprise ended in a fiasco.

Thereafter, conditions in Jerusalem (which, because of a lack of local resources, depended upon open trade routes) further deteriorated. The Knights Templars, Hospitalers and other organizations which had been founded to protect the homeland and defend the pilgrims en route, did not suffice to meet any serious challenge. Within a few decades such a challenge was posed by Sultan Saladin, a Moslem general and statesman as gentle and gallant as he was energetic and capable, who reunited the divided Moslem East under his banner. In 1187, he defeated the Christians in a fierce battle at Tiberias, and conquered Jerusalem. The news of the fall of the city shocked the Christian world. Its three mightiest rulers, Emperor Frederick Barbarossa, King Philip Augustus of France, and Richard I of England, promptly composed their differences and decided to hurry to the aid of the fallen kingdom. The Church raised funds through the sale of many of its valuables; the towns equipped ships and provided needed goods; and a Third Crusade got under way. Unfortunately, Barbarossa was drowned on the journey, Philip and Richard quarreled, and the holy places were not recovered. In 1191 the whole effort had to be given up. The Crusaders conquered only the Mediterranean port of Acre in Palestine; and since the generous Saladin granted the Christian pilgrims free access from Acre to Jerusalem, the port could from then on serve both as exchange place for European and Oriental wares and as gateway to the Holy Land.

THE CULTURAL SCENE

With the twelfth century, Western culture entered upon a period of flowering. Closer contact with the Moslems—in Asia, Sicily, and Spain—contributed to the splendor. Western man's philosophy of life had slowly changed. In early Christian times, Church fathers, such as Ambrose and Augustine, had been distrustful of "reason" because it did not further man's salvation; in the twelfth century, however, reason became the chief instrument of Western intellectual and cultural activities. It enriched the scholarly disciplines, politics, and the arts. Unavoidably, it also brought new dissensions.

Religious Activities. The influence of reason was most pronounced in the area of theology, around which all other studies centered. Reason altered the trend of theological studies; it encouraged doubt. This emphasis called to the fore all the vital forces in the Church, which, in response to the challenge, reached new heights of achievement. New monastic orders were founded; mystic movements directing men toward inwardness were strengthened; and Church institutions of lasting significance were created.

SCHOLARSHIP. Among the great Church writers of the twelfth century were Peter Lombard, Roscellinus, Hugh of St. Victor, and John of Salisbury. They were "schoolmen" who taught a younger generation to use the tools of reason for doctrinal investigation, for the resolution of conflicts in the writings of the Church fathers, and for the affirmation and strengthening of faith. Other scholars included the historians Ordericus Vitalis (*Ecclesiastical History*), Otto von Freising (*The Two Cities*), and William of Malmesbury (*Chronicle of the Kings of England*). But the two outstanding figures were Bernard of Clairvaux (d. 1153), and Peter Abelard (d. 1142). Bernard was a strict man of deep devotion and purity of life. He composed treatises on Church dogma, baptism, and immaculate conception; yet he was less a "schoolman" than a great preacher and influential Church organizer. He sponsored the Second Crusade, and he fought for the election of popes of highest moral standards. As a mystic who insisted on the orthodoxy of all Church dogmas and traditions, he devoted his life to the task of inspiring and purifying the whole Church body. Abelard was a man of very different character and bend of mind. His name is familiar to many for his love affair with Héloise and its sad consequences, described in his *History of my Calamities* and in the *Letters* of Héloise. He was a rationalistic thinker, an inspiring teacher, and a pre-eminent schoolman who followed in the steps of Roscellinus. His major contributions to Western culture consisted of his philosophical ideas embodied in his work *Sic et Non*. With keen intellect, he analyzed apparent contradictions in the theology of his time and in the writings of past great churchmen. Doubt, he insisted, would lead to inquiry; inquiry to truth. And though he never thought of challenging the Church, doubt led him into conflict not only with St. Bernard but also with other interpreters of Church traditions and eventually brought official condemnation of his writings.

MONASTICISM. Two new monastic orders were formed during the twelfth century: the Premonstratensians in 1120 and the Augustinians about two decades later. Designed mainly to include in their membership the canons who were assigned to cathedrals and performed the duties of priests, both orders not only contributed to the spiritual work of the Church, but also helped to extend papal power and made a significant contribution to the maintenance of religious devotion among the people.

HERESIES. Church life was stimulated also by the impact of non-conforming religious thought. Among non-conformists, we find two particularly significant groups: one was represented by men who believed in the simple, humble, and human ways of early Christianity, the other by men who believed in the possibility of establishing direct contact with the divine. At all stages in the development of the Church, there had been many who wanted to revive the earliest Christian ways. In the twelfth century, the most important group of this type were the Waldenses (followers of Peter Waldo) who opposed the worldliness of the papacy and Church abuses such as simony, as well as some dogmas of the Church, such as the traditional concepts of the Virgin Mary, the sacraments, and the saints. Similarly, throughout Church history there had been many Christians who sought a direct mystical experience of God and therefore devoted themselves to the individualistic service of Christ. Non-conformists of this type went to extremes in religious meditation; in their search for God they found it possible to dispense with that part of the Church which served as mediator. Among these non-conformists was Joachim of Flora, who elaborated a concept of world history based on mysticism.

Universities. The spirit of independent inquiry and of unorthodox theological investigation was greatly furthered by the establishment of additional universities. The most important became those of Paris and Oxford, both of which soon grew to enormous size. Rich and poor were admitted both to the faculty and to the student body. The goal was preparation for professional life; conclusion of studies was marked by the conferring of degrees. The universities taught theology, philosophy, law, and medicine. They enjoyed such privileges as tax exemptions and autonomous jurisdiction, which were accorded by popes, kings, and princes. Some ("masters' universities"), came under the administration of professors, others (students' universities) under that of students.

The influence of the universities was immense. They fostered doubt and inquiry which led to scholarly achievement. They stimulated the entire educational system of the existing monastic, cathedral, palace, and—later—municipal schools. The number of those learning at least reading, writing, and some elements of the seven arts increased. In the twelfth century, although England apparently possessed comparatively few laymen with scholarly training, France, Germany, and especially Italy possessed considerable numbers. The influence of universities was felt in Church affairs and in the political realm. Masters and students, for their own protection, and for the purpose of gaining increased privileges, organized fraternities similar to guilds of artisans. Constituting a state within the state, they often participated in local politics and became a formidable threat to existing social institutions.

Universities benefited greatly from Arabic studies of Latin and Greek and from Arabic interpretations of Euclid, Ptolemy, Hippocrates, and Aristotle. The Western students studied Arabic advances in medicine, algebra, astronomy, geography, and mapmaking; they became acquainted with the works of great men such as the philosopher Averröes and the geographer Idrisi. Arabic influence spread outside the universities, too, as the West learned much about fine arts from the richly ornamented handicrafts and architecture of the Moslems and also learned to imitate their agricultural methods and industrial work, particularly their textile and steel manufactures. Western man adopted Arabic words e.g., *cotton, check,* and various astronomical terms; and most important, he learned to use Arabic numerals including the zero, and methods of computation. He derived some useful information even from Moslem pseudo sciences and superstitions. In political affairs, he applied some of the methods of Oriental despotism. And he became more luxury-loving, more cosmopolitan, in everyday life.

Law. In addition to theology, philosophy, and medicine, the universities came to excel in the field of law. Canon law was reinterpreted and codified. Gratian (*ca.* 1140), gained lasting fame for his publication of the *Decretum,* a collection of Church laws with a commentary. Secular law was also reinterpreted. The Justinian law code was analyzed and many of its concepts were re-adopted. Cruel and superstitious ordeals, which had been used to prove the guilt of the accused, became less and less acceptable. Even though cruel punishments, including torture, continued in use and in some cases even increased, the ordeals were replaced by more adequate methods of determining guilt. To be sure, practice varied widely in the method of investigation and in the punishment of crime, and both investigation and punishment still depended tc a large degree upon the birth and rank of the accused person. Yet considerable progress was made, particularly in England, in making legal procedures more uniform and punishment more humane.

Court Life and Literature. Throughout the twelfth century, learning and art remained closely interwoven with, and often subject to, theology. But cultural endeavors along secular lines increased as well. In this development France excelled. At the courts of the highborn, notably at the court of Duchess Eleanor of Aquitaine, educated men and women frequently gathered. A gentler spirit, evinced by the growing veneration of the Virgin Mary, pervaded society; women played a more respected role. Poetry and music embellished court life, and feudal "courtly" ways were idealized. Younger sons of the nobility, who lacked a fief or a Church benefice and thus had no solid station in life, occasionally turned to intellectual endeavors and made their living by entertaining the great lords; as troubadours or wandering knights, they sang of chivalrous tournaments at arms, of the deeds of ancient heroes defying a stern fate, of the beauty of nature, and of women and courtly love. They recited heroic tales, as in olden times, and they composed new tender lyrics; they supplemented Latin poems with those in the vernacular and works for oral recital with written compositions. In France, Chrétien de Troyes wrote about the eternal love of Tristan and Iseult; other troubadours sang new *chansons de geste,* and the *Song of Roland* found its final form. Courtly ways spread to other countries. In Germany, *Minnesänger* appeared: Walther von der Vogelweide created his undying lyrics; and the powerful, moving *Nibelungenlied* was composed. England contributed romantic tales about King Arthur and his Knights of the Round Table. Everywhere there were wandering students who composed serious and tender songs, as well as raucous and libertine ("goliardic") verse, written—even though sometimes mixed with Latin—in the vernacular French, German, and Italian; and minstrels and *Spielmänner* entertained not only the noble and rich at their courts but also the common people at fairs and marketplaces.

Aside from epic and lyric poetry, numerous prose works, both in Latin and in the vernacular, originated in the twelfth century. Their value has only gradually come to be appreciated. Besides legends of the Saints, these prose works included stories about classical heroes, especially about Alexander the Great (who was often transformed in character and placed in a Christian medieval setting) and about the Greeks besieging Troy. Books were also written on numerous subjects ranging from the various sciences and pseudo sciences to hunting and history; and chronicles of noteworthy events were compiled.

Music. Recitations of poetry were generally accompanied by music, in which instruments (harps, lyres, and horns) supplemented the voice. Polyphonic music evolved. Like so many other cultural accomplishments, the most notable musical achievements originated with the Church. Some of the most beautiful liturgical and choral compositions of all time were created; partly under the influence of folk songs, the mighty *unisono* Gregorian chant (vocal music without instrumental accompaniment) developed vigorously.

Arts. In the arts, there were few new departures, but accomplishments along traditional lines were manifold and impressive. Medieval man did not aspire to originate new forms but preferred to do creative work in accordance with long-established values and patterns. The Romanesque style continued to dominate architecture, and churches in this style were built not only throughout the West, but also in eastern Europe; Romanesque influences spread as far as Novgorod and Suzdal in Russia. As men again gained increased mastery of technical problems in architecture, they built churches on the largest scale the West had seen since classical antiquity. This trend toward large dimensions indicated, perhaps, a certain decadence, a certain lack of ability to give new significance to traditional ways of artistic expression; and during the second half of the century, a new style—the Gothic—emerged. Nevertheless, a beauty seldom achieved still characterized twelfth-century Romanesque church architecture—a beauty that cannot be described in words but must be seen and experienced in reality.

Miniature painting also continued to flourish. Artists decorated books with exquisite illuminations, and pictures created in the style of Byzantine icons enriched the treasures of the West.

Social Conditions. The vigorous intellectual activity of the twelfth century was both the cause and the effect of wide societal changes. Courts, especially in Western Europe, became centers of arts and general culture as well as of military undertakings and law. Rulers and vassals, townsmen and even peasants, developed new character traits. Christianity began to shape their moral standards; law, their daily actions; sciences and arts, their manners, customs, and aspirations.

THE NOBILITY. The outlook on life of many strata of the nobility seems to have changed swiftly during the twelfth century. Although courage was demanded of the knight, as always, and loyalty to his overlord remained the basis of his social position, the concept of a contractual relationship between lord and vassal was no longer meaningful and the code of chivalry with its ceremonies began to become an empty gesture. These changes were more pronounced in some regions than in others, but everywhere noblemen seem to have turned to new objectives in life. Thus the owner of a manor might be more concerned about the work of his peasants and the prosperity of the countryside; he might take a greater interest in the type of tools used for the cultivation of his fields and try to improve his breed of cattle. He might favor the planting of new crops and the use of the three-field system. Although commercial activities still did not seem quite "honorable" among the nobles, the lords did, nevertheless, increase their participation also in trade. Often, they attempted to derive extra income from new methods of taxation. Many were inspired to adorn and beautify their surroundings.

A pronounced change also occurred in the military sphere. Many more castles, with heavy towers and walls and wide moats, which were easy to defend, were constructed. Castles remained uncomfortable, primitive, and unhealthy, but they did provide a large measure of security. Heavy plate armor (worn over the coat of mail), though costly to manufacture, gave the knights protection in battle and reduced the importance of valor. Fighting became more of a business. The collection of ransom from a fallen foe instead of killing him or chivalrously sparing his life, became the objective; and casualties were relatively few.

THE BURGHER. An increase in wealth, and thereby in power, was not limited to the nobility. The townsman, the burgher, also knew how to enjoy wealth and power. With progress in agricultural methods and steady improvement in the food situation, the number of towns multiplied. They sprang up not only on old Roman sites, but also in newly colonized regions, in central England, northern and eastern Germany, Scandinavia, Hungary, and Russia. Towns were built near castles or cathedrals, and on trade crossroads, rivers, or inlets of the sea. The towns were peopled by freemen—artisans, merchants, and day laborers—as well as former serfs who had escaped from the land to which they had been attached. Once in town, a serf found shelter and asylum, for towns needed additional hands; at the end of a definite period (often "a year and a day") he legally gained his freedom. The burghers came to constitute an important "third estate," distinct from the clergy and the nobility. They built high walls and gates around their towns to protect them from aggressive lords. To insure safe transportation on the highways, the traders travelled heavily armed, prepared to deal with robbers and robber barons. Soon, some of the lords began to realize that the towns, even though their power made them somewhat independent, could, as a source of needed revenue, offer important advantages. They therefore granted the town populations exemptions from labor services and gave them charters, privileges, and jurisdictional rights, and in exchange demanded payment of customs and other taxes or fees. Towns were thus enabled to find a place in the feudal hierarchy.

Life in town was in some respects easier than life outside. Not only did the burgher find better protection, but he also obtained a more efficient government and more equitable justice. He enjoyed a more luxurious, cultivated way of life, notwithstanding the price he had to pay in terms of noise, overcrowding, dirt, fires, pestilences, and similar causes of discomforts and dangers. Municipal government was, of course, in the hands of the most prosperous burghers, who tried to exercise control for their own benefit. Social stratification, early noticeable, differentiated among the wealthy merchant, the typical artisan, and the unskilled laborer (or carrier) whose living conditions remained pitiable. The possession of money became the criterion for rank. In Italy, with its comparatively ancient towns, the twelfth century saw the development of primitive forms of capitalism; despite Church prohibitions, there were vigorous money markets, where money changers exchanged the silver and gold coins of the various provinces at a profit and where money lenders provided loans for interest. Speculation in real estate was common and various forms of financial activities supplemented, as a source of income, industrial and agricultural activities. Christian bankers began to rival Jewish ones; and the lives of the Jews became more precarious as numerous persecutions of Jews occurred in England, France, and other European countries.

Political control in the towns was mainly in the hands of the guilds, which had been organized to protect property rights. Beginning with guilds of merchants, these protective organizations were gradually extended to embrace all the crafts. They regulated working conditions, standards of production, retail trade, and taxes; and they provided insurance and support in old age and sickness, and care for widows. They organized social life. They prescribed the artisan's path of advancement from apprentice to journeyman to master. The rank of master was reserved for those socially acceptable craftsmen who could demonstrate proficiency in their trade.

THE PEASANT. Obviously, social changes also affected the peasants. The opportunities for work in the towns enabled some peasants to leave the manorial lands and thereby avoid compulsory labor service and free themselves of serfdom. Others would find a haven of comparative freedom in recently deforested areas brought under cultivation and in newly colonized regions (particularly in eastern Europe) in which the lords could not claim ownership of all the available land. The flight of many peasants from the land to which they were attached forced the lords to ease the burdens on those who remained (e.g., converting their service obligations into payments in kind) so that they, too, gained in freedom. The life of the peasant was also made easier by technical innovations, such as wind and water mills (reflecting the growing rational and inquisitive spirit of man), the horse collar (which had actually been used on a restricted scale in the tenth century), and heavier plows. Moreover, expanding markets increased the peasant's income by providing new outlets and raising prices of agricultural products. Thus, at the dawn of the thirteenth century, the peasant, though still carrying the main burden, had in many regions improved his economic position.

CHAPTER XVI

THE "GREATEST OF CENTURIES"
(THIRTEENTH CENTURY)

THE GREAT EASTWARD colonizing movement of the West was brought to a halt in Asia during the twelfth century and in Europe during the first half of the thirteenth. But the undiminished vitality of the West continued to evince itself in so many other ways that some historians have spoken of the thirteenth century as the "greatest of centuries." Individuals who left a deep and permanent stamp on Western civilization appeared in the political and religious arena, as well as in the great universities and among the artists, poets, and scholars. The idea of a Universal Church triumphed; Europe, combining its classical heritage with Catholic Christian tradition, reached a crowning point in its intellectual and artistic evolution.

THE UNIVERSAL CHURCH

By the beginning of the thirteenth century, the Catholic Church had grown into an organization possessing both spiritual and worldly power. The Church enjoyed many advantages, but also had to deal with numerous vexatious problems—the same kinds of administrative, political and foreign issues confronting most of the European governments. Throughout much of the thirteenth century, the Church was fortunate in that the popes were men who combined a conception of their religious duties with an ability to administer effectively a large and oftentimes worldly institution.

Age of Innocent III. When the century began, Innocent III (d. 1216) was at the helm of the Church. Elected in 1198 at a youthful age, he became one of the most famous popes of all times. Like Gregory VII, he was perhaps more of a statesman than a churchman.

INTERNATIONAL CHURCH AFFAIRS. Innocent III vigorously built the worldwide authority of the Church. He acted as the arbiter in the struggle between the Hohenstaufen (Ghibelline) house and the Guelph family for possession of the throne. Innocent first helped to raise the Guelph Otto IV, Henry the Lion's son, to the imperial throne, and later defeated him with the help of the French and replaced him with his ward, the Hohenstaufen Frederick II. The pope interfered in French policies of state insisting that the French king Philip Augustus take back a rejected wife, and imposed his will through an interdict on the whole French country. By means of interdict and excommunication he forced King John of England to acknowledge papal rights in matters of clerical appointments and, contrary to John's wishes, raised Stephen Langton to the see of Canterbury. Not only was John forced to yield but also to acknowledge the pope's overlordship, whereby England became a papal fief for almost a century; English kings had to pay feudal dues to the popes. Innocent also intervened in political struggles on the Iberian Peninsula, and again he made use of interdicts to enforce his decisions. He succeeded in making the popes feudal overlords of Castile as well as of Sicily.

CHURCH ADMINISTRATION. Innocent owed many of his successes to his able administration of the papal realms. He achieved what most worldly rulers in their own countries strove for in vain: the establishment of a central governing authority which was the only final source of political power. Innocent applied the monarchical principle within the Church. He obtained recognition of supreme appellate jurisdiction for the papal see, secured control of clerical appointments in imperial and other lands, and, like Gregory VII, exercised supervision of all Church business through a corps of legates. He succeeded, at least for a time, in suppressing all interference by the Roman nobility or by foreign powers in the affairs of the papal states. His insistence on careful collection of dues and tithes (despite the fact that part of these often went to local lords) increased the revenues of the Church, and competent administration of the funds in turn increased the power of the popes.

FOURTH LATERAN COUNCIL. With equal forcefulness, Innocent III made final decisions in spiritual matters. In 1215, he convened a council at the Lateran and imposed his wishes in matters of ecclesiastical discipline. He settled debatable questions about dogma, including controversies about the sacraments. He decreed that no new monastic orders must be founded, introduced measures to regulate the position of the Jews in society, opposing their financial practices, and organized a campaign against the leading group of heretics, the so-called Albigenses.

HERESY. The Albigenses (or Cathari) were pious men and women who had adopted some tenets of the Manichaeans. Like Peter Waldo's followers, the Waldenses, so did the Albigenses condemn worldly property and many of the mores and customs (such as marriage) which constituted the foundation stones of Church and society. They became a popular group in southern France. Innocent III tried to win them back to the fold by peaceful means; but he failed, and in 1209 he sent a "crusading" army under a papal legate to extirpate them with fire and sword. When lords like Simon de Montfort, who coveted their lands, joined these efforts, most of the sect was destroyed. The survivors were dragged before an ecclesiastical tribunal which, entrusted with the task of "saving" the sinner and protecting the Church, tortured them into confessing their "guilt." The convicted Albigenses were then handed over to the civil authority, which condemned them to loss of property, exile, or death.

INQUISITION. The system of inquiring into the faith of those who were suspected of heresy—a system applied occasionally in earlier times by local ecclesiastical courts and used broadly and harshly in Innocent III's time against the Albigenses—was built in 1233 into a permanent institution under one of Innocent's successors, Gregory IX. This institution came to be called the "Inquisition." It was a tribunal, charged with inquiring into the Catholicity of the views held by individuals suspected of heresy, and with punishing nonconformists with penance or excommunication. But since no clear division existed during the Middle Ages between the duties of spiritual authorities and those of worldly rulers, Church action generally implied state action; consequently, condemnation by tribunals of the Inquisition (often the result of confessions obtained through torture) meant the infliction of the most severe penalties by state authorities. Punishment ranged from confiscation of property to imprisonment, exile, and burning at the stake.

FOURTH CRUSADE. Several Crusades were sponsored by Innocent III. Soon after he became pope (in 1198), the Fourth Crusade was undertaken. The death of Saladin in 1193 had revived the hopes of the Christian world; religious fervor still existed. Prayers were offered for the success of the Crusade, almost a third of the Church income was set aside for it, Jewish money lenders were forced to cancel debts and interest, and merchants were warned against providing the Moslems with supplies. But all was in vain, for the Crusade, begun in 1202, was destined to end in failure. When the armies assembled in Venice, funds were already exhausted, and the Crusaders, in order to secure transportation, had to submit to conditions which Venice imposed with the aim of gaining profits rather than saving souls. The Venetians demanded that the Crusaders first conquer the Christian town of Zara, an Adriatic seaport which was a commercial rival of Venice. This the Crusaders did. After proceeding from Zara, they were diverted a second time from their aim when a claimant to the Byzantine throne persuaded them to attack Christian Constantinople. The Byzantine Empire was in a state of disintegration and internal discord. The conquered Balkan Slavs had risen against it; the Turks assaulted it from the east; and the Italian towns of Pisa, Genoa, and Venice used it as a battleground on which their own commercial interests were advanced. The Crusaders yielded to temptation; they besieged and conquered Constantinople, and the pope reconciled himself to this act with the thought that the members of the schismatic Greek-Orthodox church might be brought back into the Catholic fold. While the road to the Holy Land was forgotten—except by pillaging knights and soldiers in search of relics, genuine or spurious, which could be turned into money—a Latin Empire of Constantinople was founded. Baldwin of Flanders became its emperor, and Frenchmen and Venetians seized the provinces. The great city of Constantinople itself was ruined. It lost its place as the foremost market on the East-West trade routes, and Venice secured the benefits of its remaining commercial functions.

CHILDREN'S CRUSADE. The Fourth Crusade was followed by the strange enterprises known as the "Children's Crusades." They represented an attempt to compensate for the sins and failures of the

EUROPE IN THE TIME OF THE CRUSADES

adults who had not recovered the Holy Land; innocent children, it was hoped, would succeed. Thus, in the year 1212, long columns of boys and girls (French children led by a boy of twelve named Stephen and German children led by a boy of sixteen named Nicholas) marched from their native lands through European countries, over the Alpine passes, and down to Mediterranean ports. Even the sick and crippled joined the procession. But the Crusades, which had begun in an atmosphere of unhealthy, psychopathic rapture, ended with thousands dying en route, other thousands sold by Christian and Arab shipowners into Moslem slavery. Innocent III promptly started preparations for another Crusade but died before they could be completed.

Successors of Innocent III. Innocent's ability to promote the political influence of the Church proved in the long run to be a danger to the papacy itself. He had established precedent for future popes to attempt tasks extraneous to the proper functions of the Church. Nevertheless, for more than half a century, his successors managed to maintain the dominant position gained by Innocent. They kept the Church's monarchical structure intact; they enforced their jurisdictional rights; and they brought the conflict with the imperial house of Hohenstaufen to a successful conclusion by ending the threat to the papal states from North and South, which the union of Germany and Sicily by virtue of Henry VI's marriage with a Norman princess had posed. Innocent's successors failed, however, in their efforts to regain the Holy Land through crusades— just as Innocent had failed. They likewise did not succeed in their attempts to turn the capture of Constantinople (in 1204) into a real victory; for the Orthodox patriarch who had moved from that city to Nicaea in order to remain independent, continued to refuse, despite pressure from Rome, to submit to the authority of the papal see, and in 1261, the Latin Empire itself collapsed. The Greeks under Michael Palaeologus reconquered Constantinople, the Byzantine Empire was revived, and the patriarch resumed his work in the capital.

New Monastic Orders. The stirring events outside the Church and the devotion engendered by the activities within it led to the founding of new monastic orders. Innocent III, disregarding the ban on new monastic orders issued by the Fourth Lateran Council, had eventually allowed their organization. The new orders were the Franciscans, the Dominicans, and the Carmelites.

ST. FRANCIS AND ST. DOMINICK. The Franciscan Order was founded by St. Francis of Assisi (d. 1226). Son of a wealthy merchant, he gave up all worldly ambitions, "married Lady Poverty," and preached the gospel of love. Followers—later called "Friars Minor"—gathered around him; like St. Francis, they lived in complete poverty, begged for their daily bread (for this reason they were called mendicants), devoted their lives to comforting the poor and the ill, and aided the needy through love and deeds. The spirit of compassion with all the world is most beautifully expressed in Francis' *Little Flowers* and his "Canticle of the Sun." The Spaniard St. Dominick was Francis' counterpart, and although he possessed little of Francis' gentleness and child-like innocence, he shared the same intense desire to serve the Christian cause. As a priest, he devoted his life to preaching and missionary work, and in order to spread the Christian faith he encouraged learning and worldly knowledge.

THE ORDERS. The Franciscan and Dominican friars, as well as the Carmelites, founded no cloisters. The Dominicans devoted themselves to intellectual endeavors. Through sternness and discipline of mind and body, they soon became, like their founder, outstanding teachers and preachers. They also came to be the leading agents of the Inquisition. The Franciscans, in contrast, became known for their simple, loving, tender methods. They were little concerned with the widespread cultural work which monks belonging to traditional orders pursued through their artistic, scientific, legal, and classical studies. They did not stress educational, agricultural, and political work, but, living unattached, they preached to the poor and helped and nursed all supplicants. Unfortunately, the standards of the great founder were not long maintained. The Franciscans amassed wealth and sank rapidly into idleness. To meet the resulting danger to the order and forestall conflicts with the official Church, which were likely to ensue if the Franciscans resumed their extreme opposition to all worldly possessions, the Franciscan rule of complete poverty was changed by Francis' disciple and biographer, Bonaventura (d. 1274), and a limited ownership of property was officially permitted to the order. This trend was opposed by some, who seceded and were later called "Spiritual Franciscans." In accordance with the ideals of the founder, these friars not only adhered to "Lady Poverty" but also favored mystical tendencies which eventually caused many of them to be branded as heretics. Such deviations from ecclesiastical policy did not, however, prevent the Franciscans, Dominicans, and Carmelites from serving Church and papacy admirably for hundreds of years.

THE EMPIRE AND THE NATIONS

Developments in the thirteenth century showed clearly how much the political world had grown away from the feudal concepts of the tenth and eleventh centuries. A new age dawned; it was foreshadowed by men like the Hohenstaufen Emperor Frederick II and the French kings Philip Augustus and Saint Louis; events and institutions such as the *Interregnum* in Germany and the signing of the Magna Charta in England; and the defeats of the Swedish and German knights in Russia. Law represented by bureaucracies triumphed over vague concepts of "honorable" relationships between the various estates or classes as promoted by a feudal nobility.

The Empire. As so often in the history of Germany, the transition from one stage of development to the next was abrupt. During the last two decades of the twelfth century, the Empire had reached a new apex of its power; it dominated the entire center of Europe as far south as Sicily. Then, after less than half a century, it declined so rapidly that it became powerless, and for almost twenty years no emperor at all could gain recognition. When the Empire was revived, it resembled the old Empire more in form than in content. Yet in the meantime, the house of Hohenstaufen had produced in the person of Frederick II one of the most remarkable, inexplicable figures of the Middle Ages.

Frederick II. Henry VI's son Frederick II (d. 1250) had grown up in Sicily where Christians, Mohammedans, Byzantines, and Jews lived side by side; where peoples, languages, and cultures had mixed; and where sciences and arts as well as different religions flourished. Frederick learned from these varied cultures and grew to be a man of extreme independence of mind who hardly fitted into the age in which he was born. He became a skeptic, an individual thinker said to have rejected all religions as frauds, a willful and brilliant ruler, a poet, and a scientist. As a freethinker he tried to organize society and build a state on a rational basis. He wrote a book on birds and studied animals and human races with detached curiosity. He is justly known as *stupor mundi*, "the amazement of the world." But his work was out of tune with the spirit of the age and it is not surprising that before he died (in 1250) the edifice he had created was already crumbling.

ITALIAN AND GERMAN POLICIES. After the death of Henry VI, Pope Innocent III, who feared the combined might of Germany and Sicily, attempted to separate the two areas by securing the election of the Guelph Otto IV as emperor. This plan failed, for Otto (d. 1218) was as insistent on the German emperor's rights in Italy as any Hohenstaufen. The pope himself therefore turned eventually to Frederick II, who had become king of Sicily; and after Otto had suffered, in 1214, a severe defeat at the hands of the French, Frederick could not be prevented from gaining also the German throne. He spent, however, only a few years in Germany and allowed the administration and jurisdiction there to slip into the hands of the princes and great lords. These nobles gained the right to leave their fiefs as an inheritance to their children without regard to the services implied, and to decide matters of taxation without consulting the emperor. In the meantime, Frederick focussed his attention on Italy and Sicily. In northern Italy he sought, though with inconclusive results, to revive full imperial authority over the Lombard towns; in southern Italy he successfully built a modern bureaucratic, centralized government with an efficient and well-balanced tax system. His plans were astonishingly modern in their conception, and his achievements were great even though they hardly survived him.

SIXTH CRUSADE. During most of his lifetime, Frederick was handicapped by incessant strife with the popes, who excommunicated him no less than five times. The main conflict began in 1228 when, after many delays, Frederick set out upon a Crusade which he had long promised to undertake. This crusade had become the more urgent as a "Fifth Crusade," which had attempted to reach Jerusalem via Egypt, had ended in 1221 in failure. Although under the ban of excommunication because of his delays, Frederick proceeded. And it was he, the excommunicated emperor, who succeeded where fervent Christians had failed. Through diplomacy, not through valor, he acquired Jerusalem from the Egyptian al-Kamil and made himself its king. The West was to retain the Holy City until 1244. After his return, his struggle with the popes continued, the principal issue being that of control over northern Italy and Sicily. It was not solved in Frederick's lifetime.

FREDERICK II's SUCCESSORS AND THE INTERREGNUM. Frederick's heirs were unable to continue his work, and in 1268, after many reversals, the house of Hohenstaufen died out. Its last member, Conradin, a young grandson of Frederick, was decapitated by order of a French duke, Charles of Anjou, who had seized the kingdom of Sicily during Conradin's minority. In the meantime, Germany remained without an emperor. Though various foreigners laid claim to the crown, no final election took place, and thus an *Interregnum* of almost twenty years ensued. As a result the medieval concept of emperorship was undermined. Ecclesiastical and lay princes as well as imperial towns were able to stabilize their independent power. Because of the international tasks of the emperor Germany had always tended toward decentralization, and now during a period when there was no emperor these trends grew stronger.

France. During the thirteenth century, as in the twelfth, political developments in France took a course very different from that in the Empire. While both areas gradually abandoned feudal institutions, Germany and Italy moved in the direction of a multiplicity of independent units dominated by great lords or oligarchies of rich burghers, and France moved in the direction of a centralized state under the authority of the king.

PHILIP AUGUSTUS. During the reign of Philip Augustus (d. 1223), who came to the throne in 1180, centralized authority over the vassals was strengthened and the forces of disruption, which had prevailed under his father Louis VII, were checked. Philip revoked many of the privileges which had been granted by Louis to the great nobles in exchange for their support against England. Moreover, escheated or forfeited fiefs were not allotted to new vassals, for, whenever possible, Philip kept them as his personal domains to increase his revenue; and he created "bailiffs" and "seneschals" who administered them for him and dispensed his justice. He used the income to hire troops which were often put under the command of the seneschals. Not only minor lords, but the great ones as well, had to acknowledge his supreme authority. Philip Augustus vigorously, though not always successfully, carried on the war against England; and when John of England, after the death of Henry II and Richard the Lion-Hearted, refused to acknowledge the French king's superior jurisdiction over English possessions in France, Philip declared all these possessions forfeit. He occupied Normandy, Anjou, and Artois and, shrewdly using Church approval to weaken his enemies, successfully defended himself against England as well as against England's German ally, Otto IV, whom he decisively defeated at Bouvines in 1214.

ST. LOUIS. Philip's work was continued by his grandson Louis IX (1226–1270), who was canonized because of his kind, chivalrous, and deeply religious character. He prevented the great nobles, who had begun to use the same effective political strategy as the king himself, from again becoming too powerful. Bailiffs, *enquêteurs* or *missi* were appointed to build the prestige of the royal court. Justice was dispensed more honestly. Roman law was studied and the *parlement,* a permanent institution charged with deciding final appeals, supplanted law courts formerly attached to the king's household. Louis secured peace within his realms by promulgating a "Truce of God," which forbade all feuds for certain periods during the year. In the same spirit of moderation, he also promoted peace with England, giving up some of the territorial gains which Philip Augustus had won.

SEVENTH AND EIGHTH CRUSADES. It was in Louis' times that the mighty movement of the Crusades, which had spanned two centuries, came to a close. The so-called "Seventh Crusade" was led by Louis in 1248, four years after Jerusalem had been reconquered by the Moslems. But on the way, while passing through Egypt, Louis was captured and had to be ransomed at inordinate costs to the French. The Eighth Crusade in 1270 was also undertaken by Louis. It got no farther than Tunis, where Louis died. Not long thereafter, the last Western stronghold in the Holy Land, the fortress of Acre, was captured by the Moslems.

England. In England, as in France, central control grew stronger in the course of the thirteenth century. But in England not only did the monarchy aspire at centralization, but the nobility itself furthered it because, during the long absences of the kings on their campaigns in France and elsewhere, it was able to reap the advantages of centralization.

JOHN AND THE MAGNA CHARTA. The incapable Richard the Lion-Hearted was followed on the throne by his brother John, who was more able, but arrogant and much disliked for his brutality. His power and prestige, at first enhanced by his determined exercise of his royal prerogatives, suffered after he met with military defeats in France and with opposition from the Church. His position was further weakened when in order to carry on his undertakings abroad he increased his monetary demands on his English vassals.

The barons, supported by Archbishop Langton, revolted and coerced him, in 1215, into signing a "Magna Charta." This document (which the pope later declared not binding) stipulated that the barons should not be tried except by their peers, that they should not be arrested arbitrarily, and that they should not be subjected to any levies excepting the customary ones without their consent. The Charta in no way replaced feudal concepts with modern democratic ideas—indeed, it enhanced and reaffirmed the barons' feudal rights. Its significance lies in the fact that it subsequently enabled various groups and classes of the population to appeal to the principles it embodied—especially those of "due process of law." What had been granted the barons could also be asked for by others.

HENRY III. The Magna Charta, instead of bringing peace, led to new civil strife, which continued under John's successor, Henry III (d. 1272). Since Henry's long reign was a weak one, the nobles went on sharing the governmental powers with the king. But a change was foreshadowed as also the middle class began to make its voice heard in politics.

Spain. Owing to Spain's continued preoccupation with the Moslems Spain's political role in European affairs remained limited during the thirteenth century. The struggle against the Moslems entered a new stage, though, when after a brief revival of their strength a lasting decline set in. The kingdoms of Castile, Leon, Aragon, and Portugal—despite continued internecine strife—were as a result able to further expand. In 1234, the Spaniards took Valencia and in 1248, Seville. Before the century was over, they reached the southern shores of the Iberian Peninsula and began to turn their attention to overseas territories. They seized the Balearic Islands and placed an Aragonese prince on the throne of Sicily in 1282, and they thus laid the basis for future maritime greatness.

Eastern Europe. From the times of Charlemagne on, Western civilization had progressed eastward—starting on the Rhine and reaching successively the Elbe River, the Oder, the Vistula, and finally the Baltic Sea up to the Finnish Gulf. In the course of the thirteenth century, Western political expansion eastward came to a final standstill.

THE BALTIC AREA. The Christianization and colonization of the Baltic lands had been carried on by Germans, Danes, and Swedes. Their drive, designed to enlarge their territories in order to acquire new agricultural lands and new fiefs, was combined in the times of

Innocent III and his successors with a drive of the papacy aiming
at expanding Rome's authority and reuniting not only "schismatic"
Orthodox Greeks in Constantinople but also Orthodox Slavs in
Russia with the Catholic Church. New gains for the West were
actually made when the Order of the Teutonic Knights, which had
been established, like the orders of the Templars and of the Hospitalers, to protect the Holy Land, had transferred its activities to
the Baltic region. While the Teutonic Knights were colonizing and
Christianizing Prussian lands on the lower course of the Vistula,
another order, the Brethren of the Sword, who had established themselves at the mouth of the Düna River, colonized Livonia. Simultaneously, the Danes and Swedes were expanding their possessions
in Estonia and Finland. Wherever knights and missionaries went,
merchants followed. But in 1240, a halt was called to Western
progress. In the great battles of the Neva (1240) and Lake Peipus
(1242), the Russians, led by young Alexander Nevsky, defeated
the Swedes and Germans, and the Western nations had to give up
their plans for further territorial expansion.

RUSSIA. At the very time, however, when Russia was successfully
defending herself against the Catholic West—and shortly thereafter
also against the aggressive pagan Lithuanians—another great Eastern invasion was begun. The Tartars, under the leadership of
Genghis Khan, moved westward after conquering much of Siberia
and China. In 1223 they crossed into Europe and defeated the opposing Russian forces. Russia was temporarily saved from subjection, however, by the opportune death of Genghis Khan. Deprived
of his leadership, the Tartars retreated, only to return in 1237. By
1240 all Russia was at their mercy and only with difficulty were
they stopped at Germany's borders. Europe proper was saved, but
for more than two hundred years Russia remained under Tartar
rule. Although Tartar control was limited—the Tartars concentrated on levying tribute, drafting Russians as Tartar soldiers, and
occasionally plundering the countryside—it had a lasting effect on
the entire Western world. It recalled the dangers to which the West
had been exposed by successive waves of Mongolian conquerors—
Huns, Avars, Magyars, Tartars—and enhanced a feeling of common destiny. On the other hand, it tied Russia more closely to the
East, helped to promote the power of the subservient Moscow granddukes at the expense of Western Russia, and retarded the cultural
growth of the conquered lands.

COMMERCE AND SOCIETY

The thirteenth century weakened the homogeneity of society which had its origins in the rather undifferentiated agricultural economy of the past. Differences between regions as well as classes became more pronounced. Population growth and the development of industry and commerce speeded up the changes. The specialization of labor increased, and it was stimulated by the growth of towns. In the past, towns had generally tried to fit themselves into feudal social and economic patterns, but, owing to their own dynamics, they undermined feudalism and emphasized values alien to a feudal society. These changes occurred even though only a small fraction of the entire population lived in towns.

Towns. Towns flourished throughout Europe. In Italy, Milan, Venice, and Genoa were the leading centers of trade, Florence became a center of textile manufacturing, and Siena, through its connections with the popes, became a banking center. In Spain and Portugal, the seaports of Barcelona and Lisbon flourished. In France, Marseilles, Lyons, and Paris, became important merchant communities as did London, Bristol, and York in England. In the Netherlands and Germany, Bruges, Ghent, Lübeck, and Danzig gained fame as seaports, Frankfort and Cologne became known for their fairs, and Nürnberg gained a reputation for its manufactures. In Bohemia and Poland, Prague and Cracow prospered. Because of their wealth, some of the towns were able to secure almost complete independence. They hired their own soldiers and sailors and joined to form leagues, thus gaining political power superior to that of many princes. Among the leagues were the Lombard League in Northern Italy and the Hanseatic League of northern German towns. Both received wide privileges from worldly and ecclesiastical lords. As the towns grew in wealth and power, the burgher gained prestige; social differentiation, though increased between rich and poor, decreased between nobles and merchants, and intermarriage between these two classes became common.

Commerce. Lack of source material makes it difficult for the historian to get a reliable picture of the importance of retail trade in the thirteenth-century economy. It may be conjectured that retail trade remained comparatively insignificant since most of the population continued to live in the country and provided for its own modest needs. Only in urban centers, such as those of northern Italy, can it have played a major role. It is different with international and overseas trade, which can be traced through a study of the documents in the archives of many commercial towns. Historians have shown that in the period of the Crusades shipping, exchange of commodities, and financial institutions had received a strong impetus. Links then established with the East remained after the failure of the Crusades. Trade in one area stimulated trade in others, so that mercantile activities increased far more rapidly than agricultural activities. Merchants saw to it that highways and seaways were kept safe from brigands and pirates. Money was coined in increasing quantities; prices rose, and so did production. Transactions on credit became common. Business loans became available despite the opposition of the Church to taking interest (which was branded as "usury") and such loans acted as a further stimulus to business.

Numerous trade routes connected the various parts of Europe. Some of the most important extended from Venice or Milan across the Alps to southern Germany and either down the Rhine to the Netherlands or via Nürnberg, Lüneburg and Lübeck to Scandinavia; others extended via Prague or Leipzig to Eastern Europe; still others extended from Genoa or Marseilles into France, up the Rhone River into the Champagne, and on to the Netherlands and England. There were two great trade routes to the Orient, one from the Italian ports via the Mediterranean either to Egypt or to the Crimea and from these intermediary stations overland to Persia and India; the other from German ports, especially Lübeck, via the Baltic to either Riga and Reval in Livonia or to Novgorod in Russia, and from these places overland to Smolensk, Moscow, and possibly down the Volga to the Caspian Sea and Persia. By crossing Asia even distant China was accessible to the thirteenth-century traders. In many foreign cities the Italians established *fondachias,* the Germans *comptoirs* or "staple-and-exchange centers." Most famous were those of the Italians in Constantinople, Alexandria, and Kaffa (southern Russia); those of the Hanseatics in Bruges, London, Bergen (Norway), and Novgorod. European merchants exported cloth, armor, horses, quicksilver, copper, herring, and salt. They imported furs, timber, tar, honey, and wax via the Baltic, and precious stones, spices, drugs, and dyes, as well as silk, cotton, and metal objects via the Mediterranean. Because of the higher standards of the

LATE MEDIEVAL EUROPE

Cities underlined are members of Hanseatic League

Eastern world, the trade balance was in its favor, and the West was forced to make up the difference through the export of gold or silver.

Society. Commercial expansion contributed to shifts in the relative importance of the feudal classes. These shifts primarily affected the nobles and the townspeople, and to a lesser extent the peasant class.

The Nobility. The nobles remained the most important class, but they found their monopoly on arms threatened by the prospering towns and consequently faced a loss of power. Many nobles tried to make up for their losses by increased attention to their administrative prerogatives and duties and by expansion of their commercial activities as producers of agricultural goods and as entrepreneurs in mining and industries.

The Clergy. Despite an increase in papal power, the clergy as a whole lost some of its position. Its status was adversely affected by the conflicts between national governments and papacy, by the growth of monarchical strength whereby some of the privileges—and tasks—of the Church were absorbed, by a loss of jurisdictional rights in various regions, and by problems arising from the difficulty of reconciling worldly ambition and grasping, competitive economic enterprise with the tenets of Christianity. Only to a limited extent was it possible for these losses to be compensated by the widening of the clergy's educational functions and influence.

The Burgher. The townsmen gained more than any other class from the changes which were taking place during the thirteenth century. They amassed wealth which bought them influence, and in exchange for aiding the monarch in his struggles with the nobility and providing the major part of the taxes, they were accorded additional rights. Soon they, too, began to occupy important administrative offices. Moreover, in a world where money came to be essential, they had the means to pay for luxury goods and services. Those who profited most were not the producers and artisans, but the merchants. They were the ones who controlled the funds; they employed the artisans and reaped the profits of business.

The Peasant. During the thirteenth century, the economic and social condition of the peasants was somewhat better than in preceding or subsequent centuries. In many regions, the process of liberating the peasant from the obligation of feudal services continued. In other regions where the status of the peasant did not change because lords of manors turned to commercial farming and could not dispense with the serf's labor, the peasant was often better rewarded for his work. Better care was taken of them in order to secure larger harvests and profits.

Travel. The entire medieval period is characterized by travel. Streams of pilgrims flowed from Scandinavia, England, Germany, France, and Hungary to the Christian shrines in Jerusalem, Rome, and Compostella in Spain. Journeymen crisscrossed European lands. Kings and courts moved from one castle to another, scholars and students taught and studied in university after university, and knights, soldiers, musicians, and magicians traveled from court to court and from fair to fair. Increased trade added new groups of travelers. On trips lasting for years they crossed endless seas, steppes, and forests. The most famous of the distant journeys was that of the Venetian Marco Polo, who spent twenty years with the Tartars and the Chinese. The Franciscan friar Orderic Pordenone and Louis IX's ambassador Guillaume Rubriquis visited the East. Missionaries such as John of Plano Carpini were sent by the pope to Russia and Tartary; John of Montecorvino (d. 1328) became the first Archbishop of Peking in China.

SCIENCES AND ARTS

Historians of the nineteenth century emphasized the unity of medieval thought and culture, as contrasted to the multiplicity of modern civilization. Later research, however, has revealed an infinite variety in the culture of Western civilization also in the thirteenth century. Advances in the scientific study of nature were made in an age when belief in magic and witchcraft was common; the Christianization and humanization of legal and political concepts were furthered in an age of brutality and growing disregard of honor and loyalty. Classical scholarship was re-introduced at the same time that there was a re-emphasis on early Christian ways opposed to pagan traditions. Economic standards based on other-worldly concepts and feudal conditions existed side by side with standards reflecting a materialistic outlook and a spirit of commercial enterprise. No *summa,* that is to say, none of the encyclopedic works, such as were written by several geniuses of the thirteenth century to summarize all contemporary knowledge and views, actually succeeded in so doing; each of those works merely reflected the prevailing theological point of view which came increasingly under attack by new forces.

Science. One of the most intriguing aspects of thirteenth-century culture was the enlargement of the Western world's intellectual horizon—a result of external factors such as travel and war and of internal factors such as ideas and individual genius. Evidence of this enlargement can be found in the numerous scientific works which reveal a more profound understanding of nature than was revealed in any earlier work produced in Europe since classical times. New knowledge gained—though often pseudoscientific—was combined with knowledge inherited from Arabs and Greeks. Geographical studies and reports appeared, based on voyages as well as on descriptive writings of the Greek Ptolemy and of Idrisi and other Moslem writers. Astronomy, algebra, botany, and zoology were studied, and new textbooks on these subjects were written. Aristotle's scientific works were edited and explained by scholars who used not only Greek but also Arab sources such as the works of Avicenna and Averröes. Robert Grosseteste wrote commentaries on the Arab works, Albertus Magnus composed a compendium of knowledge about many scientific subjects; and Roger Bacon, in his *Opus Majus,* discussed the methods and results of rational investigation. In medicine there was progress in the study of herbs and some improvement in therapy. Many technological advances were made in the fields of optics and chemistry. Methods of papermaking were improved, and gunpowder was developed. Instruments such as the compass, the magnifying glass, and the chemical clock were invented or adapted from models devised by other civilizations. Agricultural implements such as the scythe, iron plow, and horse harness were increasingly used. Iron ore and iron tools became more important in production.

Scholasticism. Economic necessity as well as intellectual curiosity led to the establishment of many schools. While the guilds took over systematic training in trades, the universities encouraged intellectual endeavors. New universities were founded, such as those of Naples, Salerno, and Padua; and the number of students increased everywhere. Students devoted themselves principally to the study of theology or philosophy; the achievements of "Scholasticism" became one of the great glories of the age.

REALISM AND NOMINALISM. Scholasticism was built on the heritage of Ancient Greece and Early (patristic) Christianity. It attempted to reconcile faith and reason and sought salvation through both. Although the "schoolmen" subordinated their reasoning to tradition, revelation, and the teachings of the Church, they weighed the contradictory statements of earlier authorities in the attempt to solve, with the help of the dialectical method, the most complex theological problems. They tried to find through science and faith a final proof of God's existence, of the immortality of the soul, and of the truth of individual Church dogmas. In pursuit of their studies, they were driven into opposing directions. The "Realists," deriving their stand from Plato, believed in the existence of universal essences (beyond conception by the human mind). What we perceive through the senses or comprehend by reason was to them no more than a reflection of the real; in "universals" they saw that which existed in reality. The "Nominalists," preferring Aristotle's position to that of Plato, divined reality in the multiplicity of the world of individual objects. They denied the reality of universals which were to them but names and they insisted that the human mind cannot conceive of anything but the "particular." Roscellinus and Abelard in the twelfth century, and Duns Scotus in the thirteenth, were Nominalists, whereas Bernard of Clairvaux and Thomas Aquinas (the thirteenth-century philosopher known as the greatest of all schoolmen) were closer to the realist position.

THOMAS AQUINAS. Thomas (d. 1274) is most famous for his *Summa theologica*.[1] A Dominican, a preacher and scholar who was also a poet and writer of hymns, Thomas surveyed again the whole field of contemporary knowledge. With authority and logic he presented thirteenth-century Catholic views not only of faith and Church, but also of most other aspects and activities of man. Thus, he analyzed the foundations of law, particularly the attitudes of the Ancients and the Christians toward natural law; he investigated the problems of worldly power, of kingship, and of the limits of secular rule; he dealt with economics, with questions of property, fair price, profit, and usury; he examined the question of heresy and its punishment; and he discussed dogma. In all his work, he tried to reconcile Aristotelian logic with Catholic tradition and the tenets of St. Augustine and other Church fathers. In a sense, he

---

[1] Notable "summas" had been written by Alexander of Hales, by Thomas' great teacher (an Aristotelian scholar) Albertus Magnus, and by Vincent of Beauvais. They included not only theological investigations, but also commentaries on classical philosophy and studies of nature and social institutions.

codified the contemporaneous Catholic views, thereby establishing standards for future scholars even if, by defining them, he also exposed the views to criticism.

Mysticism. The scholastic and logical trend in theology was counterbalanced by a strong trend toward mysticism. There were elements of mysticism in Thomas' writings and in the works of other great schoolmen, who quite generally maintained that revelation takes precedence over reason and logic. But the true mystics went farther. Like their twelfth-century predecessors, they hoped to know the superhuman—the divine—and to have communion with it during this life on earth. They felt that in man there is a spark of the divine which in times of contemplation or ecstasy (when the demands of reason and the preoccupations of daily life are overcome) can provide direct communion with God. The Church continued to look askance at these mystics who seemed to advocate communicating with God without the mediation of the Church, but, unlike the great scholastic theologians, saw in reason little aid to faith. Nevertheless, mysticism developed rapidly during the thirteenth century. It reached its climax toward the end of the century with Meister Eckhart (d. 1327) in Germany. In Italy, Francis of Assisi and his successor, St. Bonaventura, were outstanding representatives of mysticism.

Arts. It is to be expected that an age so imbued with religious fervor, so devoted to old and new paths of learning, so active, so contemplative, and so inspiring to individual genius would naturally bring forth great works of art. One of the crowning achievements of the thirteenth century was the Gothic cathedral which embodied the noblest aspirations of the age. Through pointed arches which gradually replaced Romanesque roundness, through perpendicular structure which emphasized height rather than massiveness, through flying buttresses and tall spires, the attention of man was directed away from this world and upward toward heaven. As symbols of the thirteenth-century Church, the cathedrals combined unity and multiplicity. The construction of the cathedrals was made possible by the growing wealth of Western towns and by great collective efforts; architects (the names of few of them are known today) proved masters of the slowly accumulated building techniques. Some of the cathedrals were several centuries under construction; plans and styles changed and mixed. As in Romanesque churches, beautiful sculptures which adorned the outside and inside walls related to the illiterate churchgoer stories of the Bible and mythological tales or depicted kings and queens, churchmen and noblemen. But frescoes, which often embellished Romanesque churches, were rare, for Gothic churches had little wall space. Instead, huge stained-glass windows were placed between the mighty pillars that supported a high roof. The devotion of the artist to his work and a spirit of sacredness which guided him have found their lasting expression in the masterpieces of Gothic art.

The Gothic style originated in France and spread to most countries north of the Alps. South of the Alps, particularly in Italy, it did not become so well established as in the north. The Gothic style was also employed for secular buildings, for city halls and burghers' homes; and it was reflected in various arts and crafts—in painting, miniatures, tapestries, and everyday utensils such as swords, chairs, doorknobs, and clothing.

Literature. Although it has been said that the cathedral was the chief artistic expression of the thirteenth century, lasting works of literature were also produced—notwithstanding widespread illiteracy even among the upper classes. In addition to many theological books written by schoolmen, the literature of the age included numerous scientific and legal treatises. Some of the most beautiful of Church hymns were composed, such as the "Stabat mater" of Jacopone da Todi and the "Dies irae" of Thomas of Celano. For Church literature, Latin remained the dominant language; but for other types of literature the vernacular was used more and more frequently. Among the secular works created (in their final form) during the thirteenth century were Wolfram von Eschenbach's *Parsifal,* Gottfried von Strassburg's *Tristan and Iseult* (which surpassed Chrétien de Troyes' model), the Icelandic *Edda* of Snorri Sturluson, the French *Roman de la Rose,* new *chansons de geste,* and the Spanish *Cid;* there were also prose tales of chivalry or of ancient heroic deeds, chronicles of past and contemporary events, and travel accounts. Of course, besides Church literature, traditional songs, epics, and learned treatises, there were many works of poetry and prose which were composed in a lighter vein: romances, fables, and stories, sung or told by students and professional entertainers who carried themes and traditions from place to place and thus contributed to a broad cultural exchange. Their productions were sometimes original, sometimes imitative; often they merely ridi-

culed earlier traditions. Finally, the drama, long neglected as an
art form, made its reappearance; so-called "miracle" and "mystery"
plays were written and were performed at certain times of the
year in the marketplaces in front of cathedrals.

Thus, the thirteenth century contributed a wealth of cultural
achievements rarely equaled in the history of Western civilization.

CHAPTER XVII

THE EVE OF THE RENAISSANCE
(1275–1350)

THE RENAISSANCE—that great age of outstanding human achievement which marked the transition from medieval to modern times—is dated by historians from approximately the year 1350. The period preceding it—from about 1275 to 1350—is one of the most contradictory in history. Countries which had advanced farthest on the road to the national-state idea and to central government were thrown back into anarchy; others which had promoted the idea of universal Christian government had to give up this ideal, yet found no other to take its place. The papacy which had raised its pretensions to the highest level found itself falling into the depth of the "Babylonian Captivity" in Avignon and into ensuing schism. Reason and faith, so recently wedded by the greatest of thinkers, demonstrated the irreconcilability of their positions. Faithful Christians and churchmen who attempted Church reforms along lines successfully followed by earlier reformers found themselves accused of treason and heresy. The unity of Western culture to the extent to which it had existed previously was undermined; and if generalizations are difficult for any period in history, they become utterly impossible for that of the eve of the Renaissance.

DISINTEGRATION OF THE MEDIEVAL SYSTEM

In 1270, the eighth and last major Crusade had taken place, which had got no farther than Tunisia and had brought the death of the

French King Louis IX. A chapter in world history closed. Historians have tried to evaluate the "results" of the Crusades. They have pointed out that many noblemen had perished and others had been impoverished, and that this had led to a strengthening of royal power, to at least a partial cessation of the petty feuds which had disturbed peace and reduced prosperity, and to a leveling process such as results generally from great wars. They have shown that during and after the crusades peasants saw opportunities for breaking some of the feudal chains which had tied them, as serfs, to their lords. They have emphasized the fact that connections with the Moslem world promoted the growth of towns, trade, and worldly thought and affected the Church adversely. Faith diminished; and weakened by huge expenditures, frustrated idealism, and failure to carry the crusades to a successful conclusion, the Church lost prestige and authority. But whatever influence we may attribute to the crusades, it is impossible to deduce so many fundamental changes, which transpired on the eve of the Renaissance, from just the one set of historical events culminating in the Crusades. Innumerable other factors, some traceable but others beyond reach of historical investigation, contributed to the social and cultural changes; and it may be well to remember that the crusades spanned a period of nearly two hundred years (1095–1291) and that the world around 1300, naturally, looked different from the world around 1100.

The Papacy. Toward the end of the thirteenth century, the Church found herself apparently at the peak of worldly power. Imperial might had been broken, and everywhere papal authority was recognized as supreme. Yet, underlying trends were unfavorable. Secular forces had taken over, or had claimed, many of the functions that had been traditionally those of the Church; the crusading spirit had spent itself and could not be revived despite vigorous attempts by Rome; the Moslems had made new inroads on the Christian world; and Orthodox and Catholic areas were as divided as at the beginning of the crusades. Indeed, the Latin Empire of Constantinople, which had been founded to re-establish Christian unity under the popes, had fallen. Negotiations at two Councils, held in 1245 and 1274 in Lyons, brought out old dissensions rather than a new will for unification.

BONIFACE VIII. In the face of existing trends, Boniface VIII—an arrogant and selfish man who became pope in 1294 and whose personal conduct as a churchman was not beyond suspicion—should have exercised the greatest restraint. Instead, in Rome, he antagonized the nobility, and particularly the powerful family of the Colonnas, by filling offices with members of his own family; abroad, he challenged the rights of kings to tax the clergy, and he used various penalties (such as excommunication) to defeat political antagonists. He displayed both greed for revenues and lust for power and sought to extend papal control by investing the Roman See with additional legal and administrative rights. In 1300, he declared a "Jubilee Year," but used this also for mercenary purposes by securing donations and funds from pilgrims coming to Rome. He reached the climax of papal pretensions when in 1302 he issued a bull, *Unam Sanctam,* in which he not only asserted full papal jurisdictional rights over the clergy, but also put forward general claims to supreme authority in secular as well as spiritual matters. Perhaps this bull did not add anything new to views long held by the Church, but its wording and timing became Boniface's own undoing. It was specifically directed against the French monarchy, and Philip IV, king of France, as well as the English King Edward I and other princes, vigorously rejected Boniface's claims. Quickly, Philip called together representatives of the various estates of his realms and secured from them authorization for his own jurisdiction over clerics. Then, he and other rulers accused the pope of various misdemeanors and summoned him before a council. Agents were sent out to bring Boniface, by force if necessary, before the council; and although (despite an assault on the pope and his arrest in the town of Anagni) this objective could not be carried out, the papal position received an irreparable blow. Boniface himself died soon after these events.

AVIGNON. The early fourteenth century thus witnessed the collapse of the papal status as envisaged by Gregory VII or Innocent III. Within a few years of Boniface's death, the French king secured the election of a French pope. This pope did not even take up his seat in Rome, but chose to reside instead just across the French border in Avignon on the Rhone. Thus began the "Babylonian Captivity" of the popes, which was to last for seventy years. In Avignon, the popes became to a certain extent subservient to French interests, and the popes' international standing was lost. Too often did they display extravagance and love of luxury. Enormous sums were needed not only to finance the Church's proper tasks of teach-

ing and charity but also to satisfy political and personal demands
and to maintain armies in the field for the purpose of the recovery
of the papal states in Italy. This need for money, in turn, increased
attention to administrative affairs and led to sacrifices of moral
standards and of spiritual authority. Opposition grew within the
Church as well as from without and gave the Empire and the various kingdoms opportunities for greater self-assertion.

The Empire. Even before the fall of Boniface VIII and the
Babylonian Captivity of the Church, the Empire had begun to
revive. In 1273, the election of Rudolf of Hapsburg (a family of
petty princes) as emperor ended the *Interregnum,* and this period
of lawlessness and political disintegration was terminated.

RUDOLF OF HAPSBURG. The new emperor was a man of moderation and considerable ability. He knew how to keep peace in his
realm, checkmate the robber barons, and regain dignity and authority for the office of emperor. He extended his own territorial
possessions, adding Austria to his other holdings, and finally became
strong enough to reassert imperial rights in Italy as well. But he
did not become strong enough to introduce an efficient central
government; nor could he change the precedent that emperors had
to be elected. This system served to perpetuate the preponderance
of the German princes who, at the time of an election, could impose conditions of their own and thereby keep imperial authority
weak. As a result, after Rudolf's death, the development of political
power in Germany continued along lines different from those in
most Western countries. Rulers from various houses (Hapsburg,
Bavaria, and Luxemburg) followed each other in the imperial
dignity, and each paid primary attention to enlarging, through war
or marriage, his own *Hausmacht,* i.e., the landholdings, power, and
influence of his own family, rather than the strength of the empire.

DIET OF RENSE. Nevertheless, two important steps toward reorganization were undertaken. The first occurred in 1338, during
the reign of Louis the Bavarian. The German princes (whose choice
of emperor the popes, at French instigation, tried to direct each time
an imperial election took place) declared at the Diet of Rense that
an emperor derived his rank from God, not from the pope, and
that it was unnecessary for him to be crowned by a pope, once he
had been duly elected in Germany. This important step reflected
both the weakness of the Church during the Avignonese papacy
and the change in the general attitude toward secular offices. With

the decline of feudalism, the positions held by monarchs had steadily gained in importance, and even many churchmen had come to acknowledge the divine origin of kingship and therewith its independence from papal authority. Among these churchmen were two prominent thinkers who came to live at Louis' court. One was Marsilius of Padua, who wrote a book, *Defensor pacis,* in which he opposed Church interference in secular affairs; these, he insisted, were the responsibility of the Christian peoples and of the emperors, who had a Christian obligation toward their subjects and should defend peace even against a pope. The other was William of Ockham, who insisted on abolition of Church abuses and, in connection with this, wished to restrict the popes to their spiritual duties.

Golden Bull. The second step toward reorganization of the Empire was embodied in the "Golden Bull" of 1356, promulgated by Emperor Charles IV. This edict while falling short of making the emperorship hereditary, at least provided for a new method of electing emperors. It restricted the right of election to seven princes of the Empire, four of them secular, and three ecclesiastical. The seven gained thereby the most important positions in all Germany; their lands were declared indivisible so that the eldest son (or, in the ecclesiastical cases, the clerical successor) would always inherit them intact. The electoral college of the seven was supplemented by a *diet* (a parliament comprising high clergy, noblemen, and representatives of the towns, and vested with legislative powers), and later by an imperial law court. By these measures the Empire was prevented from falling apart, internal wars were checked, central authority was increased along with that of the seven electors, and eventually Germany was started on the road to new importance.

Italy. After the *Interregnum,* imperial influence in Italy declined. Gradually, Italy reverted to its previous division into three distinct parts: Sicily and the South, the papal states, and central and northern Italy. In Sicily and the South, the French under Charles of Anjou had established themselves after the end of the Hohenstaufens; but they could not long maintain their status. Provoked by the brutality of Charles' forces, his financial demands, and his ambitious plans for expansion at the cost of the Byzantine Empire, the outraged Sicilians rose. In the "Sicilian Vespers" in 1282 they massacred the French garrison. Spanish princes from Aragon then took possession of Sicily, and the Anjous were confined to southern Italy. In the papal states, the popes and Roman nobility fought over control—a struggle solved essentially in favor of the latter when the popes moved to Avignon. In the central parts and the North, numerous individual city-states emerged. Most of them recognized a vague overlordship by the emperor, but they chose their own governments, whether "Ghibelline," as parties sympathizing with the Hohenstaufen (or Ghibelline) tradition and often allied with the merchant class were called, or "Guelph," as their opponents became known who since the times of the Guelphs Henry the Lion and Otto IV had, generally, promoted the patrician and the papal causes. Often, real power came into the hands of despots who seized the government illegally.

SWITZERLAND. Very special conditions developed in Switzerland, the small area which controlled a number of major Alpine passes and thereby formed the most important link within the Empire between Germany and Italy. Much of this area belonged to the Hapsburgs, and their governors administered it harshly. Early in the fourteenth century, when the peasants and a number of dissatisfied noblemen staged a successful revolt, Hapsburg domination was virtually abolished in central Switzerland and a confederation of districts (*cantons*) was established. Through a common diet, it gained a measure of self-government unknown in other contemporary countries with a predominantly agricultural economy. Progressive laws sharply reduced the service obligations of the peasant population.

France. The death of St. Louis in 1270 did not interrupt the growth and consolidation of the monarchy in France. His son Philip III proved inefficient and unsuccessful in foreign as well as domestic affairs, but he did succeed in retaining most of the royal prerogatives and he greatly increased his royal domain by acquiring considerable additional territories through shrewd diplomacy and marriage alliances with wealthy families. His successor, Philip IV "the Fair," pursued similar policies.

REIGN OF PHILIP IV. Philip IV was an able man, though of questionable character. Unlike most of the other kings during this era, he realized the power of money and did everything possible to strengthen his treasury. He reorganized the financial system, increased taxes, and confiscated the wealth of the Jews. He promoted the growth of towns and included representatives from towns and country seats along with the clergy and nobility in a consultative assembly, called "Estates General," which he instituted and which resembled the English Parliament. He made use of the Estates General not only as a means of gaining the support of wealthy townsmen for his financial policies, but also as a political instrument. With its help, he gained the right to tax the French clergy, notwithstanding the protests of Boniface VIII. In foreign affairs, though Philip failed to conquer Flanders, he succeeded in seizing territory in Burgundy. He likewise succeeded in annexing parts of southern France after driving out the knights of the Order of the Templars, who had established themselves there when the Holy Land was reconquered by the Turks. Under the pretext that they neglected their duties, concentrated on the administration of their lands, occupied themselves with banking activities, led a life of luxury, and even were guilty of heresy, Philip—greedy for their wealth and their position as international financiers—attacked them and crushed them in a bitter and brutal war.

GROWING TENSIONS. The concentration of authority and wealth in the hands of the king, the acquisition of many new domains by Philip Augustus, St. Louis, and Philip IV, the steady enlargement of the functions of the court and of the king's bureaucracy, and the activities of this bureaucracy which served as the chief tax-collecting agent but was independent of the feudal hierarchy—all these factors strengthening the royal position provoked jealousy and resistance. In particular, the great vassals were antagonized. Battling a trend, which actually was to bring them in 1346 the loss of their right to strike money, in 1349 that to levy troops of their own, and in 1357 that to wage private wars, they did their utmost to prevent any further increase of royal authority. In imitation of the king's procedures, they themselves started to annex the lands of minor vassals and to organize bureaucracies. The townspeople, too, turned against the Crown when they realized that the king's bureaucrats had assumed such broad functions that the king could use them to deprive the people of their traditional liberties. Under these circumstances, the conflicts between the king and the several estates became each year more acute and eventually, during the reign of Philip VI (1328-1350), led to disaster; for when in 1337 the intermittent war with England was resumed, the Crown found itself without the necessary support.

OUTBREAK OF THE HUNDRED YEARS' WAR. The immediate cause for the resumption of hostilities was the decision of Philip VI to confiscate Aquitaine. A pretext for this decision was furnished by the procrastination of the English King Edward III (who held Aquitaine as a fief of the French king) in rendering due homage to his overlord and by his neglect to fulfill his feudal obligations. The struggle over the act of homage was one of long standing, and in the time of Edward III such an act was, indeed, almost obsolete. But larger issues between France and England were at stake. There were grave dissensions over the borders of Aquitaine, and—still more important—issues of an economic nature entered into the question; for the wine trade of Aquitaine and the wool trade of Flanders with their profits for the French and English merchants were affected. The action of the French king led to a war which was to last for more than a century and became known as the Hundred Years' War (1337–1453). At first, skillful French diplomacy, papal intervention, and lack of money and resulting bankruptcy on the English side aggravated the English position. But Edward succeeded in countering the dangers by imposing a boycott on Flanders, whereby he deprived the Flemish artisans of their livelihood and thus created social unrest in this French territory. He followed up his advantage by laying claim, in 1340, to the French crown which, he insisted, was lawfully his on the basis of marriage and inheritance rights. As a result, a division in the allegiance of the French vassals occurred, and gradually the position of Edward improved. In 1346, he also scored, at Crécy, a great military victory. Dismounting their cavalry and depending mainly on infantry and archers equipped with the unchivalric longbow, the English succeeded in defeating the French who persisted in their antiquated feudal strategy. In the same year, the English took the harbor of Calais. French losses led to peace negotiations, but when no settlement was reached, new English expeditions, often supported by dissatisfied French nobles, were equipped; and under the leadership of the so-called "Black Prince," the south of France was fearfully plundered. These disasters, combined with the pestilence of the Black Death which had begun to ravage France in 1348, further diminished the French military potential, and in 1356, at Poitiers, the French forces were again sharply defeated; their king, John, was taken prisoner. Not until 1360 could he be ransomed, and then only at a huge cost in money, territory, and royal authority. Thus, the first period of the Hundred Years' War ended in disaster for France.

England. Political trends in England subsequent to 1275 were similar to those in France. In England, as in France, as the authority of the king expanded the powers of numerous royal officials to control national finance, law, and administration multiplied. The English Parliament, analogous to the Estates General in France, became important and influential as the king's advisory body. After the outbreak of the Hundred Years' War, however, the political evolution of England began to differ increasingly from that of France.

EDWARD I. The transition period from 1275 to 1350 began with the reign of Edward I. Edward had to face political problems quite similar to those confronting his contemporary rival, Philip IV of France, and in trying to solve them he relied, like the French king, on a bureaucracy which grew steadily more and more numerous. In order to reduce the power of the nobility, Edward subjected many lords to inquests, deprived them of illegally acquired land-holdings and privileges, and restricted their authority. At the same time, he reorganized the judicial institutions of the country by increasing the number of local courts, extending the jury system, and providing stricter royal supervision over the judiciary. New statutes based on existing common law gave prevailing legal practices a more precise and binding form.

The expansionist policies of Edward I appealed to slowly growing nationalistic sentiments among the upper classes of the population. The English forces subjected Wales and even conquered Scotland. (After Edward's death, in the decisive battle at Bannockburn in 1314, the Scotch under Robert Bruce regained, however, their independence.)

PARLIAMENT. The evolution of Parliament was perhaps the most significant development of the period from 1275 to 1350. Gradually this assembly of the various estates replaced the *curia regis* of former English kings. Parliament in England differed in many respects from the French Estates General; it was not merely a law court and an advisory body but rather an assembly of delegates representing the diverse propertied groups of the population. It conveyed to the government the wishes of these groups (including those of the "commoners") on a variety of matters, and it made its voice heard on the subject of taxation, particularly whenever taxes beyond customary limits were proposed. It even carried weight in the drafting of laws and the settling of grievances against royal officialdom. In 1295, the so-called "Model Parliament" was convoked, and thereafter Parliament functioned as a permanent institution.

During the reigns of the successors of Edward I—that is to say, under Edward II (1307–1327) and especially during the long reign (1327–1377) of Edward III—the influence of Parliament grew; for both kings depended upon its cooperation (hard pressed financially as they were owing to the expenditures and debts incurred by Edward I) and neither of them possessed the necessary astuteness to establish his leadership. Edward III, in particular, showed little ability at retaining control over Parliament. Interested in duplicating the exploits of the feudal knights of old, he had little understanding of the social changes which accompanied the transfer of power from the numerous vassals to the wealthy lords, squires, and burghers. Moreover, his absence from the country on military campaigns (during his reign the Hundred Years' War broke out) permitted Parliament to expand the scope of its activity. At this time the two Houses (the House of Lords, with its hereditary peerage and the higher clergy, and the House of Commons, with its Knights of the Shires and wealthy burghers) no longer functioned as one indivisible body as it had during the regime of Edward I, but instead had got into the habit of discussing their respective problems separately. Soon the House of Lords dealt mainly with judicial matters and concentrated on its traditional task of advising the king, whereas the House of Commons devoted its attention to taxation and trade, later extending its scope to political issues and questions of war and peace. As the reign of Edward III drew to a close, the two Houses had achieved their permanent status as an indispensable part of the English government.

Eastern Europe. The imperial and constitutional developments in fourteenth century central and western Europe, which foreshadowed the decline of feudalism, had no parallels in eastern Europe. In Prussia, Livonia, Lithuania, Poland, and Hungary, political and economic feudalism based on agriculture and landholding persisted, industries failed to develop on any large scale, and social stratification was not appreciably modified. Living standards were lower than in the West, cultural contributions relatively minor. Much of the area of central eastern Europe was torn by internal strife, for the divisions between Orthodox Slavs, Catholic Slavs, Germans, and Baltic (particularly the pagan Lithuanian) peoples were strong; and a powerful commonwealth was nowhere established.

The situation in Russia differed from that her neighbors. Although the country remained subject to Mongol rule and was divided into numerous principalities (such as Novgorod, Moscow, Tver, and Smolensk), a nation of great significance began slowly to emerge. Gradually, Muscovy came to assume the role of leading principality. The city of Moscow became the seat of the Russian Metropolitan, and the granddukes of Moscow won a prominent role among the Russian princes. The grand dukes, being shrewd businessmen, catered to the Tartars (whom they served as tax collectors) and amassed wealth which enabled them to get more power. Under their autocratic government, a feudal system such as had long prevailed in the West failed to develop. Most of the people lived in villages under various kinds of collective systems, and the institution of serfdom as familiar to the West was hardly known; rarely did the nobility hold "fiefs" in exchange for service, and a relationship based on honor such as the Western concepts of vassalage presupposed was not found in Russia. Towns and trade in most of the country were insignificant. What little trade there was consisted chiefly of local business in agricultural products—grain, wax, and honey. Inasmuch as trade was to a large extent controlled by the nobility and the monasteries, the basic conditions for the development of a middle class, a bourgeoisie, were lacking, and only the towns of western Russia had an active class of burghers. The most prominent of these towns was Novgorod, which owed its importance to its geographic location near the Baltic Sea. Novgorod became the leading exchange market for the chief Russian export products of timber, furs, wax, and honey. It constituted a republic in which the princes had little influence; and an assembly (*veche*) of freemen decided governmental policies under an oligarchic charter.

TURKEY. In the fourteenth century, Turkey was added to the roster of European states. Early in that century a new great conqueror, the Turk Osman (d. 1326), led the Moslems against the Eastern Roman Empire, seizing all the Asiatic possessions of Byzantium and thus breaching the walls protecting Europe in the East. In 1353 the Turks crossed into Europe and quickly conquered Gallipoli. They took large numbers of Christian boys from their parents, trained them as Turkish soldiers (the so-called "Janissaries") and thus strengthened they seized large parts of the Balkans. Although a century of intermittent wars was to precede their conquest of Constantinople, they already then became a threat to the West comparable to the menace of the Huns, Arabs, and Tartars in earlier centuries.

ECONOMIC AND SOCIAL CONDITIONS AND THE ARTS

Historians have traced the widespread "effects" of the Crusades not only upon the political, but also upon the social and cultural sectors of Western civilization. They have emphasized the stimulating influence which contacts with the Moslem world exercised upon the intellectual life of the West—particularly upon the development of the sciences, such as geography, astronomy, history, and medicine; and they have called attention to the new products and skills which reached Europe and transformed Western ways and standards of living. Yet, as in the political, so in the social and cultural spheres, innumerable other factors contributed to the changes which occurred. The historian can assert only that by the end of the thirteenth century new patterns of thought and societal structure, differing from those typifying the feudal Middle Ages, had become evident. The capitalist, the banker, the merchant, indeed the townspeople as a group—all the members of the "Third Estate"—had gained political and social influence, and they owed this gain not to the power of the sword but to the power of wealth. Furthermore, wealth came to consist of movable goods and money as well as land, which had constituted the chief capital of the nobleman. The third estate, even though it remained a small minority for centuries to come and generally was anxious to accept old established traditions and customs, actually introduced new standards of morality and new patterns of behavior. Soon, the members of the nobility and clergy modified their own attitudes and activities to make allowance for this new development.

Business Organization. The outstanding characteristic of economic enterprise during the first half of the fourteenth century was its infinite variety. Land still provided by far the most important source of income, but in some areas trade and industry had become dominant factors. They, too, varied greatly. Side by side with the old established enterprises of skilled craftsmen existed new pre-capitalistic enterprises. The concept of a "just price" was slowly undermined,[1] and likewise undermined was the view that the lending of capital did not entitle the owner to a reward in the form of interest. Even the Church, which had condemned all interest-taking as usury, began to allow exceptions. Corporations were formed—originally lasting only for the duration of one specific enterprise, but later in some instances becoming permanent institutions designed to perpetuate themselves for the sake of carrying on successive business ventures. The actual management of a corporation was often in the hands of one investor, or perhaps some hired manager; the other participants, who did not obtain their rewards by contributing services, merely invested capital and received a profit—if the business made a profit.

FORMS OF ENTERPRISE IN ITALY. Italy pioneered in working out new forms of business enterprise. In that country double-entry bookkeeping, letters of credit facilitating exchange, stable currencies (e.g., the Florentine gold florin), and insurance organizations were introduced. Kings and popes stimulated economic growth by investing in enterprises using these new facilities and methods. The new practices of the Italian townspeople spread northward to cities in Flanders, Holland, Germany, England, and France.

FORMS OF ENTERPRISE IN NORTHERN EUROPE. Though it was not so progressive as in Italy, business enterprise in European towns north of the Alps also prospered and expanded. The main northern contributions to economic development were the organization of great fairs and the establishment of important mining industries. Fairs were not new to Europe; they had long been outstanding examples of northern entrepreneurial spirit. The best-known fairs had been those held in the Champagne (France), where Oriental and southern European goods had been exchanged for the products of northern Europe. These fairs had declined in importance by the turn of the fourteenth century, but others, especially those in Frankfort, Leipzig, and in Scania (Denmark), replaced them as centers of trade and contributed significantly to business expansion. Even more beneficial than the fairs to business ventures in the north was the notable increase in mining and related manufacturing; raw materials and metals, in both of which the Orient and Italy were lacking, were thus increasingly made available.

---

[1] "Just price" was the concept that a producer or a merchant should ask no more for his wares than was justified by the value of his labor plus a moderate profit, irrespective of the market value of the merchandise.

Some of these activities were sponsored by kings and princes, but most of them were carried on by merchants—and most successfully by the members of the Hanseatic League. This association eventually enrolled merchants from as many as some seventy-two German towns under the leadership of Lübeck, and although it was rather conservative in point of view, its large size and far-reaching influence constituted an altogether new factor in trade and commerce. It was during the twelfth century that the North German merchants had developed a new type of ship, the cog, which was capable of navigating in stormy waters too risky for other types of vessels; after founding the League they achieved a nearly monopolistic control of the herring fisheries, and then they had become active in mining. They had interested themselves in the rich central German mines—especially salt mines, for salt was needed in the herring trade; and early in the thirteenth century, after the vigorous enterprise of the Vikings had dwindled, they had begun to develop Swedish and Norwegian mining resources, especially iron and copper. Meeting regularly in diets to discuss problems of common concern, the Hanseatic merchants had achieved a degree of cooperation with one another unknown in the strongly competitive Mediterranean area. As a result of their activities, not only did the balance of trade in northern Europe, not unlike that of southern Europe, swing more and more in favor of the West, but also the balance of power shifted so that from that time on Europe had less to fear from Eastern invaders.

Agricultural Organization. As usual, agricultural changes were slower in coming than those in trade and industry. Yet, in agriculture, too, the late thirteenth and early fourteenth centuries brought numerous innovations. In some regions, to be sure, rather primitive, traditional methods of exploiting landed wealth continued; but in other regions, such as England, many estates having been cut down in size, either had to be cultivated more intensively or had to be rendered suitable for the production of profitable industrial crops. In England, increased wool production led to the building of a textile industry. Despite the inferior quality of the English woven goods as compared with those of Flanders, by the middle of the fourteenth century the English producers, with the help of Flemish artisans lured to England, had overtaken their competitors. In other countries, other economic shifts occurred

Thus, grain production shifted eastward and slowly brought Prussia, Poland, and Livonia to the fore.

Social Organization. Necessarily, in those regions where business and agriculture underwent reorganization, the status of the various classes of the population changed. Whereas in the twelfth and thirteenth centuries the serfs had made considerable progress and had attained increasing independence, progress in this direction came to a standstill in the fourteenth century. When production for industry expanded, the nobility saw an advantage in having compulsory labor at their disposal; and as a result, no longer did the practice spread of commuting labor services of peasants for money payments. To be sure, this slow-down in the emancipation of the serfs was at first confined to those regions where urbanization was rapid; but in rural areas as well, social relationships changed markedly, widening the gap between the living standards of the noble and the peasant. In the towns, likewise, the economic and social conditions changed; differences between the wealthy burgher and the poor artisan or unskilled laborer increased.

Military Organization. Changes in social relationships were accompanied by changes in power relationships. Weapons with superior firepower had been developed after the formula for making gunpowder had become known, and arms like the cannon (hand firearms were to follow later) rendered obsolete the defenses of the typical castle and the traditional combat tactics of the knights. Since few noblemen possessed the means to produce, buy, and use such new weapons, military control passed into the hands of those who could do so—kings, princes, and towns. They hired "mercenaries" or "soldiers," i.e., fighters who served for money wages and did not care about chivalry. Armed with the new weapons, these soldiers could easily defeat those who continued to rely on personal prowess; frequently they joined in bands under a *condottiere* or leader who made war his business and lent the services of the whole group to the highest bidder.

Besides changing the existing power relationships, this new type of military organization gave an impetus to many industries, necessitating the expansion of iron and steel production and stimulating rapid progress in inventions and military techniques. It even influenced styles of architecture, as, for example, in the construction of fortresses, towers, and castles.

Cultural Climate. Simultaneously with military, technical, and economic changes came a new self-consciousness and self-reliance in intellectual and ideological matters. Early in the fourteenth century, scholastic investigations threatened to end up in sterile disputes. Such controversies were gradually replaced by new interests. The nominalist point of view, which was reinforced by the intensive study of natural events, gained prestige at the expense of Realism. Canon or Church law as well as civil and common law were given ever-increasing attention. In England, Germany, and France, important legal codes were compiled taking into consideration the results of the renewed studies of Roman legal thought and the *Corpus juris civilis* of Justinian. Attitudes toward political institutions also changed, as evinced not only by Marsilius of Padua, William of Ockham, and other advocates of imperial rights, but also by lawyers and writers in the Western kingdoms. Older Church authorities had often considered the necessity for political organization as evidence of man's sinfulness; political institutions now came to be regarded rather as inherently just, designed to promote the rights of the individual and the salutary evolution of a society based on mutual obligations.

The fine arts, too, reflected new perspectives. In the small area comprising the region of Florence, Siena, and Pisa in Italy an artistic center of lasting influence emerged. Painters and sculptors in this region were leaders in the emancipation of the arts from scholastic attitudes and liberated themselves from the patterns set by the Byzantine and Gothic styles. Although deeply imbued with a Christian spirit, they emphasized a new naturalistic approach in their work and thus paved the way for the ideals of the Renaissance. Great painters like Cimabue (d. 1302), Giotto (d. 1337), and Duccio (d. 1339) appeared; the latter two masters in particular concentrated on a more realistic representation of nature than their predecessors. They studied perspective and anatomy and interested themselves in depicting also everyday life experiences. Nevertheless, they never lost their sensitivity for sacred values, nor did they allow their naturalism to overshadow their primary objective of expressing the deepest emotions and aspirations of mankind. With them a new age began.

Dante. At this crossroad of Western civilization there now appeared one of its greatest figures, the Italian poet Dante (d. 1321). He may be regarded as either the last great man of the Middle

Ages or the first of the new age. His literary work, which included grave political treatises and exquisite sonnets, reached its apex in his masterpiece, the *Divine Comedy*. In this grandiose poem, Dante describes his journey through Hell, Purgatory, and Paradise and expounds the philosophical views and moral tenets of his age. He renders stern judgment on his contemporaries and on many preceding generations—their moral character, aspirations, achievements, and failures. In a survey of immense scope, depth, and beauty, he thus created a "summary" of an era which was slowly approaching its end.

CHAPTER XVIII

THE EARLY RENAISSANCE (1350–1453)

IN 1348, A TERRIBLE bubonic plague known as the "Black Death" swept over Europe. Like the Crusades, the Black Death has been held responsible—and perhaps with better justification—for numerous social and cultural changes which subsequently occurred. The Black Death was a single event, not a movement spanning two hundred years, and it was a sudden terrible event whose consequences are to a certain extent measurable. It killed from one tenth to one quarter of the populations of many European areas, ravaging western Europe more severely than eastern Europe. The resulting manpower shortages contributed to emancipation movements of agricultural laborers and to rebellions in the towns, to changes in power relationships between countries, and also to changes in social habits and mores. Class stratification became, at least temporarily, less rigid. The Black Death influenced man's scientific endeavors, his philosophy, his outlook on life, and his art. It induced in many people a feeling of gloom and pessimism, a fear of God's wrath; this mood was expressed in art and literature—for example, in the numerous artistic representations of the "Dance of Death" or in morality plays like "Everyman." It gave others a new thirst for life, imbued them with defiance of religious tenets, and whetted their desire for worldly pleasures; this mood was expressed in artistic representations of classical pagan topics or in books such as Boccaccio's *Decameron*. It should be noted however, that many of the changes occurring subsequent to the outbreak of the Black Death (the plague reappeared periodically later in the century) were under way long before the first epidemic and that the plague occurred during a period of religious doubt, of political unheaval, of artistic revaluation, and of economic expansion.

THE STATES OF EUROPE

Unlike the marvellous artistic and scholarly developments during the first half of the Renaissance (which means approximately the hundred years following the first outbreak of the Black Death) the political scene between 1350 and 1453 contained little of special interest. Political theory and practice in the Empire, in Italy and in the western European kingdoms followed along lines laid down earlier. Within the German Empire, each individual component territory consolidated its power in opposition to imperial authority; Italy brought the city-states to full flowering; France and England devoted much of their energy to the Hundred Years' War; and the various Iberian kingdoms continued to fight the Moslems and to expand their overseas possessions. Only in the north and east did innovations of special historical interest occur. In the Baltic region, two great unions of states were created; and in the Balkans, the East Roman Empire came to an end when the Turks captured Constantinople.

The Empire. Reorganization in 1356 helped to preserve the Empire but failed to strengthen its central authority. The weak emperors who succeeded Charles IV insisted on continuing the policy of increasing their family holdings at the expense of broad imperial or national aims. Good chances for restoring the imperial prestige were dissipated when—at a time of greatest weakness of the emperors' chief rivals, the popes—Sigismund (Charles' younger son who was emperor from 1411 to 1437) was called upon to convene a Church Council and, like a second Constantine, to preside over it, but failed to exploit the situation in favor of the Empire. Although the Council under his guidance re-established Christian unity, he gained neither abroad nor in Germany the prestige which his role could have given him. After his death began the long uninterrupted rule of the House of Hapsburg, which was to last until the end of the Empire in 1806. The Hapsburgs restored stability to the imperial office, but central authority remained in a weakened condition. The Diet and the Imperial Law Court lost through inactivity what little prestige they had retained. Foreign powers seized some of the German border areas. Political planning and determined action were confined to the courts of the territorial princes and the governments of the great imperial cities. It was thus through local rather than central, imperial efforts that the basis for a prosperous economic development was laid, which characterized many industrial regions of fifteenth-century Germany.

Italy. The decline of central imperial authority was most sharply felt in Italy. The country remained divided, with largely contrasting institutions in its various parts. Sicily and southern Italy continued under Aragonese rule; they stagnated politically and economically. So did the Papal States which, during the popes' residence in Avignon, were in addition torn by party strife that brought misery to all the population. The north continued to develop the city-states and acknowledge imperial overlordship, but actually achieved independence. Many of the city-states flourished. Local governments remained republican in form, even though only in Venice, with its elected doge, did this form possess substantial meaning. Actual power in Venice was exercised by a council of the wealthiest merchants; and after the conclusive defeat of the Genoese who had been their greatest rivals, a period of abundant prosperity for supporters (and of great misery for all opponents) of the ruling factions began. In other city-states, quasi-democratic or republican institutions paved the way for despots or tyrants—some of them recruited from among the *condottiere,* others from the ranks of the merchants, financiers, or landed nobility. These dictators depended upon three sources of power; first, their own wealth; second, the services of mercenary armies; and third, support from the lower strata of the population to whose wishes they catered. They often ruled wisely, even though many were arbitrary and demagogic. Frequently, the exercise of power became a family affair: in Milan, first the Visconti, then the Sforzas gained control; in Mantua, it was the Gonzagas; in Ferrara, the Estes; in Florence, the Medici; and in Urbino, the Montefeltres.

France. Throughout the first century of the Renaissance, most of the creative forces of France were absorbed by the Hundred Years' War with England. Early in the fifteenth century, there was an artistic revival inspired by the Renaissance in the Netherlands and Italy, but few achievements mark other facets of French life. Many badly needed governmental, military, and financial reforms were delayed. Moreover, while King John (d. 1364) was in captivity in

England, peasant revolts (the *Jacqueries*) shook the country. When these had been subdued, the incompetent kings who succeeded to the throne attempted to institute reforms, but new campaigns against England interrupted all progress. Then a struggle for power developed between the reigning family of Valois [1] and the dukes of Burgundy, vassals of the French king who had acquired a number of territories (besides Burgundy) and eventually obtained Flanders by marriage. The dukes thus attained greater power than the kings whose authority and rights they challenged. From time to time in the ensuing civil wars, they did not hesitate to join the English side, or to resort to the assassination of their enemies. Finally, the French kings suffered another bitter defeat at Agincourt (1415)—a defeat which, within another dozen years, led to the loss of half of France to England. It is possible that at this point, when England's forces were overextended and a desperate spirit of resistance was awakened among the French, a turning point was bound to come. What actually occurred however, seemed a "miracle." A young peasant girl from Lorraine, Joan of Arc, came forward to report that voices from heaven had told her she was chosen to save France. Arousing latent national sentiments and inspiring the soldiers, she succeeded in reviving the courage and loyalty of the French. The army rallied to win its first great military and psychological victory by raising the siege of Orléans, a strategic town on the Loire which English armies had surrounded. This victory made it possible for large areas in France to be liberated; Rheims was retaken, and the "Dauphin" Charles was finally crowned King Charles VII. Joan had fulfilled her mission. Soon thereafter she fell into the hands of the British who handed her over to the Inquisition; inasmuch as Charles did nothing to save her, she was burned at the stake. But the impetus which she had given to the French cause carried France through to victory. In 1435, Burgundy renounced her alliance with Britain and the English were repeatedly defeated in battle. When the war came to an end in 1453, they had been ejected from the continent, retaining only the harbor town of Calais.

England. Even during the period of continued victories over the French, England experienced disturbances similar to those which racked France. In England, too, the plight of the lower

---

[1] The Capetians had died out in 1328. The House of Valois succeeded them and ruled until 1589.

classes was so grave that revolts of the peasants occurred late in the fourteenth century. When, as in France, the rebel peasants were brutally subdued, rebellions of some of the powerful lords continued to keep the country in turmoil. In vain did young Richard II, grandson of Edward III, try to strengthen his royal authority at the expense of the unruly high nobility and Parliament; the rebels under the leadership of Henry of Lancaster deposed him in 1399, and crowned Lancaster Henry IV. Thereafter, the great lords dominated Parliament and controlled state policies. Disunited as they were, however, they merely intensified the misery of the populace. The economic and social progress of the previous era was endangered as trade shrank away, prices fell, and a cultural revival initiated at the close of the fourteenth century came to a sudden end. Moreover, during the second quarter of the fifteenth century, with final defeat in war against France, new disturbances marked the reign of Henry VI (1422–1467). But Parliament, subservient though it may have been to whosoever held the power, survived and continued to give a measure of stability to English institutions through its influence on taxation and law.

Scandinavia and Poland. No lasting contributions to the political institutions of Europe were made by the Scandinavian countries or Poland, but two interesting political unions were concluded: one between Denmark-Norway and Sweden-Finland, and the other between Poland and Lithuania. In both cases, military and economic factors induced these countries to sign treaties of unification—intended to create a new balance of power in the Baltic area, where previously the balance had favored the German Hanse and the Teutonic Knights.

SCANDINAVIA. The dependence of the prosperity of the Hanseatic League upon trade in the Baltic made it necessary for the Hanse to protect its position by building up its navy. This led in 1361 to wars with Denmark which dominated the "Sound," i.e., the Straits leading from the North Sea to the Baltic Sea, and thereby controlled the North European seaway linking East and West. In 1370, the Hanse defeated Denmark; the subsequent peace treaty at Stralsund guaranteed continuance of the Hanse's monopolistic position in East-West trade. Thereafter the Hanse reached the climax of its power and prosperity. Hanse merchants rivaled the great Venetian and Genoese houses in importance. They provided the northern countries with vital commodities—particularly salt—and contributed to the internal development of the various Baltic and North Sea countries—especially Sweden and Norway with their iron and copper mines. Yet, jealousy of Hanseatic military and economic power induced the three Scandinavian countries to compose their own differences, improve their economic collaboration, and to form a union (the Union of Kalmar, 1397). They failed to achieve their objectives, though, because nationalistic antipathies and Danish-Swedish territorial rivalries persisted, and the Union did not succeed in re-establishing the leading position which Scandinavia, and especially Denmark, had held before 1200.

POLAND. A union of a different kind was formed in 1386 when Grand Duke Jagiello of Lithuania married Jadwiga, last surviving princess of the Polish reigning house. Here, too, economic factors were involved, for Poland's steadily growing agricultural production needed export markets, and this stimulated a drive for direct access to the Black and Baltic seas on which Lithuania bordered. Moreover, dynastic, religious, and strategic objectives could be served: the grand dukes of Lithuania, becoming kings of Poland, could win greater prestige in Europe; Poland might be enabled to convert pagan Lithuania to Catholicism; and, while eliminating competition between themselves, both nations could gain a more powerful position vis-à-vis the Russians to the East and the Teutonic Knights ruling Prussia in the West. In fact, they soon launched an attack on the Teutonic Knights, upon whom they inflicted a decisive defeat at Tannenberg (1410). Thereafter, the new commonwealth (which, incidentally, benefited the Poles more than the Lithuanians) became an important power.

Russia. Of more lasting strength, however, was the commonwealth Muscovy began to build during the late fourteenth and the fifteenth centuries. By 1380, the Moscow Grand Duke Dimitri felt strong enough to challenge his overlords, the Tartars, whom he attacked and defeated in the battle of the Don. This victory was unprofitable, as it coincided with a revival of Tartar strength under the famous Tamerlane who took bitter revenge on the Russians; Moscow itself was captured and burned. But the resistance of the Muscovites increased their prestige among the various Russian principalities; and a number of internal reforms carried out by Dimitri and his successors also contributed to the strengthening of the political leadership of Muscovy. Greater political stability was gained by instituting the rule of primogeniture for succession on the grand ducal throne; the influence of the high nobility, the "boyars," was reduced; Muscovy's laws and suzerainty were extended to neighboring areas; and national feeling was strengthened by the Church, which had played a leading role in the resistance movement against the Tartars.

In addition to Muscovy, the principality of Novgorod flourished. Its trade with the Hanse gave it unequalled economic importance; even in the fine arts, remarkable achievements came out of Novgorod, reaching their climax in the work of the great icon painter Rublev.

Turkey. In the mid-fifteenth century, the developing patterns of eastern as well as western European policies were modified as a result of the military successes achieved by the Turks. Late in the fourteenth century, their progress had been temporarily halted by defeat at the hands of Tamerlane, who had attacked them, as he had attacked the Russians, from the rear. But the Turks, recovering from the losses inflicted upon them, then resumed their advance in Europe. Under Mohammed II (d. 1481), they decisively defeated (in 1444) those Christian nations in the Balkans which had not yet been subdued. They then turned against Constantinople and after a fierce siege conquered the valiantly defended city. The last Byzantine emperor was killed in battle, and after a thousand years of existence the East Roman Empire ceased to be. Many historians consider this event so important that instead of dating the beginning of Modern Times from the discovery of America or from the Reformation, they date it from the fall of Constantinople.

CHURCH AND SOCIETY

While during the first century of the Renaissance the Western world's political evolution did not make substantial visible strides, Church life and the structure of society evinced manifold modifications. The attention devoted by Renaissance man to secular affairs changed his ways of life and thought. Not that the average person, or even the outstanding genius, became irreligious; on the contrary, transcendental beliefs continued to keep a firm hold on most people. But nature and worldly aims were not regarded as temptations of the flesh, nor as impediments to salvation, to the same degree that they had been so regarded during earlier medieval periods. More tolerance was displayed toward economic pursuits, naturalism in art, reason as a guide in life, the study of pagan classical antiquity, and scientific investigations of nature. The Church itself did not escape a measure of secularization.

Avignon. After 1350, the Church, like each of her members a child of the age, was increasingly exposed to the impact of the new ideas. The popes continued to reside in Avignon and to occupy themselves largely with secular and administrative affairs—with questions of law, of jurisdiction, of politics, and with financial measures: extra tithes in addition to the customary one tenth, promulgation of indulgences, special donations and fines, and confiscation of the property of heretics. They performed many functions outside the proper scope of Church activities and even some that were contrary to Church regulations—the sale of Church offices, exploitation of the tourist and pilgrim trade, speculation in real estate, and mercantile and banking activities.

The Great Schism. All this violated the consciences of faithful Catholics as much as it antagonized worldly lords, and it provided material for criticism and unbelief. Fearful of losing his authority and disturbed by attacks from within the Church, Pope Gregory XI tried in 1377 to re-establish the papal residence in Rome. He returned there, but died within a year. His successor, Urban VI, through lack of moderation in his attempts to inaugurate drastic reforms, antagonized the cardinals who turned against him and created a new, most serious crisis by electing another pope. This pope, Clement VII, took up his residence in Avignon. Now, the Church had two heads, and the "Great Schism" began. The split involved all parts of the Church organization, brought papal authority to its lowest point, divided the nations on the basis of their adherence (for political reasons) to one or the other pope, and delayed urgently needed spiritual reform work.

Reform Movements. Necessarily, opposition to the Church hierarchy grew. With the spread of interest in science, art, and classical literature, it is not surprising that opposition came from men interested in secular affairs; but it came also from those multitudes of believers who had retained their faith in the fundamental obligations of Christians. Noting the secular preoccupations of the Church hierarchy, many churchmen spoke out courageously and vigorously.

WYCLIFFE AND HUSS. The most important advocates of reform were Wycliffe and Huss. They followed in the footsteps of Marsilius of Padua and William of Ockham, both of whom had recommended clear distinctions between spiritual and secular duties and, as adherents to the nominalist trends, had advocated separation of the realms of faith and reason. Both Wycliffe and Huss also followed the example of Marsilius and Ockham in condemning the claims of the Church to secular possessions; but they went farther by assailing some of the dogmas of the Church. Wycliffe (d. 1384) challenged the views of the Church on transubstantiation and the Church doctrine of salvation; like later reformers, he emphasized the Bible rather than Church tradition and saw to the translation of some parts of the Bible into the vernacular. John Huss (d. 1415), a professor at the University of Prague, under the influence of Wycliffe spread similar ideas about both the duties and the dogma of the Church. In particular, Huss condemned the existing system of indulgences.

MYSTICS. Of course, not all advocates of reform went so far as Wycliffe and Huss, both of whom were eventually accused of heresy. The majority sought a purification of Church life and organization rather than a revision of dogma. Among them were many mystics. In Italy, the spirit of mysticism was kept alive by the Spiritual Franciscans and by individuals, such as St. Catherine of Siena (d. 1380) and her followers; in Germany and the Low Countries, by followers of Meister Eckhart, such as Johannes Tauler (d. 1361) and, in the next century, Thomas à Kempis (d. 1471). As earnest and devoted Christians, the mystics, instead of indulging in criticism, emphasized the positive aspects of an invigorated spiritual life. As always, they advocated the individual's direct relationship to God and worked for a return to a pure Christian life free of worldly ambitions. Mystic trends spread also to Flagellants, Beguines, and other new, rather loosely organized "orders," which flourished especially in the Netherlands and practiced a Christian way of life that was in many respects consonant with the wishes of the reformers.

Conciliar Movement. In the face of such trends, the Church finally undertook steps to set its house in order. The initiative came not from the popes but from lesser members of the hierarchy. A series of councils, the first of which was held in 1409, were convened to develop a program with three objectives: restitution of faith, re-establishment of unity, and reform of morals.

COUNCILS OF PISA, CONSTANCE, BASEL. The first council took place at Pisa. This initial attempt failed. Instead of solving problems, it aggravated the situation for a new pope was elected who, although chosen to replace the two reigning popes, merely became a third one. A second council was thereupon called by the German Emperor Sigismund, who thus reasserted the supreme authority of the early emperors. This council (at Constance, 1414–18) was successful in solving one issue—that of schism. All claimants to the papal see were deposed; and there was general recognition of a new pope, Martin V, who took up his residence in Rome. The remaining issues, however, were not solved, for secular trends had become too firmly implanted and "heresies" had spread too widely. When questions of faith and reform were taken up and Huss was summoned before the council, the assembled authorities refused him any adequate hearing, and even though he had come under a guarantee of safe conduct, they had him burned at the stake. New councils were convened—at Pavia in 1423 and at Basel in 1431. But by that time, the popes were more immediately concerned with reasserting their leadership in the Church and their supremacy over the councils than with dogmatic and moral issues; taking advantage of the diverging interests of the various nations in regard to these questions, they succeeded in prolonging the discussions until 1438. By then, victory was theirs, and soon thereafter, notwithstanding continued resistance of many members of the council, a papal bull confirmed the monarchical principle in the Church.

COUNCIL OF FERRARA-FLORENCE. One more council was held in 1438 and 1439 in Ferrara and Florence. It, too, made no progress with reform. Instead, it concerned itself largely with the reunion of the Western and Eastern Churches, split since 1054. Hard pressed by attacking Turks, the emperor in Byzantium had appealed to the West for help. He and the Patriarch of Constantinople personally travelled to Florence, and the strategic moment to re-establish papal domination in the East seemed to have arrived. Nevertheless, although an agreement was reached, the persistent opposition, especially that of the Russian Church, prevented its execution; and with the fall of Constantinople a few years later, the chief incentive for the Eastern Church to submit to Western demands was gone.

OUTCOME OF THE CONCILIAR MOVEMENT. Thus ended the Conciliar Movement. It had restored Western unity under the popes; but the failure to solve the problems of faith and reform continued to endanger the structure of the Church. A deep social and economic split between lower and higher clergy remained, and likewise a deep religious and cultural split between a reform party and a politically minded hierarchy; and the gulf between Church aims and national aims widened. Educational institutions, especially the universities, emancipated themselves from Church guidance, and the secular trends of the Renaissance were but imperfectly reconciled with Christian tradition. Indeed, they soon took precedence over it.

State-Church Issues. In the course of the Babylonian Captivity of the Church, the Schism, and the Conciliar Movement, secular princes found many opportunities to further the emancipation of secular rule from interference by the Roman See. The action of the German princes at the diet of Rense regarding elimination of papal rights at elections of emperors, supported as it was by Church reformers like Marsilius and Ockham, set an example that was followed by other nations. In 1351, the English promulgated the *Statute of Provisors* which forbade papal appointments to English benefices, and in 1353 the *Statute of Praemunire,* which prohibited appeals without royal consent from local ecclesiastical courts to courts outside of England. In 1438, France issued the Pragmatic Sanction, which similarly provided for the right of the king to exercise Church jurisdiction and to nominate high clerics. The Empire soon thereafter passed the same kinds of ordinances; and the Spanish, by acting as champions of Catholicism, succeeded in making the papacy so dependent upon their support that they actually gained still greater liberties. Even popular movements, such as revolts of the lower classes which occurred in Italy, France, England, and Bohemia, evinced a change in the relationships of Church and State and demonstrated how deeply the lives and views of the peoples had begun to be influenced by national aspirations.

Societal Changes. The questioning of so many fundamental values and the disruption of accustomed political and economic life resulted inevitably in an accelerated transformation of the prevalent class structure. Perhaps the lowest classes, whose revolts proved to be premature, were less affected than the upper strata of society. In Italy, earlier than elsewhere, the hereditary nobility lost its former place and mixed with a merchant aristocracy. Soon the newly formed class surpassed the old feudal nobility in refinement of manners and took over certain activities formerly reserved for the nobility. The middle group or burghers (consisting of smaller merchants and artisans) was likewise strongly affected. Since this group lacked the wealth required for industrial development, it sank to a low economic level so that it lost much of its former independence, and many of its members had to work for wages. In the towns north of the Alps, it took longer for the wealth of the rich merchants to challenge the power of birthright. Moreover, the guilds were stronger there than in Italy, and they retained political influence and control of production and trade. But where ever very rich merchants made their appearance, as in southern Germany, eastern France, Flanders, England, and the Baltic ports, social changes did not substantially differ from those in the south.

In the rural areas, societal changes were fewer. Only in Italy was a new element introduced when prosperous townsmen began to supplant or supplement the land-owning feudal lord by buying estates. This meant a challenge to former class concepts; it gained for the rich townsman not only the economic advantages but also the prestige which the nobility had derived from the possession of land. It is true that also in northern countries the townsmen invested in landed property, but not on a scale that could endanger the status of the nobility. Nevertheless, in the north, too, rural society displayed new features. The owners of manors and the other lords began to enjoy imported luxuries as well as the products of an advanced European economy, and they rapidly devoted more attention to their pre-capitalistic business enterprises. On the other hand, the condition of the peasant deteriorated. The movement toward emancipation from serfdom came almost to a standstill when the lords, anxious to retain their serfs so that these would work the mines and attend to other commercial enterprises, discontinued the practice of commuting compulsory labor services into money payments.

Economic Changes. Despite population losses following the outbreak of the Black Death and despite the trend toward lower prices in many parts of Europe during the late Middle Ages, production and trade increased. Capital formation took place rapidly, but capital came to be concentrated in comparatively few hands. The few who possessed it seldom attempted to specialize in any particular branch of industry or trade. Notwithstanding enormous risks, they invested in a great variety of enterprises. They often participated in many ventures: banking, money-lending and exchange, mining, manufacturing, trading, exporting and importing, buying and selling real estate, building, and dealing in works of art. Some might even take on lucrative public offices, such as tax collecting for popes or secular rulers. Historians call this period an age of "mercantile capitalism." As the narrow concepts of a feudal nobility, the standards of the Christian Church regarding interest-taking, and the restrictive tendencies of guilds were gradually left behind, the way was opened for a measure or capitalistic activity. Kings as well as Italian despots saw their advantage in it—for the sake both of reducing the power of the nobility and of acquiring wealth and luxuries—and supported the merchant capitalists against the upper and lower classes. Subsequent scientific discoveries speeded the transformation of the economy. Technical improvements were introduced—in the mining industry, in milling processes, in the manufacture of textile goods, in shipbuilding, in occupations such as the distillation of salt from sea water, and in agriculture; a higher standard of living resulted.

Social Revolts. The transition from a feudal economy to mercantile capitalism was a drastic change that did not occur without some violence. All groups of the population became involved: clergy, nobility, townsmen, peasantry. From all sides came urgent demands; and attacks on any one dominant group—Church, monarchs, feudal lords, or guilds—engulfed all. Many disturbances originated with the noblemen. Robber barons and other members of the declining nobility participated in them—perhaps unaware of the underlying social trends which would irrevocably deprive them of their former positions. More important, however, were the revolts of the lower classes. In France, they came to a climax in 1358 in the *Jacqueries*. Faced during the Hundred Years' War by ruined crops and ever-increasing demands of their lords, and hoping to derive some advantage from a general disaster, the peasants asked for better laws and more equitable justice, for a reduction in their service obligations, and for personal freedom. Joined by townsmen who had been similarly damaged by war and burdensome taxation, they began to attack the nobles and to burn their castles. It required the extreme exertions of the government, which had been weakened by war with England, to subdue the *Jacqueries*. Other revolts, feeding on social grievances, occurred in numerous towns; common workers rose against the wealthy in Florence in 1378; similar uprisings followed in other Italian cities, in Paris and London, in southern Germany, and in towns of the Netherlands.

During the last two decades of the fourteenth century and throughout the fifteenth, the situation continued to deteriorate as religious reformers added their share to the general discontent. Thus, in 1381 Wycliffe's followers, the "Lollards," participated in a rebellion similar to the *Jacqueries* of France. Under the leadership of Wat Tyler in London, peasants and city workers rebelled, demanding economic improvements for the lower classes and envisaging broader use of parliamentary power on their behalf. Their revolt shared the fate of the *Jacqueries*. In Bohemia, the Hussites staged a series of revolts which spread far into adjacent imperial lands. The Hussites, like the Lollards, were both heretics and rebels; Czech nationalism gave their religious and social demands a special character and turned their revolts into extremely devastating wars. Still other outbreaks occurred in Spain and elsewhere, and not until the end of the Renaissance—and only after the great Reformation of the sixteenth century was over—was a comparatively stable social order re-established.

SCHOLARSHIP AND ARTS

There have been times, as in early Roman history, so lacking in great cultural achievements, that the interest of the historian in them has centered chiefly around political, constitutional, and social developments. During the late fourteenth and the fifteenth centuries, however, cultural events occurred that had far greater meaning for the future than the contemporary political or military events such as the various institutional modifications or the Hundred Years' War. These cultural events occurred in the central region, which constituted the focal point of Medieval civilization and which extended from the Low Countries throughout the Empire, western and southern Germany, Burgundy, and Italy down to Florence, Siena, and Rome. From this area spread the Renaissance—the mightiest and most meaningful of all the movements of the time. The Renaissance, an age of "rebirth" of interest in classical antiquity, comprised about two hundred years, approximately from 1350 to 1550, and marked the age of transition from medieval to modern culture. It was distinguished by a spirit of confidence in man's achievements and possibilities, by an extension of secular activities, of ambition and competition, by a joyful love for worldly attractions, for the beauty of nature, by towering achievements in art, and by a redirection of thought towards rational objectives characteristic of classical antiquity. It was an age of reform.

Humanism. Basic to the cultural achievements of the Renaissance was the philosophy and attitude of "humanism" as developed in Italy. Humanism meant occupation with "things human" as opposed to transcendental questions and problems of the "other world." Humanism emphasized the "dignity" of man and sought the full development of his personality. It took as its guideposts, not the thoughts and metaphysical speculations of the great medieval philosophers, but those of the classical authors. Humanists therefore studied with renewed fervor the works of antiquity— chiefly those of Latin authors (such as their cherished Cicero) which they preferred to the works of the Greeks. Their pursuits necessitated careful investigations of source material, based on thorough linguistic knowledge. Owing to their zeal, numerous ancient texts were rediscovered. Humanistic attitudes were soon also adopted by leading thinkers who, in opposition to scholastics with their overly subtle dialectics, applied the methods of classical scholarship to the writings of the Church fathers and who rethought Christian theological problems. Christian Humanism supplemented Classical Humanism.

ITALIAN HUMANISM. At the beginning of the era of Humanism and of the Renaissance stands the great Italian poet Petrarch (d. 1374). He personified the new spirit, and he interested himself, despite sincere allegiance to the great medieval tradition, in the affairs of nature and everything human. A famous letter of his describing his excursion on a mountain, Mont Ventoux, symbolizes this interest. Although St. Augustine had once warned in his writings against the temptations of nature and external beauty and although Petrarch carried a copy of Augustine's book along on his trip and reread it, he opened his eyes to the world surrounding him and reported the delights of his ascent of Mont Ventoux. Indeed, some historians have dated the beginnings of the Renaissance from Petrarch's venture.

Tendencies and secular interests similar to those of Petrarch animated his friend Boccaccio (d. 1375). Boccaccio's great accomplishment in his own time was his propagation of the heritage of Ancient Times. Unlike Petrarch who knew some Latin but no Greek, he devoted most of the attention of his mature years to classical studies and to composition in Latin and Greek. The two authors were followed by a long list of other distinguished humanists, including outstanding men, such as Poggio (d. 1459), who combined literary interests with studies of nature and with scientific occupations. Another was Lorenzo Valla (d. 1457), who was led by his source studies to attack the authenticity of the so-called "Donation of Constantine," on which the popes based the legal title to their sovereignty in Rome. But so deeply were humanistic tendencies by then embedded even at the papal court that notwithstanding his challenging work Valla was appointed a papal secretary. At about the same time, Aeneas Silvio Piccolomini (the future Pope Pius II) gained fame for works of a secular character, including a geography. Everywhere, Humanism marked Italian cultural life. A "Platonic Academy" was founded in Florence, which attracted famous Greek scholars, especially some of those forced to flee from the Turks. Princes and cardinals, tyrants, and wealthy burghers vied for the honor of engaging the services of scholars and becoming patrons for artists, writers, and musicians.

GERMAN AND NORTHERN HUMANISM. From Italy, Humanism spread northward across the Alps. Its flowering there came in the sixteenth century, but some humanistic trends had evinced themselves in the fifteenth. Obstacles to Humanism were greater in the North since scholastic traditions were still alive and vigorous. Moreover, superstitious beliefs were stronger, and works such as the *Witches' Hammer,* dealing with witchcraft, found a wide public. Interest in astrology and magical arts was widespread. Yet in the North, too, classical studies were gradually taken up, and a modern spirit made itself felt. Biblical scholarship improved and Humanism permeated modes of thinking and writing. The mathematician, astronomer, and classical scholar Johann Müller, known as "Regiomontanus" (d. 1476), exemplified the growing importance of Humanism. Awareness of man's natural surroundings was reflected in the publication of numerous books on mathematics and astronomy, cosmogony, and geography. At the courts of the princes, particularly at the imperial court and that of the dukes of Burgundy, but also at the courts of lesser nobles and in the houses of wealthy merchants, the taste for classical and humanistic studies was evinced; and wealth was used to promote humanistic endeavors.

Renaissance Learning. The spirit of free inquiry characteristic of Humanism and the Renaissance brought manifold results. Intellectual leadership shifted from the universities, whose standards declined with the degeneration of scholasticism, to individual scholars who had no affiliation with institutions controlled by the Church. The University of Paris, once the pride of the Western World, no longer provided much stimulus; and Italian and English universities likewise failed to retain their former greatness. The German universities, more recently founded, possessed greater vitality, but they did not fill the place left vacant by the others. It was through individual efforts that studies of the Grecian heritage were broadened, and Latin, corrupted for centuries, regained some of its classical beauty. Libraries were compiled by secular and ecclesiastical princes and by other wealthy private persons in all parts of Europe, and literary and art treasures were collected. Education was given more attention; many schools were founded, especially north of the Alps, and literacy became more common. The traditional curriculum of the seven arts was gradually augmented to include studies of classical languages, law, science, and manners, and less importance was attached to dialectics and grammar. Prominent scholars, like Vittorino da Feltre, set new perspectives in learning; and thousands of humanistic students—men and women —came especially to Italy which, owing to its ancient heritage and its contemporary achievements, passed through a period rivalling the days of Ancient Rome.

Literature. Humanistic tendencies, which led to the spread of scientific and other scholarly activities beyond the Church and the universities and which necessitated schooling for larger numbers of people, gave the written word a far greater significance than it had possessed in earlier medieval times. Literature gradually took over the central role in man's intellectual endeavors, as evidenced in an abundance of works. In the second half of the fourteenth century, Petrarch published his *Sonnets;* and Boccaccio wrote the *Decameron*—a classic which with its entertaining stories reflects general human concerns as well as life in late medieval Italian society. Both of these works were composed in the vernacular language. As in Italy, so in France, Germany, and England, secular writings were enjoyed by widening circles. Stories of chivalry became popular not merely among courtiers but also among the bourgeoisie, who amplified and transformed them. Numerous chronicles were compiled, and histories were written, such as that by Froissart (d. 1410) who described the early phases of the Hundred Years' War. In England, the allegorical poem *Piers the Plowman* (attributed to William Langland) was composed; it is outstanding among the literature of the time inasmuch as it occupied itself with economic, religious, and moral problems of the lower classes. Toward the end of the fourteenth century, Chaucer wrote the *Canterbury Tales*. Not merely did this work constitute an artistic achievement; it provided also a realistic and brilliant, and yet charitable, study of human nature, of virtue and vice in their manifold aspects.

Literary works of the following (the fifteenth) century lack much of the imagination of those in the fourteenth. The output was extremely large, but much of it, especially in Italy, was dry and stilted, designed to imitate the classical style. The authors often took up pagan mythological themes, but the numerous allusions to Latin writers could appeal to only those trained in the "sophisticated" taste of the time. Exceptional was the poetry of François Villon (d. 1463), whose poetic gift, delight in life, and insight into the realities of the human condition infused his creations with the spark of originality and sincere emotion. On the whole, literature in the North, as expressed in legends, poems, songs, and miracle and morality plays, all of which had a background of folklore, was more spontaneous than the aesthetic, refined writings of Italy.

Art and Architecture. The greatest glory of the Renaissance was its art—painting, sculpture, and architecture. These works of art must be enjoyed through direct experience of them, for no description can give an adequate impression of the lasting beauty created by the great masters.[2] Individual men of genius constituted the source of Renaissance greatness. A society appreciative of beauty, allowing men to develop their own, individual, and many-sided personalities, and receptive to the works created by them, supported their endeavors.

ITALIAN ART. In Italy, no longer did Florence and the central Italian region stand alone in producing great works of art; their example spread to Rome, Milan, Venice—everywhere. Outstanding among the Italian painters were Fra Angelico (d. 1455), Masaccio (d. 1428), Fra Filippo Lippi (d. 1469), and Gozzoli (d. 1497); among the sculptors, the della Robbia family, Ghiberti (d. 1455), and Donatello (d. 1466); among the architects, Brunelleschi (d.

---

[2] Perhaps the most inspired picture of the whole age is that given by Jakob Burckhardt in his *Civilization of the Renaissance in Italy*.

1446). While devoting themselves to religious as well as worldly subjects, they combined classical beauty and simplicity with some medieval Gothic elements, and imbued these with the spirit of the Renaissance and their own aesthetic feelings. They paid increasing attention to a realistic representation of nature and daily life, in which they took joy. They attached new importance to observation, to what their senses told them; and through the study of anatomy, of perspective, and of light and shadow, the foremost painters improved the desired rendering of naturalistic features. They painted on canvas as well as on wood or walls (frescoes) and used chemically perfected pigments. In architecture, the great masters applied new and daring building techniques. Nevertheless, it was not through their technique but through their inspiration, imagination, and workmanship that they achieved masterpieces enduring in human history.

NORTHERN ART. The northern countries followed closely the example set in Italy; at least Germany and the Netherlands produced achievements worthy of the age. A late flowering of the Gothic style was evident; the great trading towns with their rich merchants took pride in adorning their surroundings with marvelous buildings. Wood carving was brought to a perfection unknown to Italy (which lacked timber), and carved and painted altars and statues beautified thousands of small country churches as well as great cathedrals. Another branch of artistic work, the woodcut (which was used for illustrations in books), was also more highly developed in the North than in Italy. The themes of the northern artists were less secular, or pagan, than those of the Italians. Lacking some of the joyful spirit of the South, the northern artist persisted to a large extent in the pessimistic mood of earlier times; his work centered around death and the dangers of worldliness and sin; he called man to repentance rather than to indulgence in worldly affairs and their enjoyment.

As to northern painting, a Renaissance style can be traced earliest in the Netherlands—particularly Brabant and Flanders, two provinces which in the fifteenth century formed a political part of the Burgundian realm. Closely connected economically with the great Italian ports in the Mediterranean area as well as with the Hanseatic towns on the Baltic, the cities of the Netherlands had become centers of a prosperous burgher society. Their accumulated wealth was invested in daring commercial enterprises, in luxurious living, and in imposing works of art. It was there that painters flourished like the brothers van Eyck (d. 1426, 1441) and Roger van der Weyden (d. 1464). Their loving devotion to every part, every detail of nature's and man's creations, and the intensity and simplicity of their presentation, combined with deep religious feeling, give an unparalleled appeal to their works. In many technical aspects, the Netherland masters became teachers of all of Europe—including Italy.

Music. Interestingly, it was the Netherlands which also made special contributions in the field of music. Church chant and secular songs, cultivated by Cathedral choirs, artisan guilds, students, and performers at the courts of princes, flourished during the fifteenth century in many regions of northern Europe. The Netherlands broke with tradition in instrumental and vocal music, introduced innovations in choral singing when developing the art of the canon, and contributed to the evolution of the polyphonic style. It was from there that some of the finest composers came, including Dufay (d. 1474), and it was Netherland masters who influenced most parts of Europe.

The Printing Press. At the very end of the first half of the Renaissance, at almost the same moment when Constantinople fell, another event of fundamental importance occurred: the development of the printing press with movable type by the German printer Johann Gutenberg (d. 1468). He also introduced the use of type made of lead instead of wood. Soon, the Gutenberg press in Mainz was supplemented by the Aldine press of Manuzio in Venice and other presses. It is difficult to overestimate the significance which scholarship and the written word were to assume owing to Gutenberg's invention, and the influence they were to exercise on the cultural climate and social structure of the Western world.

CHAPTER XIX

ON THE THRESHOLD OF THE MODERN AGE
(1453–1492)

THE FORTY YEARS which elapsed between the capture of Constantinople by the Turks and the discovery of America—the "last forty years" of the Middle Ages—are remarkable for the beauty and vigor which mark European civilization. Italy, Germany, and the Netherlands continued to produce works of art unsurpassed in other ages. Botticelli (d. 1510), Verrocchio (d. 1488), Leonardo da Vinci (d. 1519) are just a few names which illustrate Italian accomplishments in painting and sculpture, while Memling (d. 1494), Schongauer (d. 1491), and Riemenschneider (d. 1521) are among the many names of great artists in the Netherlands and Germany. The composer Okeghem (d. 1492) was outstanding in the field of music. Pico della Mirandola (d. 1494), a man of universal interests and far-reaching ability, a classical scholar and an accomplished writer, brought Italian Humanism to perhaps its finest stage. No new aspect of civilization was, however, introduced by these men; perhaps none was called for as long as what had been evolved during the early Renaissance showed so much vitality and continued to bring forth so many distinguished accomplishments. It was different, though, with regard to the political and economic situation of the Western world. Disruptive forces had triumphed between the middle of the fourteenth and the middle of the fifteenth centuries; the time for reconstruction had come. Increasing national pride in various countries of Europe provides the background against which this reconstruction must be viewed.

WESTERN EUROPE

Two aspects characterize the political conditions in Western Europe toward the end of the Middle Ages: the national state idea which meant the triumph of loyalty to the nation over the previously prevailing ideal of Christian unity; and the monarchical idea, which meant the triumph of royal power over feudal nobility.

Spain and Portugal. The most spectacular developments took place on the Iberian peninsula. From comparative insignificance, Spain and Portugal emerged to become, within less than twenty-five years, the foremost powers of the Western world. For more than a hundred years, Portugal, Castile, and Aragon had explored the seas, extended their rule over territories beyond the seas—eastward to the Balearic Islands, Sardinia, Sicily, and Naples, and even to parts of Greece; westward to the Azores and the Canary Islands; and, under the sponsorship of the Portuguese Prince Henry the Navigator (d. 1460), also southward along the African coast as far as the Equator. At home, all three countries had in unrelenting struggle put an end to the unruly behavior of the nobility; and their rulers, supported by the Church (which, in turn, received aid from them), had gradually gained in strength. During the last part of the fifteenth century, this long and slow evolution led to a sudden climax, marked by three great events: (1) the marriage, in 1469, between Ferdinand of Aragon and Isabella of Castile, which led to a unification of these two kingdoms and therewith to the establishment of modern Spain; (2) the success of Portuguese and Spanish discoverers—of Diaz who in 1486 reached the Cape of Good Hope at the southern tip of Africa, of the Genoese Columbus who served the Spanish monarchs and in 1492 landed in America, and of Vasco da Gama who in 1498 reached India by sailing along the Cape of Good Hope; and (3) the liquidation in 1492 of the kingdom of Granada, last of the seven-hundred-year-old possessions of the Moslems in Spain. In order to forestall future dangers from the south, the Spaniards expelled most of the Moslems and Jews living there, and the Inquisition was used to convert by force those who stayed, and to establish uniformity in the newborn empire.

France. For France, the chief problem after the end of the Hundred Years' War consisted in the re-establishment of effective government and of her place among the European nations. Her victory over the English meant more than mere territorial gains; it meant that France's feudal age, which had brought the involvements with the English, was over. To be sure, the country remained divided, owing to the independent position of the dukes of Burgundy; and regional differences, especially between north and south, remained strong. But a national spirit triumphed and the king rather than the nobility or the Estates General became its representative. France entered the Modern Age early.

At the beginning of this age stood the cruel and cunning figure of Louis XI (1461–1483)—a most remarkable and capable ruler. He had the good fortune of seeing his chief rival, Charles the Bold, brilliant duke of Burgundy, defeated, and in 1477 killed, during an attempt to extend Burgundy's rule into Switzerland. Even though after Charles the Bold's death the rich Netherlands, part of the Burgundian realms, escaped Louis because Charles' daughter and heiress, Mary, married the German Prince Maximilian, Louis could now in safety pursue French internal reforms. He established a nearly absolute rule. The country was cleared of roaming and pillaging soldiers and brigands, and the army was reduced and subjected to strict control. Supreme jurisdiction was monopolized by the court, and the treasury was rebuilt through extreme parsimoniousness; royal domains were expanded at the cost of the remaining nobles, among whom the king shrewdly sowed discord; and the administration, confined to the hands of appointees of the king, was subjected to a previously unknown, extremely careful personal supervision.

England. England emerged from the Hundred Years' War in a more precarious position than France. Not only had she lost her Continental possessions except for Calais, but royal power was seriously undermined. Parliament, which continued to function and which exercised increasing control over the bureaucracy, veered in its actions in accordance with the changing fortunes of the great lords who fought for control of the government. The loot brought back by the English from France and Flanders was soon exhausted, and a soldiery accustomed to pillaging and in search of employment made the whole land insecure. The situation worsened when war broke out between two contending branches of the royal house (York and Lancaster)—the so-called "Wars of the Roses." In its course, both sides stained themselves with the ugliest acts of brutality, murder, and betrayal. Not until 1485 did the almost three-decade-long conflict end with the Battle of Bosworth Field. The last York king, Richard III, was killed; he had been a capable administrator who understood the trends of the times, the importance of the burghers, and the need for adjustment to new economic and international conditions. But political acts of treachery cost him his throne and life. His successor was Henry VII of the House of Tudor. Cunning and parsimonious like Louis XI of France, he regained power and authority for the crown. Peace returned; the abuses of protectionism, bribery, and nepotism were reduced; and the country was gradually opened to new economic prosperity and to the arts of peace which flourished on the Continent.

The Netherlands. Emphasis on trade and the emergence of a mercantile-capitalistic society particularly benefited the Netherlands. Despite their small size, the Low Countries had for a long time played a prominent role in the European economy, owing to the favorable location of their harbors and the importance of the Flemish textile industries. After the decline of Bruges toward the end of the fourteenth century, Antwerp had become one of Europe's greatest commercial centers. Lively connections extended from there to Venice, Milan, and Florence, to Nürnberg, Augsburg, and Frankfort, to Paris and Lyons, to London, Hull, and Bristol, and especially to the Hanseatic ports of Hamburg, Lübeck, and Danzig. Under the rule of the ambitious and luxury-loving Burgundian dukes, the Low Countries further improved their position. By the time the Modern Age began, Netherlands ships were leading in numbers on the northern East-West trade route, Netherlands merchants were among the richest of Europe, and Netherlands towns rivalled the Italian towns not only in business enterprise but also in style of living, in arts and music, and in the development of a refined Renaissance society.

CENTRAL AND EASTERN EUROPE

The circumstances which altered the political patterns in Western European countries did not have an equally strong effect on Central and Eastern Europe. Germany, Italy, Scandinavia, and Poland continued along more traditional lines and did not yet enter the "Modern Age" which Western Europe approached; and Russia could only begin to chart a national policy after she had gained independence from Tartar domination in 1480. Moreover, economic dislocations (caused by rising prices and depreciation of money) and the resulting social upheavals, which characterized the Western European economy in the second half of the fifteenth century, also affected Central and Eastern Europe. These difficulties were not counterbalanced by the advantages which nations on the Atlantic seaboard enjoyed.

The Empire. In Germany, expansion of mining and industry and pursuance of traditional trade objectives kept economic activity for the time being at a comparatively high level. Great banking enterprises were built up in southern Germany, masterful craftsmanship distinguished the goods produced in many towns (such as Nürnberg), and the ventures of the Hanseatic merchants still proved lucrative. Cultural interests also broadened. But conservatism, evinced by merchants and craftsmen, prevented, especially in the North, a timely conversion to modern methods. Competition of Netherlands ships reduced the share of the Hanse in the Baltic trade, and guilds and other medieval institutions retarded the growth of that type of business organization which proved successful and suitable for modern developments. Moreover, political conditions remained unfavorable. Not centralization but decentralization made headway. The electoral and other princes, as well as individual "free imperial towns," jealously watched over their old-fashioned liberties, while an emperor, Frederick III (d. 1493), ruled who lacked the qualities needed for his office. His was, unfortunately for Germany, the longest rule of any emperor. During his time, internal strife continued; foreign enemies infringed on the Empire's borders; and at one time the emperor had to give up even his own capital, Vienna. Only one political achievement can be traced to Frederick's reign—an achievement intended to increase the wealth and power of his family, but turning out to add enormous prestige also to the Empire as a whole and laying the basis for an unexpected restoration of Germany's leading position: the marriage of Frederick's son Maximilian to Mary, heiress of Burgundy. Through this marriage the rich Netherlands was added to the Hapsburg possessions.

Italy. The extraordinary evolution of the city-state, which Italy had witnessed since the end of the Crusades, came to its peak during the last decades of the Middle Ages. Perhaps the times of Venice's greatness (except for Renaissance art which flourished in

Venice later than in other parts of Italy) were already over; conservatism in business methods was as strong in Venice as among Hanse merchants, and the effects of the reorientation of overseas as well as of Continental trade and trade routes reduced Venice's prominence. But other cities—Milan and especially Florence—only then attained the full glory of their development. Tyrants continued to direct affairs through wealth, demagoguery, and intrigues; and though their methods were often divorced from accepted standards of Christian ethics, they were successful where wisdom and moderation prevailed. All of Europe was to learn from the examples they set—whether from a Sigismondo Malatesta of Rimini (d. 1467) who failed because he relied on mere force and artful display, or from a Giovanni de Medici (d. 1427) in Florence and his heirs Cosimo (d. 1469) and Lorenzo the Magnificent (d. 1492) who succeeded because a sober sense of reality directed their actions. As a "modern" entrepreneur as well as a politician, Giovanni had risen to the eminent position from which he could direct Florence's fate. While keeping up a pretense of popular control and adroitly managing public opinion, the Medici House directed the government unofficially for almost a century. Under its patronage, the arts flourished as well as business. In external affairs, the Medici exploited the rivalries of neighboring city-states, of the papacy, and of outside interests of German emperors and, later, of the French kings, and supported a system of "balance of power." This enabled the various Italian city-states, and especially Florence herself, to preserve their independence of the large powers.

Other parts of Italy, where city-states and the peculiar system of despots did not prevail, were less prosperous and set few examples. Southern Italy (under the Aragonese) and the Papal States continued to stagnate politically and economically, although Rome became a center of Humanism and of Renaissance art.

Eastern Europe. The Renaissance spirit spread from Italy and Germany eastward to Poland-Lithuania. Close cultural connections between this area and the West had long existed; the common Catholic faith had constituted a link, and thousands of German artisans had settled in Poland where, through their skills and habits, they had fertilized the civilization of numerous towns. Unlike the situation in Poland, however, almost no reflection of Renaissance culture can be traced in Orthodox Russia. Cultural achievements there were scarce.

POLAND-LITHUANIA. In the last part of the Middle Ages, Poland reaped the benefits of her union with Lithuania. In 1466, at Thorn, she could impose on the Teutonic Knights a peace which forced them to cede parts of western Prussia and to recognize Polish overlordship. Poland thereby became, at least for a while, Catholic Europe's eastern bulwark against Russian expansion—just as Hungary under its able king Matthias Corvinus (d. 1490) served after Constantinople's fall as a buffer against the Turks. The powerful German Hanse town of Danzig, which controlled the exit to the Baltic Sea and therewith the key to Poland's increasingly important grain trade, while retaining its German allegiance and its traditional German liberties, began to orient itself toward Poland. Unfortunately, social progress in Poland did not equal the country's political advance. A thin but important stratum of society was produced which was receptive to, if not very creative in, Renaissance scholarship and art. But this stratum, composed of a rich and luxury-loving nobility, an extravagant and arrogant clerical hierarchy, and a small merchant aristocracy, was faced by a large illiterate, destitute lower nobility, by poor, unlearned country priests, and a miserable and oppressed peasantry and town proletariat. These masses gained as little from political conquests as from the economic benefits which the expansion of the Polish grain market brought.

RUSSIA. At the end of the Middle Ages, Muscovy was ruled by Tsar Ivan the Great (1462–1505). Under him, the basis for Russia's future greatness was laid. Gradually, he incorporated one neighboring principality after another, also seizing the great port of Novgorod (Novgorod's trade was, however, ruined by the expulsion of the Hanse merchants). He asserted his authority over Church and nobility, carried out clerical reforms, and had a new law code drafted. Through a marriage with a Byzantine princess, he raised the prestige of his country; and through invitations to foreign craftsmen, doctors, and merchants, he introduced Western skills and techniques and improved the military strength and the wealth of his country. After putting an end to what was still left of Tartar control and suzerainty, he entered into diplomatic relations with Western powers. Nevertheless, Russia continued to develop along lines different from those of the Western world. Townsmen gained little influence; wealth remained concentrated in the hands of tsar, Church, and high nobility—all of whom maintained numerous economic monopolies. Serfdom, which decreased in the

West, was extended in Russia; and the monarchical structure there showed more similarity with Oriental despotism than with Western concepts.

CONCLUSION

The transition from Medieval to Modern Times was, of course, almost unnoticeable to the generations who lived through it. Like generations of all ages, they were only vaguely aware of the changes, and uncertain of the direction of existing trends; they felt the continuity more than the break. But in retrospect, the new aspects are evident. By 1500, the Western world possessed little of that unity which Roman traditions and Christian heritage had given to life and thought in the High Middle Ages. An individualistic spirit prevailed which expressed itself in the business ventures of enterprising men and the breakdown of the feudal class structure; in the growth of national feelings and the diversity of legal developments; in the challenge to traditional religious ideas and the spread of a scientific attitude toward nature; in the scholarly investigations of classical antiquity and the adoption of new standards for artistic creations; and most of all in the widening of the horizon of Western man. In the new age the West was to expand its activities beyond the borders known in the Middle Ages and to embrace, and dominate, all of the globe.

EXAMINATIONS

Careful study of precise answers to the following questions will prove helpful in preparing for examinations in almost any Western civilization course.

NOTE: Numbers in parentheses refer to pages on which pertinent information can be found.

Ancient Near East:

1. Discuss the relationship of state and religion in Ancient Egypt and in Sumer. (9–10, 14, 17, 24–25)

2. Describe the role of the Assyrians in history. (19, 26–27)

3. Describe the rise of the Persian Empire and give an account of Persian civilization. (28–29)

4. Give an account of some of the great artistic achievements of the Ancient Near East, which have survived into modern times. (13, 21, 26, 28)

5. Identify, or define; give the approximate date; and explain the significance of each of the following:
   1. Sargon of Akkad (12)
   2. The Hyksos (11, 23)
   3. Mycenae (21–23)
   4. Hammurabi (16–17)
   5. Thutmose III (24)
   6. Pyramids (8–9)
   7. Ikhnaton (23–24)
   8. Phoenicians (18–19)
   9. David (19)
   10. "Babylonian Captivity" of the Jews (29)

Greece:

6. Compare the religious concepts of the Greeks with those of the Hebrews and discuss the connection between Greek religion and the Greek *polis*. (29, 34, 43–44, 58)

7. Describe Greek Colonial expansion (31, 34, 61)

8. Contrast the Spartan and the Athenian systems of government. (34–39)

9. Give an account of the development of Greek science and the philosophy underlying it, pointing out essential differences between Greek and modern science. (40–41, 53–55, 65–66, 75)

10. Discuss Athenian imperialism, its extent and its consequences. (48–53)

11. Trace the constitutional developments in Athens from the time of Draco to the fall of Athens in 404 B.C. Discuss the limitations of tyranny in Athens as well as of subsequent aristocratic and democratic institutions there. (37–39, 49, 52–53)

12. Give an account of the changing social and economic patterns in Athens, including in your account a discussion of the influence which slavery, concentration of wealth, and exploitation of an empire exercised on Athenian society. (37–39, 50–57)

13. Describe the struggle for Greek unity in the fifth and fourth centuries B.C. (50–53, 60–63)

14. Identify, or define; give the approximate date; and explain the significance of each of the following:
    1. Peisistratus (32, 38)
    2. Themistocles and Aristides (47, 49)
    3. Alcibiades (52)
    4. Epaminondas (61–62)
    5. Demosthenes (63)
    6. Phidias (56)
    7. Praxiteles (64)
    8. Alcaeus (42)
    9. Euripides (57)
    10. Aristophanes (57)
    11. *Laocoön* (74)
    12. Delphic Oracle (44)
    13. Messenian Wars (34)
    14. Battle of Marathon (47)
    15. Delian League (50)
    16. Seleucid Empire (71)
    17. The "Hellenistic" Age (67, 72)

Rome:

15. Give a picture of Etruscan civilization and describe how it was gradually fused with that of Rome. (78, 79)

16. Describe the territorial expansion of Rome. (81–82, 83–84, 88, 90–96, 101, 106–108, 119, 123)

17. Discuss, step by step, the transformation in Rome of republican into imperial institutions during the century from the Gracchi to Augustus. (99–108, 111–113)

18. Trace the growth of a bureaucracy in Ancient Rome. (80, 82–83, 85–87, 102, 107–108, 111, 118, 125, 135–136)

19. Write an essay on, and illustrate by examples, the influence of Greek and Hellenic civilization on the political and cultural life in Rome. (97–98, 109–111, 115–116, 120, 127–129)

20. Contrast the social and economic order of Roman society in the times of the "good emperors" with (a) that in the times of Cicero, and (b) that in the times of the Republic around 300 B.C. (125–127, 130; 108–109; 85–88)

21. Discuss the forces helping to undermine the strength of the Roman Empire in the third and fourth centuries A.D. (130–132, 134–136, 138, 141)

22. Identify, or define; give the approximate date; and explain the significance of each of the following:
    1. The *Aeneid* (77, 115)
    2. Equestrian Order (96, 101–102, 104–106, 114, 118, 125–126)
    3. Centuriate Assembly (80, 87)
    4. Tribunes (82, 87, 99)
    5. First Triumvirate (106–107)
    6. Tarquin Superbus (77, 79)
    7. Coriolanus (77–78)
    8. Pyrrhus (90)
    9. Hamilcar (91)
    10. Gaius Gracchus (99)
    11. Titus (118, 121)
    12. Lucretius (110)
    13. Battles of Pharsalus, Philippi, and Actium (108, 111)
    14. Battle of the Teutoburg Forest (113)
    15. Edict of Milan (137)
    16. "Pax romana" (114, 123)
    17. Stoicism and Epicureanism (75, 116, 120, 128)

General:

23. What is the legacy which the Ancient World has left to Western civilization?

24. Arrange in chronological order and identify: (See Chronology, Tables of Memorable Statesmen, etc., and Index)

1. Homer, Vergil, Tacitus, Thucydides, Sappho, Cicero, Pindar, Horace, Sophocles
2. Pericles, Hammurabi, Caesar, Solomon, Ikhnaton, Darius the Great, Constantine the Great, Alexander the Great, Hannibal
3. Archimedes, Galen, Hippocrates, Euclid, Thales, Ptolemy, Pythagoras
4. Aristotle, Seneca, Buddha, Plato, Epicurus, Socrates, Apostle Paul, Confucius

MEDIEVAL TIMES

Early Middle Ages:

25. Describe the "barbarian invasions" of the Roman Empire, their impact upon the Empire, and the organization and fate of the new barbarian states. (141, 143–148, 152)

26. Trace the development of monasticism in the Christian Church. (140, 151, 161, 167–168)

27. What achievements of Charles, son of Pepin the Short, account for his being called "Charlemagne" or Charles the Great? What has survived of these achievements? (158–160)

28. Describe the rise of the political power of the Moslems and their territorial conquests. (152–155, 164)

29. Identify, or define; give the approximate date; and explain the significance of each of the following:
    1. Emperor Justinian (149)
    2. Council of Nicaea (137)
    3. The Huns (141, 143–144)
    4. Gregory the Great (151)
    5. Saint Jerome (150)
    6. Saint Benedict (151)
    7. Saint Boniface (155)
    8. Alcuin (161)
    9. Treaty of Verdun (160)
    10. The Vikings (162–165)

High Middle Ages:

30. What do we mean by "feudalism"? Discuss its political, social, and economic aspects during the tenth and eleventh centuries. (168–173, 202–205, 222, 243)

31. Describe the eastward expansion of the German Empire from the age of Otto the Great to that of Frederick II of Hohenstaufen. Point out both territorial and cultural aspects. (166, 176, 190–191, 195, 217–218, 251, 271)

32. Write an essay on the Crusades—their origins, their course, and their outcome. (186–188, 196–197, 209–210, 214, 216, 230)

33. Discuss in detail the internal political developments in France during the reign of King Philip II Augustus and in England under Henry II. Point out similarities and differences. (192–194, 215–216)

34. Write an essay on the intellectual developments of the twelfth and thirteenth centuries. (197–202, 224–228, 244–245)

35. Give an account of the policies of Innocent III, of his achievements and goals; then describe the policies of Boniface VIII and their fate; and finally, compare the position of the Catholic Church at the death of Innocent III in 1216 with that of a century later, after Boniface VIII's death. (207–209, 211, 214, 217, 225–226, 230–232)

36. Give a survey of thirteenth-century international trade and commerce; describe their organization, the great trade routes, the chief types of commodities, the exchange facilities, etc. (219–221, 223, 240–242)

37. Identify, or define; give the approximate date; and explain the significance of each of the following:
1. Otto the Great (165–166)
2. Frederick Barbarossa (191)
3. Eleanor of Aquitaine (192, 194)
4. Philip IV (the Fair) (234–235)
5. Edward I (237–238)
6. Cluny (167–168, 177)
7. Investiture Struggle (177, 179, 190, 193)
8. The Cistercians (186)
9. The Inquisition (208–209)
10. Albigensian Crusade (208)
11. "Ministeriales" (176, 191–192)
12. Magna Charta (217)
13. Scholasticism (183, 198, 224–225, 244–245)
14. Abelard (198)
15. Marco Polo (223)
16. Troubadours and Minnesänger (201, 227–228)
17. Romanesque and Gothic Architecture (184–185, 202, 226–227)

Late Middle Ages:

38. Describe the civil wars in France, England, and Bohemia in the fourteenth and fifteenth centuries, their social and religious background, and their outcome. (249–250, 253–254, 256, 258–259)

39. Give an account of the legal and constitutional development of England from the times of King John to those of Henry IV. Compare it with the contemporary developments in France. (215, 217, 234–236, 237–238, 248–250)

40. Describe the decline of serfdom in the late Middle Ages (204–205, 222–223, 242–243, 246, 256–259)

41. Discuss the political conditions in Italy from the outbreak of the Black Death to the times of Lorenzo de Medici. (248, 270–271)

42. How can we justify the expressions "Waning of the Middle Ages" and "Dawn of a New Era" when applied to the political and cultural life of the West in the fourteenth and fifteenth centuries? (245–247, 252–253, 256–257, 259–261, 265–267, 269–270, 273)

43. Identify, or define; give the approximate date; and explain the significance of each of the following:
1. Boniface VIII (230–231)
2. "Babylonian Captivity" of the Church (231–232, 253–255)
3. Council of Constance (254–255)
4. Guilds (203–205, 222, 240–242, 250–252, 270–272)
5. Hanseatic League (219–220, 242, 250–252, 270–272)
6. "Golden Bull" (233)
7. Hundred Years' War (235–236, 238, 243, 248–250, 257–258)
8. Wars of the Roses (268–269)
9. Giotto (244)
10. Petrarch (260)
11. "Renaissance" (247, 252, 259–265)
12. Fall of Constantinople (252, 272)
13. Gutenberg (265)

General:

44. Trace the history of "heresy" from the times of Bishop Arius to those of Huss.

45. Numerous changes occurred in the course of the five centuries from the eleventh to the fifteenth in the political structure of Europe and in the conditions of the feudal nobility, the Church, the townsmen, and the peasants. Describe these changes and show how they contributed to the gradual shift from an agricultural, feudal, ecclesiastical culture to an urban, national, and secular culture.

46. Write an essay on the influence of Church and religion on the art and architecture, and on education, literature, philosophy, and science of the Middle Ages.

47. Give an account of the artistic and literary legacy which the Middle Ages left to Modern Times.

48. Arrange in chronological order and identify: (See Chronological Tables Tables of Memorable Statesmen etc., and Index)

A. Saint Augustine, Thomas Aquinas, Wycliffe, Master Eckhart, Saint Francis, Bernhard of Clairvaux, Roscellinus.

B. Frederick II of Hohenstaufen, Saint Louis of France, William the Conqueror, Saint Vladimir, Gregory VII, Sultan Saladin, Gregory the Great, Lorenzo de Medici, Charlemagne.

SOME MEMORABLE RULERS, STATESMEN, SCHOLARS, AND ARTISTS

B.C.	Greek and Hellenic			Roman		Various
	Rulers and Statesmen	Scholars and Poets	Artists	Rulers and Statesmen	Scholars and Poets	
IX Century		Homer Hesiod				
VIII Century				[Romulus]		Isaiah
VII Century	Draco [Lycurgus]	Alcaeus Sappho				
VI Century	Solon Peisistratus Cleisthenes	Anacreon Anaximander Thales Pythagoras		Tarquin Superbus		Jeremiah Zoroaster Confucius Lao-tse Buddha
V Century	Miltiades Aristides Themistocles Cimon Pericles Alcibiades	Pindar Herodotus Aeschylus Sophocles Euripides Thucydides Socrates Anaxagoras Empedocles Heraclitus	Phidias			
IV Century	Dionysius I of Syracuse Epaminondas Philip II Alexander the Great	Plato Aristotle Hippocrates Democritus Euclid	Praxiteles			

Century						
III Century	Ptolemy I Seleucus Pyrrhus	Epicurus Zeno (Stoic) Archimedes		Scipio the Elder		Hannibal
II Century		Polybius		Cato the Elder Tiberius and Gaius Gracchus	Terence Plautus	.
I Century				Marius Sulla Pompey Caesar Antony	Catullus Cicero Lucretius Horace Vergil	
A.D.						
I Century				Tiberius Nero Vespasian	Ovid Livy Seneca	Apostles
II Century		Ptolemy Plutarch Galen		Trajan Hadrian Marcus Aurelius	Tacitus Juvenal Suetonius	
III Century				Aurelian Diocletian	Ulpian	Origen Tertullian Cyprian
IV Century				Constantine Julian the Apostate Theodosius		Eusebius John Chrysostom St. Anthony St. Basil

283

SOME MEMORABLE CHURCHMEN, SCHOLARS AND ARTISTS

A.D.	Theology—Philosophy, Science History	Literature	Painting Book-Illust.	Architecture Sculpture	Music
V Century	St. Augustine St. Jerome St. Patrick				
VI Century	St. Benedict Gregory the Great	Boethius Gregory of Tours			
VII Century		Isidore of Seville			
VIII Century	St. Boniface	Bede Paul the Deacon (*Beowulf*)			
IX Century		Alcuin Einhard Strabo Johannes Scotus	(*Carolingian* Renaissance)		
X Century	Gerbert of Rheims		(*Ottonian* Renaissance)		(Musical Notation)
XI Century	Gregory VII Lanfranc Anselm of Canterbury	Avicenna (Arab) Roscellinus (*Chanson de Roland*)	(*Romanesque* Style)		

Century				(Painting)	(Sculpture)	(Music)
XII Century	St. Bernard Abelard Hugh of St. Victor Joachim of Flores	Otto von Freising Ordericus Vitalis Edrisi (Arab) Averroës (Arab) Maimonides (Jew) William of Malmesbury	Chrétien de Troyes Bertran de Born (Troubadour) (Nibelungenlied)	(Romanesque Style)		Thomas of Celano Jacopone da Todi
XIII Century	St. Francis St. Dominick Innocent III Albertus Magnus St. Thomas	Villehardouin Saxo Grammaticus Matthew Paris Roger Bacon	Walther von der Vogelweide Wolfram von Eschenbach Gottfried von Strassburg	(Gothic Style) Cimabue	Niccolo Pisano	
XIV Century	Master Eckhart Wycliffe	Marsilius of Padua William of Occam	Dante Boccaccio Petrarch William Langland Chaucer	(Gothic Style) (Early Renaissance Style) Duccio Giotto	Giovanni Pisano	
XV Century	Huss Thomas à Kempis	Ibn Khaldun (Arab) Froissart Nicolas of Cusa Johann Müller Regiomontanus	Francois Villon Gutenberg (Printer)	(Renaissance) Masaccio Fra Angelico Botticelli Leonardo della Robbia van Eyck Memling Rublev (Russian Icons)	Ghiberti Donatello Brunelleschi Verrochio	Dufay

285

SOME MEMORABLE RULERS

A.D.	Germanic Kingdoms		England	Eastern Europe	Popes	Various
V Century	Alaric (Visigoths)				Leo the Great	
VI Century	Theodoric (Ostrogoths) Clovis (Franks)			Justinian (East Rome)	Gregory the Great	
VII Century	Pepin of Heristal (Franks)					
VIII Century	Charles Martel (Franks) Pepin the Short (Franks)			Leo the Isaurian (East Rome)		
IX Century	Charlemagne		Alfred the Great		Leo III	Harun al-Rashid (Arabs)
	Germany Holy Roman Emp.	**France**				
X Century	(House of *Saxony*) Otto the Great	Hugh *Capet*		St. Vladimir (Russia)		

Century						
XI Century	(House of *Franconia*) Henry III Henry IV		Canute the Great William the Conqueror	Yaroslav the Wise (Russia) Boleslav the Bold (Poland) St. Stephen (Hungary)	Gregory VII	
XII Century	(House of *Hohenstaufen*) Frederick I Barbarossa Henry VI	Louis VI	Henry II	Vladimir II (Russia)	Alexander III	Saladin (Turks)
XIII Century	Frederick II Rudolf of *Hapsburg*	Philip II Augustus St. Louis	Edward I	Alexander Nevsky (Muscovy)	Innocent III Boniface VIII	Genghis Khan (Tartars)
XIV Century	Charles IV	Philip IV Philip VI of *Valois*	Edward III	Jagiello (Lithuania) Dimitri Donskoy (Muscovy)		Tamerlane (Tartars)
XV Century	Maximilian I of *Hapsburg*	Louis XI Charles VIII	Henry IV (*Lancaster*) Richard III (*York*) Henry VII (*Tudor*)	Matthias Corvinus (Hungary) Ivan the Great (Russia)	Martin V Pius II Sixtus IV	Ferdinand and Isabella (Spain) Lorenzo de Medici

CHRONOLOGY

Man's limited faculties make it difficult for him to grasp the sequence of events, to recognize their interrelationships and, possibly, to gain a glimpse of "evolution" and "causes and results" in history. He has therefore attempted to arrange his material with the help of dates. Dates reveal connections and parallels; they furnish us with a basis for comparisons, which make historical studies meaningful and exciting.

The following Chronological Tables should be used in connection with the index (which refers the reader to the pages on which the persons and events here mentioned are described at greater length) and particularly also in connection with the Tables of Memorable Rulers, Statesmen, Scholars, and Artists.

B.C.

3200–2300 EGYPT'S "EARLY KINGDOM"

ca. 3200	Reign of Menes (First Dynasty) of Egypt

ca. 3000 UNIFICATION OF MESOPOTAMIA (SUMER)

ca. 3000	Development of Wheel (in Sumer?)
	Development of Cuneiform Writing
3000–2200	EARLY MINOAN CIVILIZATION (Crete)
ca. 3000	Building of First Pyramid (Imhotep)
ca. 2800	Egyptian Calendar
ca. 2650	Reign of Cheops (Fourth Dynasty) of Egypt
ca. 2600	Reign of Messanipada of Sumer
ca. 2500	Reign of Eannatum of Sumer
ca. 2350	Reign of Sargon of Akkad
ca. 2300	Reign of Pepi II (Sixth Dynasty) of Egypt
2300–2000	Time of Troubles in Egypt
2200–1600	MIDDLE MINOAN CIVILIZATION

2000–1800 EGYPT'S "MIDDLE KINGDOM"

ca. 2000	Reign of Dungi (Shulgi) in Mesopotamia
	Early Codex of Law and Epic of Gilgamesh in Mesopotamia

B.C.

2000–1200	HITTITE EMPIRE
1950	**Babylonian** Invasion of Sumer
ca. 1900	Early Semitic Writing developed
1800–1100	ACHAEAN, IONIAN, AND DORIC INVASIONS OF GREECE AND AEGEAN ISLANDS
1800–1500	Minoan Culture at Peak
1792–1749	Reign of **Hammurabi** (Law Code) in Mesopotamia
1700–1570	Hyksos Rule in Egypt

1570–1085 EGYPT'S "NEW KINGDOM"

ca. 1570	Reign of Ahmose I (Eighteenth Dynasty) of Egypt
1550–*ca.* 1150	Babylon under Hittite Rule
ca. 1490–1436	Reign of Thutmose III of Egypt
ca. 1411–1375	Reign of Amenemhet III of Egypt
ca. 1400	Crete invaded by Mycenaeans
1400–1184	MYCENAEAN CULTURE
ca. 1369–1353	Reign of **Ikhnaton** of Egypt
ca. 1352–1344	Reign of Tutankhamen of Egypt
ca. 1300	Hebrews leave Egypt, invade Palestine
ca. 1292–1225	Reign of Ramses II (Nineteenth Dynasty) of Egypt

ca. 1247   ASSYRIANS TAKE AND DESTROY BABYLON

ca. 1200–800	INDEPENDENT STATE OF PHOENICIANS
ca. 1195–1167	Reign of Ramses III (Twentieth Dynasty) of Egypt
1184	Conquest of Troy by Achaeans
ca. 1100	Phoenician Alphabet developed
1114–1078	Tiglath-pileser I of Assyria
ca. 1005–965	Reign of **David** of Israel and Judah
ca. 965–925	Reign of Solomon of Israel and Judah
ca. 900	EARLY ETRUSCAN CIVILIZATION IN ITALY
ca. 883–859	Assyrian Conquest of Syria and Palestine
ca. 850	Carthage founded by Phoenicians
ca. 800	**Homer** and Hesiod

776   FIRST OLYMPIC GAMES (legendary) IN GREECE

767–686	Isaiah, Jewish Prophet

B.C.

753 LEGENDARY FOUNDING OF ROME

745–727	Reign of Tiglath-pileser III of Assyria
725–705	Sparta subdues Messenians
722	Israel conquered by Assyrians
722–705	Reign of Sargon II of Assyria
709	ASSYRIANS TAKE BABYLON
705–681	Reign of Sennacherib of Assyria
668–633	Reign of Ashurbanipal III of Assyria
663–609	Reign of Psamtik I (Twenty-Sixth Dynasty) of Egypt
641–586	Jeremiah, Jewish Prophet
625–605	Reign of Nabopolassar of Babylon
ca. 621	Draco's Legislation in Athens
612	Nineveh taken by Babylonians (Chaldaeans) and destroyed
604–562	Reign of Nebuchadrezzar of Babylon
ca. 600	Legendary Legislation of Lycurgus in Sparta

594 SOLON'S LEGISLATION IN ATHENS

586	Judaea conquered by Babylonians; Jews abducted into Captivity
569–546	REIGN OF KING CROESUS OF LYDIA
560–527	Rule of **Peisistratus** in Athens
549–529	Reign of Cyrus II of Persia
546	Death of Thales
545	Cyrus II of Persia conquers Greek Asiatic Settlements
539	Cyrus II of Persia conquers Babylon
536	Return of Jews from Babylonian Captivity
529–522	Reign of Cambyses II of Persia
525	CONQUEST OF EGYPT BY PERSIANS
521–486	Reign of Darius I of Persia

510 EXPULSION OF PEISISTRATUS' SON FROM ATHENS

509 LEGENDARY EXPULSION OF TARQUIN SUPERBUS FROM ROME

508	Reforms in Athens under Cleisthenes
507	Death of Pythagoras

B.C.

492–479   GREEK-PERSIAN WARS

490	Battle of Marathon (Miltiades)
485–465	Reign of Xerxes of Persia
483	Aristides ostracized
480	Battle of Thermopylae (Leonidas)
	Battle of Salamis (**Themistocles**)
479	Battle of Plataea (Pausanias)
478	DELIAN LEAGUE FOUNDED
470	Themistocles ostracized
ca. 466	Naval Battle of Eurymedon
464	Earthquake in Sparta
461	Cimon ostracized
458	Cincinnatus, Roman Dictator
456	Death of Aeschylus
ca. 450	"Twelve Tables" Legislation in Rome
449	Death of Cimon
447	Athens' Defeat at Coronea
	Office of Quaestor established in Rome
445	"Thirty Years Peace" between Athens and Sparta
	Intermarriage of Patricians and Plebeians permitted in Rome
443	Office of Censor established in Rome
438	Death of Pindar

431–404   PELOPONNESIAN WAR

429	Death of **Pericles**
428	Death of Herodotus
ca. 422	Battle of Amphipolis (Cleon)
421	Truce of Nicias
420	Quaestorship opened to Plebeians in Rome
417	Death of Phidias
415–413	SICILIAN EXPEDITION OF ATHENS
410	Enslavement for Debt prohibited in Rome
406–367	Reign of Dionysius I, Tyrant of Syracuse
406	Battle of Arginusian Islands (Alcibiades)
	Death of Sophocles and Euripides
405	Battle of Aegospotami (Lysander)
404	FALL OF ATHENS
404–403	Rule of "Thirty Tyrants" in Athens
400	Death of Thucydides

B.C.

399 DEATH OF SOCRATES

392	Veii taken by Romans
390	ROME TAKEN BY GAULS
387	"Academy" of **Plato** founded in Athens
385	Death of Aristophanes
377	Death of Hippocrates
371	VICTORY OF THEBES AT LEUCTRA
367	New Social Legislation in Rome; Plebeians admitted to consulship
362	Battle of Mantinea; Death of Epaminondas
359–336	Reign of **Philip II** of Macedonia
348	Roman Trade Treaty with Carthage
347	Death of Plato
347–341	First Samnite War
338	Battle of Chaeronea; *End of Greek Independence*

336 – 323 REIGN OF ALEXANDER THE GREAT

334	Alexander defeats Persians at the Granicus
333	Alexander defeats Persians at Issus
	Conquest of Egypt by Alexander
331	Battle of Gaugamela; Conquest of Persia by Alexander
330–325	Alexander's Campaigns in Central Asia and India
330	Rome begins to coin Money
326–304	Second Samnite War
323–322	Lamian War; Greeks rebel against Macedonia (Antipater)
322	Death of **Aristotle**
ca. 310	Death of Praxiteles
305–283	Reign of Ptolemy I in Egypt
305–281	Reign of Seleucus I in Asia Minor
301	BATTLE OF IPSUS
298–290	Third Samnite War
281–261	Reign of Antiochus I of Seleucid Empire
287	Secession of Roman Plebs; Legislation put in hands of Assembly of Tribes
ca. 285	Death of Euclid
282–275	Pyrrhic Wars
271	Death of Epicurus

B.C.

B.C.

86	Revolts in Italy; Death of Marius
83	Return of Sulla; Civil War, Proscriptions

82–79 DICTATORSHIP OF SULLA

80–72	Revolts in Spain (Pompey against Sertorius)
74–63	Second Mithradatic War
73–71	SPARTACUS RISING
69	Victory over Mithradates at Tigranocerta (Lucullus)
67	**Pompey** destroys Pirates on the Mediterranean
64	Subjection of Judaea
63	Consulate of **Cicero**
63–62	Rising of Catiline
63	Conquest of Pontus by Pompey

60 FIRST TRIUMVIRATE (POMPEY, CAESAR, CRASSUS)

58–51	Caesar's Conquest of Gaul
54	Death of Catullus
53	Defeat against the Parthians at Carrhae; Crassus killed
49	CAESAR CROSSES THE RUBICON AND SEIZES ROME
48	Battle of Pharsalus; Pompey defeated, flees, and is killed in Egypt
48–47	Caesar and Cleopatra; Incorporation of Egypt
47	Caesar Dictator; Suicide of Cato the Younger
46	Introduction of Julian Calendar

44 ASSASSINATION OF CAESAR

43	*Second Triumvirate* (Octavius, Antony, Lepidus)
	Murder of Cicero
42	Battle of Philippi; Brutus and Cassius commit suicide

31 BATTLE OF ACTIUM; OCTAVIUS DEFEATS ANTONY AND CLEOPATRA

30	Egypt becomes a Roman Province
27	Octavius becomes "Augustus"

B.C.

19	Death of Vergil
8	Death of Horace
4	Birth of Christ

A.D.

9	ROMAN DEFEAT IN GERMANY (TEUTOBURG FOREST)
14	Death of Augustus
14–37	Reign of Tiberius
17	Death of Livy
	Death of Ovid
37–41	Reign of Caligula
41–54	Reign of Claudius
43	BRITAIN BECOMES A ROMAN PROVINCE
54–68	Reign of Nero
64	Fire in Rome; Persecution of Christians
65	Death of Seneca
69–79	Reign of Vespasian
70	Destruction of Temple in Jerusalem by Titus
79–81	Reign of Titus
79	Eruption of Vesuvius; Death of Pliny the Elder
81–96	Reign of Domitian

98–117 REIGN OF TRAJAN

101–106	DACIAN WARS
114–117	PARTHIAN WARS
117	Death of Tacitus
117–138	Reign of Hadrian
ca. 120	Death of Plutarch
130	Death of Juvenal
131–134	War against the Jews; Destruction of Jewish State
138–161	Reign of Antoninus Pius
ca. 140	Death of Suetonius
ca. 160	Ptolemy, the Geographer
161–180	Reign of **Marcus Aurelius**
180–193	Reign of Commodus
193–211	Reign of Septimius Severus
199	Death of Galen

A.D.

211–217	Reign of Caracalla
222–235	Reign of Alexander Severus
228	Death of Ulpian, the Jurist
230	Death of Tertullian
249–251	Reign of Decius
249–250	PERSECUTION OF CHRISTIANS
253	Germanic (Gothic) Invasion of the Empire
254	Death of Origen
258	Death of St. Cyprian
270–275	Reign of Aurelian
284–305	Reign of **Diocletian**
301	Diocletian's Price Edict
303	Persecution of Christians
307	**Constantine** becomes "Augustus"
312	Battle of the Milvian Bridge

313 EDICT OF MILAN

324–337	Reign of Constantine as sole Emperor

325 COUNCIL OF NICAEA

340	Death of Eusebius of Caesarea
356	Death of St. Anthony
361–363	REIGN OF JULIAN THE APOSTATE
373	St. Ambrose becomes Bishop of Milan

375 INVASION OF EUROPE BY THE HUNS; MIGRATIONS OF THE GERMANIC PEOPLES

378	Battle of Adrianople; Visigoths invade Roman Empire
378–395	Reign of Emperor Theodosius
381	Council of Constantinople
395	FINAL DIVISION OF ROMAN EMPIRE
397	Death of St. Ambrose
410	Sack of Rome by Visigoths
420	Death of St. Jerome
429	Vandals invade Africa
430	Death of **St. Augustine**
440–461	Reign of Pope Leo I, the Great
449	ANGLES AND SAXONS SETTLE IN ENGLAND
ca. 450	St. Patrick in Ireland
451	Council of Chalcaedon

451	Defeat of Huns on the *Catalaunian Fields*
452	Invasion of Italy by Huns
471–526	**Theodoric,** King of Ostrogoths

476   END OF WEST ROMAN EMPIRE

481–511	Reign of **Clovis,** King of Franks
486	Franks conquer Gaul
488	Ostrogoths begin conquest of Italy
507	Visigoths in Spain
524	Death of Boethius
527–565	Emperor **Justinian** of the East Roman Empire
534	Justinian's Law Code completed
	End of Vandal Kingdom in Africa
543	Death of St. Benedict
ca. 555	END OF OSTROGOTH KINGDOM IN ITALY
568	Invasion of Northern Italy by Lombards
590–604	Reign of Pope Gregory the Great

622   THE "HEGIRA"; FLIGHT OF MOHAMMED FROM MECCA TO MEDINA

626	Defeat of Persians by Heraclius
632	Death of Mohammed
636	Moslems conquer Syria
638	Moslems conquer Jerusalem
642	Moslems conquer Egypt
687–714	PEPIN OF HERISTAL, MAYORDOMO OF THE FRANKISH KINGS
698	Moslems seize Carthage
711	MOSLEMS CROSS GIBRALTAR INTO EUROPE
713	End of Visigoth Rule in Spain
714–741	Charles Martel, Mayordomo of Frankish Kings
717–741	Reign of Leo III, the Isaurian, in East Rome; Iconoclasm
732	BATTLE OF TOURS AND POITIERS; RETREAT OF MOSLEMS
735	Death of St. Bede
751	**Pepin the Short** becomes King of the Franks
754	Donation of Pepin (Papal States)
	Death of St. Boniface
768–814	Reign of Charlemagne

774	Conquest of Langobard Kingdom by Charlemagne
775–815	Expansion of Carolingian Empire into Bavaria, Saxony
795–816	Reign of Pope Leo III

800 CHARLEMAGNE CROWNED EMPEROR

809	Death of Harun al-Raschid (Bagdad)
825–870	VIKING INVASIONS OF IRELAND AND ENGLAND
827	Moslems establish themselves in Sicily

843 TREATY OF VERDUN; DIVISION OF CAROLINGIAN EMPIRE

862	Vikings (Northmen) in Russia; Rurik in Novgorod
870	Treaty of Mersen; Charlemagne's Empire redivided
871–899	Reign of Alfred the Great in England
885	Vikings at the Gates of Paris
906	MAGYAR INVASION OF CENTRAL EUROPE
910	Founding of Cluny Monastery
911	Viking Rule of Normandy
919–936	Reign of Henry I (of Saxony) in Germany
936–973	Reign of Otto the Great in Germany
955	DEFEAT OF MAGYARS ON THE LECHFELD
960	Beginnings of a Polish Kingdom

962 OTTO THE GREAT OF GERMANY CROWNED EMPEROR

987–996	Reign of Hugh Capet in France
988	INTRODUCTION OF CHRISTIANITY IN RUSSIA (ST. VLADIMIR)
992–1025	Reign of Boleslav I of Poland
997–1038	Reign of Stephen I of Hungary
ca. 1000	Introduction of Christianity in Norway
1015–1054	Reign of Yaroslav the Wise of Russia
1016–1035	Reign of Canute the Great in Denmark and England
1035	Establishment of Kingdoms of Aragon, Castile, and Leon in Northern (Christian) Spain
1039–1056	Reign of Emperor Henry III (House of Franconia)

1248	Christian Spaniards take Seville
1248–1254	Seventh Crusade
1254–1273	"INTERREGNUM" IN GERMANY
1259	BEGINNINGS OF RISE OF HANSEATIC LEAGUE
1261	End of Latin Empire of Constantinople
1266	Charles of Anjou becomes King of Sicily
1270	EIGHTH CRUSADE; DEATH OF ST. LOUIS
1271–1295	**Marco Polo's Travels** in Asia and China
1272–1307	Reign of Edward I of England
1273–1291	Reign of Emperor Rudolf of Hapsburg
1274	Death of **Thomas Aquinas**
	Second Council of Lyons
1282	Sicilian Vespers
1285–1314	Reign of Philip IV of France
1291	Beginnings of Swiss Confederation
	Fall of Acre, last Christian Bastion in the Holy Land
1294–1303	Reign of Pope Boniface VIII
1295	"MODEL PARLIAMENT" CONVOKED IN ENGLAND
1302	Papal Bull: *Unam Sanctam*
	Convocation of States General in France
1307–1314	Destruction of Order of Templars in France

1309–1377 "BABYLONIAN CAPTIVITY" OF THE CHURCH (AVIGNON)

1314	Scottish Victory over English at Bannockburn
1320	Kiev conquered by Lithuanians
1321	Death of **Dante**
1327	Death of Meister Eckhart
1328–1350	Reign of Philip VI Valois in France
1337	Death of Giotto
1337–1453	"HUNDRED YEARS' WAR" BETWEEN FRANCE AND ENGLAND
1338	Diet of Rense regulating Imperial Elections in Germany
1340	English King Edward III claims throne of France
1346	Defeat of the French at Crécy
	Sale of Estonia to the Livonian Knights by Denmark
1346–1378	Reign of Emperor Charles IV

1348 OUTBREAK OF THE BLACK DEATH

1353	Statute of Praemunire in England
1356	Defeat of French at Poitiers
	"Golden Bull" issued by Emperor Charles IV
1357	Turks conquer Adrianople
1358	Outbreak of Jacquerie in France
1370	PEACE OF STRALSUND BETWEEN HANSEATIC LEAGUE AND DENMARK
1374	Death of **Petrarch**
1378	Revolts in Florence
1380	Defeat of Tartars on the Don River
1381	Beginning of Revolts of Peasants and Lollards in England
1384	Death of Wycliffe
1385	Pragmatic Sanction published in France
1386	UNION OF POLAND AND LITHUANIA
1397	UNION OF KALMAR BETWEEN DENMARK, NORWAY, AND SWEDEN
1399–1413	Reign of Henry IV (Lancaster) in England
1400	Death of Chaucer
1409	John Huss, Rector of the University of Prague
	COUNCIL OF PISA
1410	Defeat of Teutonic Knights at Tannenberg
1414–1418	COUNCIL OF CONSTANCE
1415	Huss burned at Stake

1417 END OF SCHISM IN CATHOLIC CHURCH; POPE MARTIN V ELECTED

1420–1436	Hussite Wars
1426	Death of Hubert van Eyck
1429	St. Joan: Siege of Orléans raised
1431	**St. Joan** burned at Stake
1431–1449	COUNCIL OF BASEL
1434–1464	Cosimo de Medici, Ruler in Florence
1438–1439	COUNCIL OF FERRARA-FLORENCE
1438	Pragmatic Sanction in France; Rights of the Gallican Church asserted
1440	*Platonic Academy* founded in Florence
1440–1452	Introduction of Printing with Movable Type (**Gutenberg**)
1450–1466	Francesco Sforza, Ruler in Milan

1453 CAPTURE OF CONSTANTINOPLE BY THE TURKS

1453	End of Hundred Years' War; English surrender at Bordeaux
1455	Death of Ghiberti and Fra Angelico
1455–1483	WARS OF THE ROSES IN ENGLAND
1458–1490	Reign of Matthias Corvinus in Hungary
1458–1464	Reign of Pope Pius II (Aeneas Silvio Piccolomini)
1460	Death of Prince Henry the Navigator of Portugal
1461–1483	Reign of Louis XI of France
1462–1505	Reign of Ivan the Great of Russia (*Muscovy*)
1466	Death of Donatello
	Peace of Thorn between Poland and Teutonic Knights
1469–1492	Rule of Lorenzo il Magnifico of Medici in Florence
1477	Death of Charles the Bold of Burgundy; Marriage of Mary of Burgundy and Maximilian of Hapsburg
1479	UNION OF ARAGON AND CASTILE UNDER FERDINAND AND ISABELLA
1480	End of Tartar Rule in Russia
1485	Richard III of England killed; Henry VII (Tudor) becomes King
1487	Diaz rounds Cape of Good Hope

1492 COLUMBUS DISCOVERS AMERICA

BIBLIOGRAPHY

The following bibliography is confined to the listing of a few general history books and a few others of perhaps uncommon interest. It includes only works in English which are rather easily available. It should be used in connection with the bibliographies given in the various textbooks which are listed in the correlating tables on pp. x–xvii. Most of these bibliographies are subdivided to render orientation easy, and some also discuss the merits of the works listed.

ANCIENT HISTORY

A. BIBLIOGRAPHY:

A. Nairn's Classical Hand-List, ed. B. H. Blackwell. Oxford, 1939.

B. SOME GENERAL HISTORIES:

Albright, William F. From the Stone Age to Christianity. Baltimore, 1940.
Breasted, James H. Ancient Times. Boston, 1935.
———. Dawn of Conscience. New York, 1934.
Cambridge Ancient History.
Cary, Max et al. Oxford Classical Dictionary. Oxford, 1949.
Rostovtzeff, Mikhail. A History of the Ancient World. 2 vols. New York, 1926–29.
Scramuzza, Vincent M., and P. L. MacKendrick. The Ancient World, New York, 1958.
Swain, Joseph W. The Ancient World. 2 vols. New York, 1950.
Thomson, J. O. History of Ancient Geography. Cambridge, 1948.
Trever, Albert A. History of Ancient Civilization. New York, 1936.

C. SOME HISTORIES BY REGIONS:

Near East:

Albright, William F. The Archaeology of Palestine. London, 1949.
Breasted, James H. History of Egypt. New York, 1935.

Chiera, Edward. *They Wrote on Clay*. Chicago, 1956.

Delaporte, Louis J. *Mesopotamia: The Babylonian and Assyrian Civilization*. New York, 1925.

Frankfort, Henri. *The Birth of Civilization in the Near East*. London, 1951.

Glotz, Gustave. *The Aegean Civilization*. New York, 1925.

Guerney, O. *The Hittites*. Harmondsworth, 1952.

Meek, Theophile J. *Hebrew Origins*. New York, 1936.

Mylonas, George. *Ancient Mycenae*. Princeton, 1957.

Moscati, Sabatino. *Ancient Semitic Civilizations*. New York, 1957.

Olmstead, Albert T. *History of Assyria*. New York, 1923.

――――. *History of the Persian Empire*. Chicago, 1948.

Wilson, John A. *The Culture of Ancient Egypt*. 1951.

Greece:

POLITICAL HISTORY:

Bury, John B. *History of Greece*. New York, 1951.

――――. *The Hellenistic Age*. New York, 1923.

Michell, Humphrey. *Sparta*. New York, 1952.

Robinson, Charles A. *Hellenic History*. New York, 1956.

Tarn, William W. *Hellenistic Civilization*. New York, 1952.

ECONOMIC AND SOCIAL HISTORY:

Glotz, Gustave. *The Greek City and its Institutions*. New York, 1930.

Jones, Arnold H. M. *Athenian Democracy*. Oxford, 1957.

Larsen, Jakob A. O. *Representative Government in Greek and Roman History*. Berkeley, 1955.

Michell, Humphrey. *The Economics of Ancient Greece*. New York, 1940.

Rostovtzeff, Mikhail. *The Social and Economic History of the Hellenistic World*. 3 vols. Oxford, 1941.

Zimmern, Alfred E. *The Greek Commonwealth*. Oxford, 1931.

HISTORY OF ART, MUSIC, AND LITERATURE:

Beazley, John D., and Ashmole, B. *Greek Sculpture and Painting*. Cambridge, 1932.

Dinsmoor, William B. *The Architecture of Ancient Greece*. New York, 1950.

Gardner, Ernest A. *A Handbook of Greek Sculpture*. London, 1915.

Plommer, Hugh. *Ancient and Classical Architecture*. London, 1956.

Rose, Herbert J. *A Handbook of Greek Literature*. London, 1948.

Sachs, Curt. *The Rise of Music in the Ancient World*. New York, 1943.

History of Religion, Philosophy, and Science:

Burnet, John. *Early Greek Philosophy*. New York, 1930.

Grube, Georges M. A. *Plato's Thought*. London, 1935.

More, Paul E. *Hellenistic Philosophies*. Princeton, 1923.

Mure, Geoffrey R. G. *Aristotle*. New York, 1932.

Nilsson, Martin P. *A History of Greek Religion*. Oxford, 1949.

Sarton, George. *A History of Science*. Cambridge, 1952.

Taylor, Alfred E. *Socrates*. Boston, 1951.

Biography:

Mackenzie, Compton. *Pericles*. London, 1937.

Robinson, Charles A. *Alexander the Great*. New York, 1947.

Sources:

Loeb Classical Library. Cambridge, Mass.

The Oxford Book of Greek Verse in Translation. Oxford, 1938.

Rome:

Political History:

Boak, Arthur E. R. *A History of Rome*. New York, 1955.

Charlesworth, Martin P. *The Roman Empire*. New York, 1951.

Jones, Henry S. *The Roman Empire, 29 B.C. to 476 A.D.* 1908.

Marsh, Frank B. *A History of the Roman World, 146–30 B.C.* London, 1951.

Mommsen, Theodor. *A History of Rome*. New York, 1958.

Pallottino, Massimo. *The Etruscans. Harmondsworth,* 1955.

Salmon, Edward. *A History of the Roman World, 30 B.C. to 138 A.D.* London, 1950.

Economic and Social History:

Carcopino, Jerome. *Daily Life in Ancient Rome*. New Haven, 1940.

Frank, Tenney *et al. An Economic Survey of Ancient Rome.* 6 vols. Baltimore, 1933–40.

Johnston, Mary. *Roman Life*. Chicago, 1957.

Rostovtzeff, Mikhail. *Social and Economic History of the Roman Empire*. 2 vols. Oxford, 1957.

History of Art, Music, and Literature:

Anderson, William J. *et al. The Architecture of Ancient Rome.* 1927.

Bieber, Margarete. *The History of the Greek and Roman Theater*. Princeton, 1939.

Duff, John W. *A Literary History of Rome*. 2 vols. New York, 1953.

Plommer, Hugh. *Ancient and Classical Architecture*. London, 1956.

Walters, Henry B. *The Art of the Romans*. New York, 1911.

Sachs, Curt. *The Rise of Music in the Ancient World*. New York, 1943.

HISTORY OF RELIGION, PHILOSOPHY, AND SCIENCE:

Cowell, Frank R. *Cicero and the Roman Republic*. New York, 1948.

Radin, Max. *Handbook of Roman Law*. St. Paul, 1927.

Rose, Herbert J. *Ancient Roman Religion*. London, 1948.

Sarton, George. *A History of Science*. Cambridge, 1952.

BIOGRAPHY:

Baker, George P. *Hannibal*. London, 1930.

Buchan, John. *Augustus*. Boston, 1937.

———. *Caesar*. London, 1936.

Burckhardt, Jakob. *The Age of Constantine the Great*. New York, 1949.

Scramuzza, Vincent M. *The Emperor Claudius*. Cambridge, 1940.

Sedgwick, Henry D. *Marcus Aurelius*. New Haven, 1922.

SOURCES:

Loeb Classical Library. Cambridge, Mass.

Early Christianity:

Alföldi, Andras. *Conversion of Constantine and Pagan Rome*. Oxford, 1948.

Craig, Clarence. *The Beginning of Christianity*. New York, 1943.

Enslin, Morton S. *Christian Beginnings*. New York, 1938.

Goodenough, Erwin R. *The Church in the Roman Empire*. New York, 1931.

Katz, Solomon. *The Decline of Rome and the Rise of Medieval Europe*. Ithaca, 1955.

Kidd, Beresford J. *A History of the Church to 461*. Oxford, 1922.

Latourette, Kenneth S. *A History of Christianity*. New York, 1953.

Morey, Charles R. *Christian Art*. New York, 1935.

MIDDLE AGES

A. BIBLIOGRAPHY:

L. J. *Paetow's Guide to the Study of Mediaeval History*. New York, 1931.

B. SOME GENERAL HISTORIES:

Artz, Frederick B. *The Mind of the Middle Ages*. New York, 1954.

Dawson, Christopher. *The Making of Europe*. New York, 1945.

Hoyt, Robert S. *Europe in the Middle Ages*. New York, 1957.

Lamonte, John L. *The World of the Middle Ages*. New York, 1949.

Stephenson, Carl. *A Brief Survey of Mediaeval Europe*. New York, 1941.

Strayer, Joseph R., and D. C. Munro. *The Middle Ages*. New York, 1959.

Taylor, Henry O. *The Mediaeval Mind*. 2 vols. New York, 1927.

Thompson, James W., and E. M. Johnson. *An Introduction to Medieval Europe*. New York, 1937.

C. SOME HISTORIES BY PERIODS:

Early Middle Ages:

Bury, John B. *The Invasion of Europe by the Barbarians*. London, 1928.

Deanesly, Margaret. *A History of Early Medieval Europe, 476–911*. London, 1956.

Duckett, Eleanor G. *The Gateway to the Middle Ages*. New York, 1938.

Margoliouth, David S. *Mohammed and the Rise of Islam*. New York, 1905.

Pirenne, Henri. *Mohammed and Charlemagne*. New York, 1939.

Rand, Edward K. *Founders of the Middle Ages*. Cambridge, 1928.

Turville-Petri, Gabriel. *The Heroic Age of Scandinavia*. New York, 1951.

Wallace-Hadrill, John M. *The Barbarian West, 400–1000*. London, 1952.

High Middle Ages:

Baldwin, Summerfield. *The Organization of Medieval Christianity*. New York, 1929.

Haskins, Charles H. *The Renaissance of the Twelfth Century*. Cambridge, 1927.

Haskins, George L. *The Growth of English Representative Government*. Philadelphia, 1948.

Packard, Sidney. *Europe and the Church under Innocent III*. New York, 1927.

Runciman, Steven. *A History of the Crusades*. 3 vols. Cambridge, 1951–54.

Tellenbach, Gerd. *Church, State, and Christian Society at the Time of the Investiture Contest*. Oxford, 1940.

Walsh, James J. *The Thirteenth Greatest of Centuries*. New York, 1909.

Late Middle Ages:

Burckhardt, Jakob. *The Civilization of the Renaissance in Italy*. New York, 1929.

Cheyney, Edward P. *The Dawn of a New Era, 1250–1453*. New York, 1936.

Ferguson, William K. *The Renaissance*. New York, 1940.

Gilmore, Myron R. *The World of Humanism*. New York, 1952.

Huizinga, Johan. *The Waning of the Middle Ages*. London, 1924.

Sellery, George C. *The Renaissance: Its Nature and Origins*. Madison, 1950.

Thompson, Faith. *A Short History of Parliament*. Minneapolis, 1953.

D. SOME HISTORIES BY NATIONS:

Barraclough, George. *The Origins of Modern Germany*. Oxford, 1947.

Diehl, Charles. *Byzantium, Greatness and Decline*. New Brunswick, 1957.

Haskins, Charles H. *The Normans in European History*. Boston, 1915.

Merriman, Roger B. *The Rise of the Spanish Empire*. 4 vols. New York, 1918–34.

Myers, A. R. *England in the Later Middle Ages*. Harmondsworth, 1952.

Petit-Dutaillis, Charles. *The Feudal Monarchy in France and England*. London, 1936.

Platonov, Sergius F. *History of Russia*. New York, 1925.

Sayles, George O. *The Medieval Foundations of England*. London, 1948.

Schevill, Ferdinand. *A History of Florence,* New York, 1936.

Thompson, James W. *Feudal Germany*. Chicago, 1928.

Tilley, Arthur A. *Medieval France*. Cambridge, 1922.

Vasiliev, Alexander A. *History of the Byzantine Empire*. 2 vols. Madison, 1952.

Von Grunebaum, Gustave E. *Medieval Islam*. Chicago, 1953.

E. SOME HISTORIES OF THE CHURCH:

Deanesly, Margaret. *A History of the Medieval Church*. London, 1954.

Elliot-Binns, Leonhard. *The Decline and Fall of the Medieval Papacy*. London, 1934.

Latourette, Kenneth S. *A History of Christianity*. New York, 1953.
Lea, Henry C. *History of the Inquisition*. 3 vols. New York, 1888.

F. SOME HISTORIES OF MEDIEVAL SOCIETY:

Boissonade, Prosper. *Life and Work in the Middle Ages*. New York, 1927.

Ganshof, Francois. *Feudalism*. London, 1952.

McIlwain, Charles H. *The Growth of Political Thought in the West*. New York, 1932.

Oman, Charles W. *A History of the Art of War in the Middle Ages*. Ithaca, 1953.

Power, Eileen. *Medieval People*. London, 1952.

Stephenson, Carl. *Mediaeval Feudalism*. Ithaca, 1942.

Thompson, James W. *An Economic and Social History of the Middle Ages*. New York, 1928.

G. SOME HISTORIES OF MEDIEVAL ECONOMY:

de Roover, Raymond. *Money, Banking, and Credit in Mediaeval Bruges*. Cambridge, 1948.

Dopsch, Alfons. *The Economic and Social Foundations of European Civilization*. London, 1937.

Heaton, Herbert. *Economic History of Europe*. New York, 1948.

Kerr, Albert B. *Jacques Coeur*. New York, 1929.

Lopez, Robert S., and I. W. Raymond. *Medieval Trade in the Mediterranean World*. New York, 1955.

Nelson, Benjamin N. *The Idea of Usury*. Princeton, 1949.

Ortigo, Iris. *The Merchant of Prato*. New York, 1957.

Pirenne, Henri. *Economic and Social History of Medieval Europe*. London, 1936.

Zimmern, Helen. *The Hansa Towns*. New York, 1889.

H. SOME HISTORIES OF MEDIEVAL PHILOSOPHY, SCIENCE, AND EDUCATION:

Clark, James N. *The Great German Mystics*. Oxford, 1949.

Copleston, Frederick C. *Mediaeval Philosophy*. London, 1952.

Gilson, Etienne H. *History of Christian Philosophy in the Middle Ages*. New York, 1955.

————. *Reason and Revelation in the Middle Ages*. New York, 1954.

Haskins, Charles H. *Studies in Mediaeval Culture*. Oxford, 1929.

Laistner, Max L. *Thought and Letters in Western Europe*. New York, 1931.

Rashdall, Hastings. *The Universities of Europe in the Middle Ages*. 3 vols. Oxford, 1936.

Sarton, George. *An Introduction to the History of Science*. Baltimore, 1927.

Thorndike, Lynn. *A History of Magic and Experimental Science*. Vols. 1–4. New York, 1923–38.

I. SOME HISTORIES OF MEDIEVAL ART, MUSIC, AND LITERATURE:

Decker, Heinrich. *Romanesque Art in Italy*. New York, 1959.

Jones, Charles W. *Medieval Literature in Translation*. New York, 1950.

Lang, Paul. *Music in Western Civilization*. New York, 1941.

Morey, Charles R. *Early Christian Art*. Princeton, 1953.

——. *Medieval Art*. Princeton, 1942.

Panofsky, Erwin. *Early Netherlandish Painting*. Cambridge, 1953.

Reese, Gustave. *Music in the Middle Ages*. New York, 1940.

Ross, James B., and Mary M. McLaughlin (eds.). *Portable Medieval Reader*. New York, 1949.

Swarzenski, Hanns. *Monuments of Romanesque Art*. Chicago, 1954.

J. SOME BIOGRAPHIES:

Hodgkin, Thomas. *Charles the Great*. New York, 1908.

——. *Theodoric the Goth*. New York, 1891.

Jörgensen, Johannes. *St. Francis of Assisi*. New York, 1922.

Kantorowicz, Ernst. *Frederick II*. New York, 1931.

Kelly, Amy R. *Eleanor of Aquitaine*. New York, 1950.

Schevill, Ferdinand. *The Medici*. New York, 1949.

Ure, Percy N. *Justinian and His Age*. Harmondsworth, 1951.

Williams, W. *St. Bernard of Clairvaux*. Manchester, 1953.

K. A SPECIAL INTERPRETATION:

Adams, Henry. *Mont-Saint-Michel and Chartres*. New York, 1913.

INDEX

Aachen, 160
Abelard, Peter (1079–1142), 198, 225
Abu-Bekr (573–634), 153
Abyssinia, 133
Achaean League, 72, 95
Achaeans, 16, 20, 23
Acre, 197, 216
Acropolis, 55
Actium, Battle of, 112
Adrian IV, Pope 1154–1159, 196
Adrianople, Battle of, 141, 143
Adriatic Sea, 91
Aegean, civilization, 16, 20–21, 23, coast, 28, islands, 32, 36, 46, Sea, 14, 20, 28, 31, 45, 51
Aegina, 50, 51
Aegospotami, 52
Aeneas, 77
Aeneid, 77, 115
Aeschines (389–314 B.C.), 63
Aeschylus (525–456 B.C.), 57
Aesop (*ca.* 620–560 B.C.), 42, 97
Aëtius, Flavius (396?–454), 144
Africa, during Ancient Times, 13, 19, 31, 60, 73, 92, 96, 100, 104, 112, 130, during Middle Ages, 144, 149, 154, 162, 267
Agesilaus (*ca.* 400–360 B.C.), 60, 61
Agincourt, Battle of, 249
Agrippa (63–12 B.C.), 115
Agrippina (15?–59), 126
Ahmose I, Pharaoh *ca.* 1580–1557 B.C., 23
Akhetaton, 24
Akkad, 11
Alamanni, 144
Alaric, King of Visigoths, 370?–410, 143, 144, 152
Alba Longa, 77, 78
Albertus Magnus (1206?–1280), 224, 225
Albigenses (Cathari), 208
Albion, King of the Lombards *ca.* 565–573, 152
Alcaeus (*fl.* 7th century B.C.), 42, 97
Alcibiades (*ca.* 450–404 B.C.), 52
Alcman (*fl.* 7th century B.C.), 36
Alcuin (735–804), 161
Aldine Press, 265
Aleppo, 5

Alexander the Great (356–323 B.C.), 29, 30, 63, 64, 67–72, 73, 74, 202
Alexander III, Pope 1159–1181, 196
Alexander of Hales (?–A.D. 1245), 225
Alexandria, 64, 69–74 *passim,* 76, 132, 139, 153, 220
Alexius I Comnenus, Eastern Roman Emperor 1081–1118, 188
Alfred the Great, King of the West Saxons 871–899, 163
Allia, Battle on the, 83
Alphabet, 19
Alps, 92 (Hannibal's crossing), 178 (Henry's crossing), 182, 185, 220 (trade routes)
Ambrose, Saint (340?–397), 140, 150, 197
Amen, 10, 11, 24, 25
Amenemhet III, Pharaoh 1837–1789 B.C., 10, 11
Amenhotep III, Pharaoh *ca.* 1411–1375 B.C., 24
America, 162, discovery of, 266, 267
Ammianus (*fl.* 4th century A.D.), 139
Amorites, 16
Amphipolis, 50, Battle of, 52
Anacreon (572?–?488 B.C.), 30, 42, 97
Anagni, 231
Anaxagoras (500?–428 B.C.), 54
Anaximander (611–547 B.C.), 41
Anaximenes (*fl.* 6th century B.C.), 41, 54
Angles, 144, 147
Anjou, 215
Anselm, Archbishop of Canterbury 1093–1109, 180, 183, 193
Anthony, Saint (250?–356), 140
Antigonus (382–301 B.C.), 72
Antioch, 5, 68, 71, 72, 139
Antiochus I, King of Syria 281–261 B.C., 69, 71
Antiochus III, King of Syria 223–187 B.C., 95
Antipater (398?–319 B.C.), 69, 71–72
Antisthenes (*ca.* 444–371 B.C.), 66
Antoninus Pius, Roman Emperor 138–161, 122
Antony (80?–33 B.C.), 111–112
Antwerp, 269
Apelles, 64

313